W9-CHL-381

PLACE IN RETURN BOX to remove this checkout from your record.
TO AVOID FINES return on or before date due.

DATE DUE	DATE DUE	DATE DUE
APR 2 6 2005	DEC 0 6 2004	AUG 1 7 2009 0 5 1 5 0 9
MAY 1 4 2012 0 3 1 8 1 2		Aug 3 19 19

c:\circ\datedue.pm3-p.1

'MAU MAU' DETAINEE

The author at work in Mr. Kenyatta's private office in Nairobi

'Mau Mau' Detainee

THE ACCOUNT BY A KENYA AFRICAN
OF HIS EXPERIENCES IN
DETENTION CAMPS
1953–1960

JOSIAH MWANGI KARIUKI

Foreword by Margery Perham

London
OXFORD UNIVERSITY PRESS
NAIROBI
1963

Oxford University Press, Amen House, London E.C.4

GLASGOW   NEW YORK   TORONTO   MELBOURNE   WELLINGTON
BOMBAY   CALCUTTA   MADRAS   KARACHI   LAHORE   DACCA
CAPE TOWN   SALISBURY   NAIROBI   IBADAN   ACCRA
KUALA LUMPUR   HONG KONG

Printed in Great Britain

Dedicated to

Kenyatta wa Muigai, our National Leader, Father
of our Nation, of the clan of Mumbui of the
Agikuyu, children of Gikuyu and Mumbi

*

The memory of Dedan Kimathi Wachiuri, Leader in
Nyandarua

*

Waruhiu Itote (General China), Leader in
Kirinyaga

*

Stanley Mathenge, wherever he may be

*

All those who were killed or crippled in our green
forests, in the 'Reserves', Prisons, and Detention
Camps for the fulfilment of the ideals they
believed in

*

Those that were spared to build a nation out of the
ashes and tribulation of the Emergency and
in the hope that they may also be inspired
to complete the total liberation of
our Mother Africa

*

The student youth of Kenya on whom so much
now depends

v

Contents

Illustrations

PLATES

The author at work in Mr. Kenyatta's private
office in Nairobi *frontispiece*

between pages 184 *and* 185

MAP

Acknowledgements

It is invidious to have to choose a few out of the many who have helped me write this book, but I would like especially to thank the following.

Jomo Kenyatta for his personal interest and guidance; 'Jaramogi' Oginga Odinga, who made my journey to London practicable; Othigo Otieno, Burudi Nabwera, Ngumbu Njururi, Karuga Koinange and the Committee of African Organizations who all helped to make possible my extended stay in England; my wife Doris Nyambura who encouraged me in difficult days; Robinson Mwangi Wanjagi, Joseph Kirira, Jeremiah Kirumwa, David Oluoch, Kirori Motoku, Kimana Wachuku, and Taddeo Mwaura who shared so much with me; Fenner Brockway, M.P., and John Stonehouse, M.P., who helped to get me out from time to time; the Movement for Colonial Freedom; Miss Margery Perham, C.B.E., for a room to work in and arguments in her lovely cottage garden; Miss Catherine Hoskyns for her hospitality and advice; Mr. and Mrs. Antony Hoskyns for their interest and help in making a jacket; Clyde Sanger for assistance with the grammar; Carl Rosberg of the University of California for his enthusiasm and kindness and the staff of the Oxford University Press for their long-suffering cheerfulness, both in Nairobi and London.

Abbreviations

C.I.D.	Criminal Investigation Department
D.C.	District Commissioner
D.D.O.	Delegated Detention Order
D.O.	District Officer
G.M.K.	Gikumbo Mount Kenya
K.A.D.U.	Kenya African Democratic Union
K.A.N.U.	Kenya African National Union
K.A.P.E.	Kenya African Preliminary Examination
K.A.R.	King's African Rifles
K.A.U.	Kenya African Union
K.C.A.	Kikuyu Central Association
K.I.S.A.	Kenya Independent Schools Association
K.K.E.A.	Kikuyu Karing'a Educational Association
K.K.M.	Kiama Kia Muingi. (Society of the People)
K.P.R.	Kenya Police Reserve
M.L.C.	Member of the Legislative Council
M.R.A.	Moral Rearmament
N.D.P.	Nyeri Democratic Party
N.P.C.P.	Nairobi Peoples Convention Party
P.C.	Provincial Commissioner
R.S.M.	Regimental Sergeant Major
Y.K.A.	Young Kikuyu Association

Foreword

MARGERY PERHAM

I MUST begin by saying that Mr. Kariuki, the author of this book, has agreed that I should be free to write what I wish in this Foreword. This was for him a considerable act of trust; it follows, of course, that he has no responsibility for what I write.

This book must have a deeply disturbing effect upon those British readers who believe its story. Those, especially in Kenya, who regard it as untrue or greatly exaggerated may deplore its publication. Yet I believe that it is right that it should be published. It records the experiences of a young Kikuyu who was detained from 1953 to 1960 as an activist in the Mau Mau movement in Kenya and who describes his periodical ill-treatment while in detention. But it also reveals what passed in his mind during this experience and there can be little doubt that, in greater or less degree, his attitude of mind is shared with thousands of other Kikuyu who, as the so-called 'hard-core' of Mau Mau, are likely to play a very active part in the future Kenya. It is also probable that his story will arouse sympathy and understanding among Africans in general and in much of the non-African world. For us British, whether in Britain or in Kenya, who were shocked by the character of the Mau Mau outbreak, to know all may not be to forgive all but it is still important to *know*, and few who read this book are likely to close it with quite the same views of Mau Mau, or, perhaps, of Africa in general, as those with which they opened it.

The effect of Mr. Kariuki's book must depend upon the extent to which it commands belief. For myself I believe that he has given a substantially true account of his own experiences. I say 'substantially' because he could not be expected to take a panoramic view of a total situation in which, beginning as little more than a schoolboy, he occupied one small and inevitably isolated part. I will return to this point in a moment. In judging the question of credibility I have had the advantage of meeting him. I had no predisposition to like a 'hard-core' ex-Mau Mau detainee, yet I quickly felt a liking for him. This was because he made an impression not only, as could be expected, of resolution, but also of modesty, friendliness, balance and humour. More surprising, he revealed a healing desire for reconciliation with those Europeans or Africans who had ill-treated him. The result of our meeting was that I decided I ought to do what lay in my power to facilitate the writing and publication of his story.

My personal impression is not enough to authenticate this record. Others will make their own decision. Most will be able to judge only from the internal evidence of this book, but others will have external evidence of the background of events. If those with intimate knowledge of this recent history can produce evidence to refute this account, either in whole or in part, that would be one important result of this publication. But we must remember that there is published evidence that some of the authorities concerned *were* guilty of acts of negligence, harshness and cruelty in dealing with the Mau Mau outbreak. In the early years of the Emergency some incidents of the torture of prisoners came to light. When I was in Kenya in 1953 I heard stories of harsh measures and I made my own protest to the Governor. The death of eleven 'hard-core' prisoners at Hola Camp at the hands of African warders in 1959 shocked British opinion and led to a searching inquiry into the incident. It also led to a more general Committee of Inquiry which found some evidence, not only of inefficiency and neglect in the detention camps, but also of violent methods being used against prisoners, abuses which were generally, but not always, committed by African warders. A list of the relevant official reports follows this Foreword.

A balanced view of the large-scale detentions and of the policy behind the administration of the camps can be attained only in the context of Kenya's years of crisis during the fifties. The Mau Mau movement was in fact a rebellion and, in the main, the rebellion of a single tribal group, that of the Kikuyu, with some kindred and neighbouring groups, the Kamba, Meru and Embu, affected in a varying but lesser degree. This Kikuyu tribe lives in the very heart of the Colony. Its lands reach close to the capital but they also stretch northwards into a large hilly and forested area which proved ideal for guerrilla war. The outbreak was utterly unexpected. It almost broke down ordered

government and its suppression cost some sixty million pounds
and a prolonged military effort with the help of British troops.
This was not all. Incitement to kill was directed against Europeans. It was not, however, very effective for, though some of
the resultant murders were peculiarly cruel, the number of
Europeans killed was surprisingly small, some thirty as against
the 1,000 reported to have been massacred in Angola in
1961. But over a wide area for several years Europeans in their
isolated farms lived day by day, and especially night by night,
in almost hourly fear of the arrival of assassins with their pangas
—heavy-bladed agricultural implements—with which victims
were slashed to death. The maiming of cattle, a device
reminiscent of Irish history, caused the European farmers an
indignation far greater than that aroused by the financial loss.
Africans, and indeed Kikuyu, suffered far more than Europeans
or Asians. As a minority of Kikuyu, especially some of those
holding responsible positions, openly supported the Government, something close to civil war developed. It is estimated
that 1,700 loyalists were killed and many others were wounded
or tortured. At a mission station in the height of the rebellion
I saw a little of the courage of the Christians as they carried
on with their work in the face of danger, ostracism and
death. When the Lari massacre by the Mau Mau of a whole
village, men, women and children, occurred, I met a friend, a
senior police officer, who an hour before had been at the scene
of the events, and he was almost unmanned by what he had just
seen.[1] On the other side some 10,000 Africans were killed by
the security forces and nearly 90,000 detained before the rebellion was brought to an end.

In the face of terrorism and counter-terrorism as employed
in the contemporary world, the would-be humane and impartial
onlooker feels a sense of moral helplessness. Such is the power
of the modern state that rebellion has become more of a
murderous than a military effort, and the most atrocious con-
flicts have generally been those, of which Algeria is an example
on the larger scale, in which a subject race rises against alien
colonizers. It was in Algeria that some French authorities seem

[1] It will be seen (p. 38) that Mr. Kariuki throws doubt upon the assumption
that the massacre was a planned Mau Mau operation. This is certainly not the
official view. As this outstanding atrocity deeply affected European opinion it may
be hoped that the incident may be further investigated.

to have legitimized the use of torture. Our author refers to some
of the brutalities committed by Africans but seems to believe,
with other African politicians, that their extent has been
exaggerated. There is a natural temptation for Africans, in
retort, to exaggerate the harshness of repression. It must be left
to historians to sift all the evidence when passions have cooled.

I have dwelt upon this aspect because it is necessary to recall
to those who read this book what can so easily be forgotten,
the pathological atmosphere in Kenya when the events described in it occurred—not only the sense of personal fear in
which Europeans and loyalists were living, but fear for the
future of white settlement, and fear even for a colony-wide
breakdown of order if an initially Kikuyu movement should
spread to other tribes. But in addition to these very ex-
plicable fears there was something more. The movement was
fostered and bound together by secret and graded oaths, and
the bestiality of the more advanced of these was so revolting
to Europeans, and not only to them, that it seemed to many
that those who used such methods ceased to be normal human
beings. It appeared that these oaths had extraordinary psychological effects upon many of those who took them. Here again
there is no certain evidence as to the prevalence of the more
extreme oaths. Our writer who, as he records, took only the
first two relatively milder oaths, has hard things to say of the
practice of pressing prisoners to confess to their oaths. The
danger of such an attempt is obvious but the intention behind
the policy was reformist and not punitive. It was an attempt to
accelerate release by breaking the spell of the Mau Mau oath
and passing men through what was known as the 'pipeline'.
This was a progression for the detainees from the more severe
to the more lenient camps until they could be detained finally
in sight of their home country, and visited by their families, in
the hope that this would complete their reformation.

I saw many of these 'hard-core' men and women in the
camps I visited and the dark look upon their faces, which seemed
to add an extra darkness to the colour of their skin, and their
look of settled hatred as they sat about motionless on the
ground, evoked something much deeper than normal fear both
for them and for those they hated. If they were sometimes
treated with brutality by officers at their wits' end in dealing

with them, the sincere attempts to apply psychological and other redemptive methods should also be remembered. I recall an incident in which an Englishwoman who was in 'moral' charge of some of the 'hard-core' women, and who had studied their customs and their language, believed she had won a group of them back to a basis of understanding and co-operation and so to the possibility of a release to which they had seemed almost indifferent. As a final proof of trust she handed to them her own very young baby and I caught my breath as they took the small white bundle and passed it around among themselves. But their looks and gestures were the universal ones of motherhood, and before long they were in a lorry *en route* for their home villages.

It should also be remembered, in considering the background of this book, that from the purely practical angle the policy of detention faced the Kenya Government with an almost impossible task. They had to build their camps quickly and with equal haste recruit such hundreds of European staff as they could find, few of whom had any experience of such work. These, in turn, had to rely upon rapidly recruited and raw African warders—14,000 was the 1954 figure—who were, as a matter of policy, in the early days chosen from non-Kikuyu tribes. Where the officials in charge were faced, perhaps in camps containing many thousands, with the defiance of these 'hard-core' prisoners, who, perhaps, just sat still refusing to work or to co-operate in any way, there was always a danger that their spirit might infect the whole vast mass of the detainees. I would assume from his own account that if the writer was called 'hard-core', and, indeed, assumed this name himself, it was because of an obstinacy derived from his strong will and not from the spiritual state of mind which the authorities discerned in the advanced oath-takers. He might not agree with me here since 'hard-core' became an honourable appellation, and a bond of unity which no ex-detainee would wish to weaken. But the root cause of Mr. Kariuki's defiance of the authorities seems to have been his determination to prove that he and his close associates in defiance were not in the grip of some remedial obsession but pursuing logical and irrevocable political aims.

I would therefore suggest that if we accept—and regret—the evidence Mr. Kariuki records of his ill-treatment, we should also give weight to the attempts that were made to deal fairly

and intelligently with an unprecedented situation. Mr. Kariuki
himself gives us plenty of evidence of ways in which humanity
tempered violence, for example by the alternation of humane
with inhumane officials, and by the opportunities for sport and
education in some of the camps. Most important, perhaps, was
his confidence that in Britain, and even in Kenya, there were
standards of law, justice and humanity to which he could appeal,
and to which he *did* appeal successfully, though to do so needed
all his courage and skill.

More widely than the issue of humanity, Mr. Kariuki's story
will be taken as a condemnation of British colonialism as
exhibited in Kenya. In this issue the outbreak should be seen
in its wider historical dimensions. For neither Mr. Kariuki nor
his Mau Mau comrades on the one side, nor the officials and
settlers who struggled with them on the other, were responsible
for the situation which suddenly forced them into such destruc-
tive antagonism. The first of the long series of events which led
up to the Mau Mau rebellion occurred not, indeed, when
Britain annexed East Africa in 1895—for the record shows how
her other 'all black' African dependencies have developed in the
main by orderly process into independence—but when the first
white settler began to farm in the largely empty highlands. For
white settlement meant confronting the tribes which patchily
inhabited this then nameless block of Africa with an alien tribe
of utterly different culture, one which, for all its small numbers,
was powerful in its civilization, wealth and unity, and therefore
in its capacity to dominate. This group was determined to take
over from Britain the control of the country as other European
colonists had done in almost every part of the world where they
settled in new lands among the native peoples. It was only
through the most strenuous efforts by opponents in Britain of
this policy that settler 'self-government' was denied and
imperial control retained. But the Africans could not continue
to remain ignorant of the significance for them of this long and
public conflict over the destiny of their territory. Nor could they
be sure that their fear that the European settlers would gain
control over the government was no longer valid. For reasons
which have been given the Kikuyu were the tribe most deeply
affected and the Mau Mau movement was the sudden culmina-
tion of their gradual political awakening.

The movement had three aspects : sociological, economic and political.

Sociologically it was the assertion of a tribe, perhaps Kenya's most able and ambitious tribe, against the dominating presence of a European colony. Its members had seen the erection upon their borders of a powerful and attractive civilization which undermined their own society while it seemed to deny their access to the new one except as its servants. Economically, as under ordered government the Kikuyu rapidly increased both in numbers and in agricultural skill and ambition, they felt that their own beautiful reserve of hills, woods and streams was inadequate to their needs, and they looked enviously at the nearby European farms upon which many of them went out to work—among them the author's family. The Kikuyu had lost only a small proportion of land to European settlement. But a loss which was spatially unimportant was, in the circumstances, psychologically oppressive. Moreover, by occupying empty land the settlers barred Kikuyu expansion. The Africans were too much dominated by the land issue to recognize that European development had created many new opportunities for employment. This is not surprising. The provisions of a welfare state for a changing society were hardly yet envisaged and Africans were faced with overcrowding and unemployment in the towns and the need for farmland to support the children, the women and the aged.

Finally, the tribe, largely through Mr. Kenyatta's leadership, had awakened to the idea that their discontents could be cured by political action. They had for long watched European and Asian political activities and had learned much from the observation. They were ceasing by the late forties to be interested in the gradualist policy of the Government. This was one of advancing their political education partly through increasing control of their own local government and partly by minority representatives in the Colony's legislature. By the late forties they were, perhaps, beginning to be moved less by the fear of the settlers achieving political control than by the determination to achieve this for themselves and win the place for the majority which, as they now knew, the rules of democracy accorded them. Their sense of increasing oppression was more psychological than reasoned : as with other revolutions they were advancing in education and economic well-being but the pace was too slow and the presence of an alien community, which regarded them as inferior, had become intolerable to many of the educated Africans. The emancipation of the Sudan, of Ghana, and of neighbouring and backward Somalia, all helped to turn hope into determination. Apart from its other interest, this book reveals the abrupt awakening of a young Kikuyu to the political facts of life and to a world now suddenly realized as one which favoured colonial emancipation.

I must confine myself to this brief reminder of the political background against which the tragic drama of Mau Mau was played out. It would take too long, and perhaps it is too soon, to discuss with confidence any closer allocation of responsibility for these events. There is a sense in which African tribes must be regarded as the innocent parties since it was the Europeans, especially in eastern Africa, who broke in upon their long isolation and took complete control of the situation. In this sense the responsibility for all that has happened since rests upon the Europeans, many of whom went out with the best intentions to build up in the wilderness a projection of their own civilization in the hope that this would benefit both races. But the time comes when the Africans lose their innocence: with western education and contact with the world they escape the simpler imperatives of tribal life and eat of the knowledge of political good and evil. In this story we can almost watch the young Kariuki partaking of this dangerous knowledge.

With the shattering of reliance upon the old tribalism and the dwindling sense of trust and confidence in British rule, a new allegiance had to be built up and attached to the new African leaders, an all-inclusive devotion which could sublimate the tribe and even be attached as far as possible to this strange new entity, the nation. This nation has still to be created, both as an idea and an institution, to fill the areas roughed out in the scramble for Africa. It is because of this that the Africans' political consciousness tends to spring directly from the tribe to the race. For it is as Negroes, as black men, that they feel they have been subordinated and despised. Yet, and this is their present dilemma, it is through their claim to self-government as nations that Africans must make their first effective demand upon their rulers and the world for recognition.

The Mau Mau movement, however, failed to extend beyond the Kikuyu and those groups closely linked with them. As a collection of clans with no pre-existing political unity, the Kikuyu needed an outstanding leadership to arouse in them a sense even of tribal unity and to direct their confused discontents into a political movement. In this record, we can see reflected in Mr. Kariuki's mind, the ready and passionate response to Mr. Kenyatta's leadership. We can see at the same time the growth both of a wider sense of race and a realization of the need for a Kenya nationalism.

Africans, victims of historical developments the pace of which has almost outrun the comprehension and control of their rational command, are almost obliged to account the strains they experience not to history, still less to themselves, but to the evil will of other men, of colonial rulers and, above all, colonial settlers. It may be long before they will distinguish the services and disservices which both have brought to Africa. Yet can we British, most concerned with the experience of making and so hastily unmaking an empire, be sure that we ourselves as yet understand the forces that have suddenly surged up to break the level surface of our rule?

It is important for us to make a rational attempt to understand these forces. They have broken in upon our preconceived policy for Kenya and radically changed its timing if not, indeed, its substance. The underlying cause of all Britain's difficulties in east and southern Africa arose from our conviction, for which we had much evidence, that the peoples of these dependencies, in contrast with the West Africans, were mostly too poor and retarded to advance quickly towards self-government. But it seems that the Kikuyu were torn between the action of two powerful forces, of alien power holding them back while a passionate desire to escape this control urged them forward. With their own society in increasing disintegration, the Kikuyu felt impelled towards insurgence. It has been one costly to themselves, to the other inhabitants of Kenya and to the British taxpayer, but—the hard fact must be faced—it has roused all concerned with Kenya to accept the need for a rapid advance to majority rule. Some of us may still believe that it would have been better for the Kenya Africans themselves if their independence could have come more gradually, and therefore that their education could have been more advanced, before the heavy responsibilities of nationhood had been undertaken. For they are a people still deeply divided tribally and all too ill-prepared for modern government, whether democratic or not. But Mr. Kariuki and his friends can hardly be expected to agree with such a view and to them the impetus given by Mau Mau to their political emancipation must seem to be its justification.

I am aware that this book will not always be read for what it is, the exceptional evidence of one African prisoner, but will be used as evidence against Britain's record in general and will provide valuable propaganda material for our critics and enemies. This is always the penalty of the healthy publicity of our democracy. But, if the British can be accused about Mr. Kariuki's treatment, they can ask who judges them and by what standards. The world has probably never seen, in relation to its population, such a high percentage of the imprisoned as in the middle years of this century. Perhaps it has never seen such deliberate and wholesale destruction of our race. But there are surely degrees of guilt between on the one side the calculated and sustained wrongs carried out generally with the maximum secrecy, according to the plans, and indeed the principles, of rulers, and on the other side the random cruelties, unsanctioned by the ruling power, committed by its agents during a few years of exceptional fear and crisis. It can be said for Britain that at least since the abolition of slavery, her people have struggled, admittedly with varying success, to maintain a standard of humanity in their empire. How far the harsh measures used were ordered, or at least condoned, by the colonial authorities, and how far they were the excesses of lower ranks in the scattered detention camps, is a question I cannot answer and it may be difficult ever to find a detailed and exact reply. There is always a difficulty, one which has often recurred in Britain's colonial history, for critics by the fireside or on the padded benches of Westminster, even when they have been able exactly to ascertain the facts, to assess correctly the degree of guilt on the part of their agents caught up in sudden danger on the frontier. But the channels of communication seldom remain completely blocked for long. In the case of the Mau Mau rebellion there was a series of inquiries into allegations of ill-treatment, including a general investigation into the whole system of detention.[1] There was a most interesting report by a medical officer skilled in psychiatry and with experience of Kenya.[2] There were visits by inquiring Members of Parliament, including some especially vigorous members of the Labour Opposition. There were numerous questions in Parliament. The Hola Camp incident of 1959 gave rise not only to two exhaustive reports[3] but also to many questions in Parliament and a Labour motion demanding an inquiry was debated.[4] The camps were also open to visiting missions from the International Red Cross.

This story reinforces the conclusion that it is always advisable for those outside prison to hear the voice of those who are inside. The political prisoner above all may suffer from being condemned, but much more, perhaps, from being forgotten. We may hope that various measures developed by Britain by which the rights of prisoners are protected will be maintained throughout the Commonwealth, including those new African states which already have their political prisoners. The Christians, above all, whose faith is traced back to a Prisoner who was unjustly tried for a political offence, flogged and tortured to death, should be especially sensitive in this matter. Those who make use of the story in this book to condemn Britain may justly be asked whether they are qualified by their own laws and customs to do so. The minimum here should be their own signature of the Declaration of Human Rights and their guarantee of the right of entry into their courts of international jurists and of the International Red Cross into their prison camps.

Mr. Kariuki might have passed in and out of the detention camps as one of an undifferentiated mass. He might have had his spirit broken. He might have developed a bitter, settled enmity towards the white man. He might have died from the effects of his imprisonment or been hanged along with the hundreds convicted after trial under the special Emergency laws. I hope that other readers will, like me, be glad, both for his own sake and for what we may learn from his story, that this prisoner, however much on some matters we may disagree with him, survived with unbroken spirit and integrity to write this African *De Profundis*.

[1] See the items under (1) in the list of books on p. xxii, especially number 4.
[2] Item 1 on the list on p. xxii. [3] See items 2 and 3 in list of books on p. xxii.
[4] *Parliamentary Debates*, 16 June 1959, V. 607. 248–384.

Notes

Mr. Kariuki mentions one or two books on 'Mau Mau'. I thought it might be useful to make a list which includes these, the Government reports to which I have referred and a few other books which might be of interest to those who may wish, after reading this book, to refer to some background material.

(1) GOVERNMENT REPORTS

Dr. J. C. Carothers, M.B., D.P.M., *The Psychology of Mau Mau* (Nairobi, 1954).

Documents relating to the Deaths of eleven Mau Mau detainees at Hola Camp in Kenya (Colonial Office, June 1959), Cmd. 778.

Record of Proceedings and Evidence in the Inquiry into the Deaths of eleven Mau Mau detainees at Hola Camp in Kenya (Colonial Office, July 1959), Cmd. 795.

Report of the Committee on Emergency Detention Camps, Supplement to *Kenya Gazette*, September 1, 1959 (Nairobi).

F. D. Corfield, *Historical Survey of the Origins and Growth of Mau Mau* (Colonial Office, 1960), Cmd. 1030.

(2) SECONDARY AUTHORITIES

George Bennett and Carl Rosberg, *The Kenyatta Election: Kenya 1960–61*: (1961).

Muga Gicaru, *Land of Sunshine* (1958).

Ian Henderson, *The Hunt for Kimathi* (1958).

Jomo Kenyatta, *Facing Mount Kenya* (1934). Republished 1961.

Dr. L. S. B. Leakey, *Mau Mau and the Kikuyu* (1952).

——, *Defeating Mau Mau* (1954).

Montagu Slater, *The Trial of Jomo Kenyatta* (1955).

F. Welbourn and K. E. M. Students' *Comment on Corfield* (the shortened version appeared in the May 1961 issue of *Race*).

(3) Two Novels

I have added these as they illustrate aspects of the emergency and are written from different standpoints.

Elspeth Huxley, *A Thing to Love* (1954).

R. C. Ruark, *Something of Value* (1955).

Mr. Kariuki and I are agreed that where he refers to any act of ill-treatment which might damage the reputation of the man concerned, the name will be suppressed. Europeans will be given the fictitious name of an English town, while Africans will be given the name of an Old Testament figure. Mr. Kariuki assures me that, as regards Africans, where some incident was well known or the individual is now restored to favour with the detainees, such a precaution is unnecessary. Where it is thought that there might be doubt in the reader's mind as to whether an individual is African or European the name is followed by an A in brackets in the case of an African, and an E in brackets for a European.

In writing this book Mr. Kariuki had some literary assistance from an English friend but, as must be obvious, the substance is entirely his own. I have had no hand in the writing, although I have added a few footnotes giving references to Parliamentary Debates, etc.

I must thank my Research Assistant, Miss Stephanie Grant, who helped me with the many tasks presented by preparing this book for publication when the author was, for much of the time, engaged upon extensive travels.

M.P.

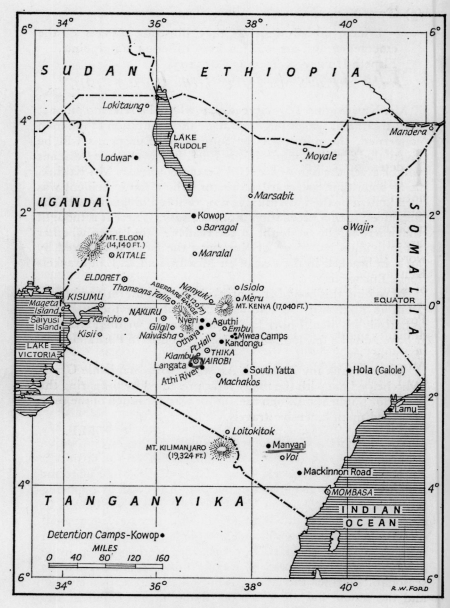

The major Detention Camps in Kenya

CHAPTER I

The Days before the Emergency began

I AM a Kikuyu who was detained in fourteen of Kenya's detention camps between 1953 and 1960. This book is largely the story of my years in these camps. It is written not in any spirit of bitterness or spite but because no one has yet told the truth about them and because they have become an important part of the history of my country. 'Manyani', the largest camp, capable of holding up to 30,000 of us, is now a word deeply entrenched in the language of every tribe in Kenya, and no one can hope to understand the present temper of Kenya African politics without some awareness of the life led by our 80,000 detainees during those Emergency years. Possibly too, some description of how we organized ourselves in difficult conditions will be of interest to those who may still be in danger of a similar fate today in other parts of colonial Africa. But to help readers judge the value of what I have to say I should perhaps begin by telling something of myself and my life prior to detention.

I was born on the twenty-first of March 1929 at Kabati-ini, near Bahati Forest in the Rift Valley Province of Kenya. My parents had left their home in Chinga in the Nyeri Native Reserve the year before to become 'squatters' on the farm of a European, known to us as *Muturi*. This is the Kikuyu word for a smith, and was given to him because of his skill at repairing farm implements. I never knew his real name. Squatters in European farms in the White Highlands were given a small piece of land to cultivate and allowed to pasture a specified number of cattle or goats. In return they were expected to be available, with members of their family, to do regular or seasonable jobs for the farmer. The wages were extremely low and the system has all the social disadvantages found in any feudal relationship. These drawbacks counted for little once our

1

people had felt the need for money, whether to buy clothes, education or bicycles. My parents, in common with many other Kikuyu and Nyanza tribesmen at a time when cash crops such as coffee, tea and pyrethrum were either prohibited or virtually unknown in the various 'Native' Reserves, strongly desired the comparative riches that could come from herding their cattle and goats in the White Highlands, where by law no African could hope to own land and where one European's pastoral farm might be bigger than a location in the Reserves containing sixty thousand people.

I was the middle child in a family of five, all the rest of whom were girls. The third daughter, Wangechi, died when she was three but my other sisters are still alive and are now all married. My mother, Mary Wanjiku, persuaded her old father to accompany us from Chinga. He was six feet four inches tall and had been a great warrior in the days before the British came to our country, raiding for cattle and women against both the Masai and the Kikuyu under the leadership of Mugo Wandiga, a famous Kikuyu General mentioned by John Boyes in his book *King of the Agikuyu*. Mugo Wabira, as my grandfather (*guka*) was called, owned at this time nearly four hundred sheep and goats, and he brought half of them with him to Muturi's farm. This was many, many more than the regulations allowed but it was not difficult to avoid detection, especially as we were careful to distribute them widely among our friends. Mugo died in 1947 and we were sad to lose such a man, one of our links with the great days before the Europeans came.

We belonged to the *Mbari ya Mbogo* (Buffalo sub-clan) of the Mungari clan, who have a traditional reputation for hard work, marital fidelity and an excessive partiality for arrowroots. Mungari, founder of the clan, was the son of Wangari, who was one of Gikuyu and Mumbi's nine daughters, each of whom is the founder of a Kikuyu clan. Gikuyu and Mumbi are the father and mother of our tribe and their home was situated at Mukurwe-ini wa Gathanga where they were sent by Mwene Nyaga (God) whom they believed had his home high among the forbidden snows of Mount Kirinyaga (Kenya). As with many of East Africa's tribes there is a legend among the Kikuyu that women once ruled us until the men became very dissatisfied and secretly conspired to make as many of the women as possible pregnant at the same time. When most of the women were heavy with child the men took over the government. Like many other Kikuyu families we also had a strain of Masai blood in us, a legacy of the old raiding days.

My father, Kariuki Kigoni, returned to Chinga in the Reserves in 1940 with his new and young second wife, Gathoni, leaving my mother and her children in the Rift Valley. My mother then went to live with Zacharia Ndung'u, taking me with her. Zacharia is now living at the Saw Mills near Njoro. He has a wife, Priscilla, and five daughters. From this time I looked on him as my father and I still help him whenever I can. I never saw Kariuki, my real father, again. He died in 1943, after wandering about for six months in a crazed condition. It was said that he had been made mad by a witch-doctor employed by some other members of our clan who were jealous of his property and land holdings. My elder sisters, Nyakio and Njoki, arranged his burial in Chinga. My mother refused to allow me to go and investigate the circumstances of his death as she felt I might well suffer the same fate myself and she said I was far too young to go on such a dangerous journey alone.

Up till the age of seven I led the normal life of a Kikuyu small boy of those days, herding the cattle and goats, learning Kikuyu customs and traditions from my grandparents, spying on the dances of my elders, stealing sugar-cane and maize and being thoroughly spoilt by my elder sisters and their lady-friends. My dearest possession was a *gathii* (goatskin cloak) embroidered with beads by my grandfather. It had the advantage that I could wriggle out of it in a trice if caught in some misdeed, leaving my captor foolishly clutching the cloak instead of me.

In 1936 Muturi asked my mother if she would allow me to work in the kitchen of the big house. He had been impressed by my lack of fear of Europeans compared with other boys of my age. The wages were three shillings a month plus food, and every Saturday Muturi's wife used to give me some sugar and salt to take home to my mother. I was forbidden to wear the *gathii* there and in its place Muturi gave me a pair of shorts and a shirt. At first it was very difficult to cope with the shorts, especially when going to the lavatory. It was best to get rid of them far away and well before the event. My work was to wash up the dishes and saucepans, to look after the cats and dogs (three of each) and to feed the ducks and chickens. The smallest dog was very friendly and we called it *Macha*, which means elephantiasis, because of its huge, fat, short legs. The largest one was spotted and frightening and was known as *Kirumi*. There is a story in Kikuyu that when a leopard's cubs are still very young the mother deserts them for a while and suddenly returns with grim aspect and fierce growls to terrify them. Those that are so frightened that they run away are called *Kirumi* while the brave ones that remain become proper leopards. Our *Kirumi* certainly had several of the less pleasant attributes of a leopard.

My immediate master was Benson (A), Muturi's cook. I never ceased to be surprised at the way in which he could swallow food at scalding hot temperatures and his mouth must have been like a piece of leather. He was a fine chef and I remember one night some visitors asked Muturi if they could see Benson personally to congratulate him on the wonderful meal they had just eaten. Like many cooks in Kenya and elsewhere Benson held that it was legitimate to take reasonable amounts of food from his employer. That particular evening, while quietly enjoying a succulent leg of lamb roasting on the stove, he heard Muturi's footsteps approaching at an hour when by all previous custom Muturi should have been drinking coffee. The illicit meat was only too visible and in a panic Benson seized it and placed it on his head under his big white chef's hat. Balancing precariously he followed Muturi to the drawing-room. The meat was very hot and burning into his skull. He was receiving, in considerable pain, the congratulations of the visitors when he felt, horror of horrors, drops of fat slowly trickling down on to each cheek. One of the guests also saw this and, exclaiming to Muturi on the sweat so apparent on his hard-working cook, he seized a napkin and, coming over to Benson, began to wipe the 'sweat' away. As Benson's head yielded to the pressure of the napkin the meat suddenly lost its equilibrium and toppled on to the beautiful carpet on the floor. In the ensuing silence the cook slowly picked it up and returned fearfully to the kitchen. Great was Muturi's anger at this episode. Not that he really minded Benson taking the meat.

What annoyed him was the deception which had given to his guests the idea that their host was a mean man and did not give his remarkable cook enough to eat. All the people on the farm laughed at this story for many weeks.

I liked Muturi and his wife very much. They treated me well and gave me toys and picture magazines. They were most kind to my mother and myself. Looking back, however, I deeply regret that they did not tell me about reading and writing and encourage me to start my education.

One day in 1938 during the planting season Obadiah Mwaniki, a relative of my mother's and a teacher in the Church Missionary Society School in Nakuru Township, came to visit us. Aged about twenty-five, he seemed to me like a young god with his smart clothes and shoes, his watch and a beautiful bicycle. I worshipped in particular his bicycle that day and decided that I must somehow get one myself. As he talked with us it seemed to me that the secret of his riches came from his education, his knowledge of reading and writing, and that it was essential for me to obtain this power. My mother, who was now about forty years old, had joined the literacy class which was run in the evenings by a Kikuyu called Evanson Ngamau. She could write her name and had learned to count from one to ten and although she never achieved much more, even this seemed miraculous to me and I begged her to teach me all she knew. She bought me a slate and a pencil and at night after my work in the kitchen was finished we struggled together with these new things. In the big house I concentrated hard on learning the English names of all the domestic utensils.

About two months after Obadiah's visit my mother persuaded me to give up my job and to enter Evanson's Day School full-time. The fee was fifteen cents (about twopence) for every term of twelve weeks. Muturi had built the school out of his own pocket and the money went to pay the teacher. I went there when I was eleven years old and I rapidly became the star pupil in my class. Because of my service with Muturi I already knew how to wear trousers and clean my fingernails, and I had begun writing and counting with my mother. My classmates were far behind. There were about forty pupils and we were taught singing, dancing, drawing, counting and scripture, in which we learned the catechism. It was not really a good school but my three years of discovery and development there were a vital part of my life.

The great war that came in 1939 between the Europeans did not much affect life on the farm. In 1940 there was an ominous rumour that Hitler was coming to kill us all and many people went fearfully down to the rivers and dug holes in the banks to hide from his troops. But the British Army did not recruit from the farms; there was no real shortage of food and we could not understand or feel deeply about the fundamental issues. After I left Evanson's School I went to several other schools in Kenya but it was very difficult to find enough money to pay the higher fees. My mother very much wanted to see me educated and used all the money she had, so that sometimes she did not have enough to eat and my sisters did not have enough clothes. There were some black wattle trees which belonged to my mother's family and I used to cut them down and take off the bark and unroll it and sell it. This tree grows on the Kikuyu hills and the bark is exported and used for tanning leather. In 1941 I joined a school at Bahati Forest. The headmaster was James Giteni, a clever and able teacher who had been trained at a Mission station in Kiambu. The school was managed by the Kikuyu Independent Schools Association (K.I.S.A.) which had been started by our tribal leaders after the split with Dr. Arthur of the Church of Scotland Mission in 1929 on the issue of female circumcision. As well as K.I.S.A., another group started, the Kikuyu Karing'a Educational Association (K.K.E.A.), and these two organizations were running the only African-managed educational systems in the whole of Kenya at this time. Before their proscription at the beginning of the Emergency these schools had provided places for many who would have failed to continue their education had we been forced to rely merely on Missions or the Government, and some of our most prominent politicians have been products of K.I.S.A. or K.K.E.A. James Giteni had taken the post because it was better paid than any job he could be offered by a Mission.

In Kenya schools were started by the Missions and religion and education have always been closely bound up together. This K.I.S.A. school at Bahati owed religious allegiance to the African Independent Pentecostal Church founded by Johanna Kunyiha, a prominent District Councillor and Court elder in

Nyeri District, who was awarded the M.B.E. in 1961. The representative of his Church in the Rift Valley was Petro Muchangariba and he sometimes came to preach to us. He was a strong speaker and openly spoke out about the evils of the colour bar and the seizure of our land by the Europeans : he was detained during the Emergency. But politics were generally unknown to the ordinary people of the area at this time, although we used to discuss our land grievances through the smoke in the huts at night.

The art of distillation was unknown to our people before the Europeans came. But the Sudanese troops ('Nubians') who came with them spread the method throughout the country. It is undoubtedly a cheap way of getting very drunk but its introduction began to spoil the social habit whereby our old men drink together the wholesome and mildly intoxicating Kikuyu beer. My mother became so skilled at making this Nubian gin that her brew became famous for miles around, and was a valuable source of extra money for us and for my education. During the early days of the war many soldiers would come out from Lanet and Nakuru to drink in our hut. There were Europeans, Africans and coloured South Africans all together. They frequently became very drunk and began to abuse and fight each other. One coloured soldier was badly hurt and we hid him in the nearby forest where he spent three days unconscious. We soon had a gramophone and other luxuries from the money earned in this way. Another benefit came to me indirectly because my disgust at this nightly-repeated scene of debauchery, vomiting and brawling was so great that I vowed never to touch alcohol and I never have. But a man called Abraham became jealous of our success and our gramophone and he betrayed us to a police informer. My mother was arrested in September 1942 and sentenced to two years' imprisonment. Although Gathoni, my father's second wife, looked after me, I was very unhappy and rapidly became thin and sick. I visited my mother in Nakuru jail once. She was well but I cried bitterly at seeing her in the white prison clothes. I gave a Sudanese wardress one hundred and twenty shillings to buy her as many extra comforts and food as possible. This was quite customary but the prison officers naturally did not know about it.

In 1944 Muturi left Kenya and we went two miles away
to a farm owned by a man named Tryon (E). He was given the
Kikuyu name of *Karimiramithi*, 'Thorn Tree Cultivator', because
he forbade the destruction of thorn trees which he said were
beautiful. We found this very strange. Tryon had two Italian
prisoners of war working there, one called Starino and the
other Giuseppi. They were friendly and talented, and also
excellent builders. Starino had a small stick with a big map of
the world wrapped inside it. I spent hours poring over it. They
made tin whistles, which I used to sell for them, on commission,
to the other young men. Sometimes in the evenings they gave
us an entertainment which included trick cycling and fine
songs. Free and easy people, the girls liked them, and they were
not apart like other Europeans. Giuseppi became a close companion of mine and when we parted he gave me his watch.

Since my mother had been sent to jail times had been hard
for me and my two unmarried sisters. We could at best hope to
earn three shillings a week picking pyrethrum flowers from
morning till evening. But this work was only seasonal and I
decided to ask Tryon to give me a regular job. When he saw
my references from Muturi he took me on as a clerk at a wage
of thirty shillings a month. Regretfully this now meant leaving
the K.I.S.A. school, which had been a wonderful thing in my
life.

My new job was to count the gallons of milk and the sacks of
maize and to prevent the farm workers stealing either. This was
very difficult for me to do conscientiously because my people
could not harvest enough for their basic needs out of their
patches of cultivation and they and their families often went
hungry. Anyway, we Kikuyu have a proverb, *Murimi ndaunagwo
guoko*, which can be freely rendered 'He who is working in the
cornfield should be fed there'. So I merely told them that they
should not take more than necessary. Once one of the milkers
called Warui Wanjeri finished milking a cow, and putting his
head in the bucket hastily gulped down some of the still warm
milk. Unfortunately Tryon saw him and a little later called him
over and accused him of drinking the milk. Warui denied it,
whereupon Tryon, leading him to a mirror, took hold of the
ends of his moustaches, brought them together and demanded
to know why they were still dripping milk if he had not been

drinking it. Warui, who had forgotten about his moustaches, shamefacedly wiped the milk off them. He was not discharged either, but was told that if he was so desperate he should at least use a cup. Tryon also pointed out that the cattle did not belong to Warui.

In my own dire need I would sometimes augment my wages by appropriating half of the skimmed milk that was supposed to be fed to the pigs and then selling it at five cents (about a halfpenny) a bottle to the people on the farm. At Christmas, in place of presents, I used to distribute bottles to all my friends free. Tryon never discovered either of these devices.

My mother was released from jail in June 1944. Many people came to our hut that evening to celebrate her release and I slaughtered a he-goat, *thenge*, for her and we were very happy. She told me that some Kipsigis women convicts had been jealous of the extra supplies she had obtained through the one hundred and twenty shillings and had tried to poison her. She had been helped and protected in this crisis by the Sudanese wardress. It seemed that my money had been well spent. She said that otherwise the prison at Nakuru had not been a bad place and the officers and warders had been kind to her. But every day she remembered her children and she had often been ill with worry about us.

After the end of the war I carried on with my job. My mother was for ever trying to persuade me to continue my education but our need for money was so great that I felt it vital to go on earning for a while. Late in 1946 I decided to take a day off at Nakuru Races. I had only been there once before and I have never been since. I took with me forty shillings from my savings and bought a two-shilling ticket in the Sweepstake, Number 124876. I prayed and clutched it tightly for an hour and then went along to look at the board on which the winning numbers were shown. Number 124876 . . .! I looked again. Number 124876. I sat down on the ground and wondered how to make sure this was not a dream. Hitting my head with my hands in Kikuyu style it seemed to be no dream. Europeans pinch themselves. I pinched myself and it hurt. Definitely no dream. I went along into the office where an official gave me 1,600 shillings . . . Sixteen hundred shillings . . . Eight bicycles . . . with lamps and bells. . . .

I rushed off to the privacy of the latrine and thought what
to do next. The whole world must know that I had won the
sweep and half the whole world must be waiting to rob me
of my winnings, which were truly vast. I wrapped the money
in my handkerchief, tied it round my belt and then put the belt
on inside my trousers. Belt, handkerchief and money were
surely now invisible and it would be a very clever robber that
would know where the money was. I was beginning to feel
a delayed-action happiness but I could not feel completely
content until I reached home safely. There were thirty-two
shillings left out of my original forty, and I spent this on a dress
for my sister and sheets and blankets and food for my mother.
I hurried home alone on foot, eight long nervous miles. I
shunned all would-be companions and refused to accept any
lifts. I reached home about half past five, gave my family their
presents and told them about the money. They were extremely
happy that night. I gleefully informed them that I would soon
own a bicycle like Obadiah's. My mother said nothing but took
fourteen hundred shillings for safe custody and allowed me to
keep two hundred. Several years later she told me that she kept
the money always in a small leather bag tied round her waist
under her clothes. We did not celebrate in any way that evening
because she said that we should not appear happy in case bad
people suspected the truth and robbed us.

The next morning my mother told me that we must now
make arrangements for my return to school and that no bicycle
was to be bought at this time. We were all strengthened in this
resolve when a young man called James Thuku Mangothi,
from Kihuri in Othaya Division of Nyeri district, came to stay
on the farm and talked to Tryon in English. I now know that
his English was very bad but it seemed to us in our ignorance
a marvellous accomplishment and it inspired me to agree with
my mother. James is now employed in Nairobi as a cook. So
in February 1946 I went to Nakuru African School to repeat
Standard V there.

Later that year we heard that there was to be a meeting
of all Africans at Njoro at which a person who had stayed in
England for many years would be speaking. It was a Sunday,
which is the day that the labourers on all the Rift Valley farms
go to market. Although the people in the area had previously

had little to do with politics, everyone was excited at the prospect of seeing the great man from London and hearing his
words, though many believed that he would not be able to
speak either Kikuyu or Swahili after fifteen years away from
his country. Many of my school friends wanted to go and so the
School Committee hired a lorry to take forty of us to Njoro.
As we came near we met many other lorries converging on the
meeting-place and we passed long files of people going there on
foot. When the meeting began, there must have been a crowd
of four to five thousand, including many children.

Two people made speeches introducing Kenyatta. They were
somewhat dull because at that time the leaders were not
practised in public speaking and crowd psychology and the
audience became restive. But then Jomo Kenyatta came to the
platform himself. He was holding a carved walking-stick loosely
in his hand and wore his big brown leather jacket. He began
by greeting us all with the special words of respect used for each
age grade. The effect of his voice and personality was immediate and magnetic so that even the smallest children became
still and quiet as Kenyatta talked to us of his doings in England
and of the future of our country. He was mixing Kikuyu and
Swahili words in a wonderful way and the doubters found that
he knew more old Kikuyu phrases than they had ever heard.

He said that he did not want the Europeans to leave the
country, but it was time that they started to behave like guests
in our house. They had come as strangers to us and we had
accommodated them and now they claimed that our house
belonged to them. In the old days we used to carry their
maidens on our shoulders and draw them in rickshaws from
Mombasa to Nairobi so that their legs should not become tired
by walking through the scrub and forests of thorn. They should
not forget that the land they tread is ours. Under an African
government Europeans would have nothing to fear in the same
way as he, Kenyatta, an African, had not feared while in
Europe under a European government. During the last war we
sent our young men to sacrifice their lives in helping the British
people to fight and conquer Germany. The white officers had
been rewarded with farms on which to settle in our land and
loans with which to stock them. The African soldiers had been
rewarded with the colour bar, unemployment and the *Kipande*

(registration card). There had been no colour bar to prevent us dying for Britain in the war.

Then Kenyatta appealed to us to unite and to forget tribalism. We should work hard and try to educate our children as well and quickly as possible so that they could take over the government of the country. As he sat down the women gave him the five *ngemi*, a trilling cry reserved in Kikuyu custom for the birth of a male child and given only to the most memorable speakers. The meeting slowly broke up, the crowd remaining for a long time in small groups debating all the marvellous things he had spoken and discussing the great future he would bring us. This was the year that Kenyatta first began to teach our people how to love their country. Those who had been stagnant in their misery now began to look for happiness. Far into the night in eating-houses, in lorries and in their homes, the people of the Rift Valley talked about their new leader from London and the new hope he brought.

I myself was fundamentally changed by his statesmanlike words and his burning personality. I vowed there and then that I would struggle with him for justice and freedom for our country and I dedicated myself to follow him in his crusade to remove the sufferings and humiliations of our people.

During the next four years my studies took nearly all my time and energy. Late in 1947 I went back to my father's lands in the Nyeri Reserve. The atmosphere there was not pleasant and the people seemed backward. They still planted all their crops mixed up together, bananas and maize, beans and cabbages. Few seemed to have any proper idea of politics. Those who had been cultivating my father's lands were not happy to see me. They had fondly hoped that I would not know about their transactions with my father and they had been certain that I would not be able to find the goats or the money to redeem the pieces of land he had transferred to them. However, I slowly redeemed all the fragments and allowed some of the farmers to continue cultivating the land as my *ahoi*, that is tenants. My education continued at Kariko Primary School in Chinga and at Karema in Othaya. I then moved on to Keruguoya Intermediate School in Embu District. All these were Roman Catholic schools and at that time I considered myself a Roman Catholic. In 1950, on the recommendation of the Keruguoya headmaster, I entered Form I at King's College, Budo, in Uganda, where I stayed until I was twenty-two. This is a secondary school in Uganda run by the Protestant Church Missionary Society.

I enjoyed my time in Uganda. While it is sometimes difficult to break through the reserve of the Baganda, I made some lasting friendships among them. They are tremendously keen on education and have many very clever young men. It is a pity that they became so interested in the survival of their own kingdom that for a time this badly hindered the speed of their advance towards independence. Most people seem to own bicycles in that country and they use them in remarkable ways : it is common to see live goats strapped on the carriers on the way to market and some bicycles carry enormous loads. One day in a village near Budo I was surprised to see a cyclist with a stove fixed to his carrier; he was cycling along peeling potatoes, cooking them and eating them without dismounting at all.

During my time in Buganda I heard with sadness of the great troubles my people were having in their struggle with the European settlers. From visitors and Kikuyu friends in Kampala I heard of the increasing frustration and bitterness growing in Kenya : I heard of the humiliations suffered time and again because of the colour bar : I heard of the shortage of land, the lack of educational opportunities, the toughness of the Administration and the refusal to admit our people into the Legislative Council. I was so intensely busy working for my examinations that I could take no part at all from Kampala in the struggle at this time. It was my clear duty first to prepare myself educationally, to arm myself with the weapons of literacy and the power of reading and writing. But all through 1951 and 1952 it became obvious that, unless the British soon gave way to some extent, we were heading for a tragic disaster. I was not surprised when I returned to Kenya on 22 October 1952 to await the results of my School Certificate examination to learn that two days previously the country had been placed under a State of Emergency by the new Governor, Sir Evelyn Baring.

CHAPTER II

K.C.A., K.A.U. and 'Mau Mau'

OVER the years there have been many versions published of the history of Kenya since the British, in the shape of Lord Lugard and others, came into the country in the 1890s. Naturally, since so few of our people were able to get education, these have nearly all been written by Europeans, tending to glorify the pioneering spirit and triumphs of such as Lord Delamere and to emphasize the majesty of the scenery and the quaintness of the 'native'. It has amused me sometimes to read aloud in the books issued to our schools the inevitable distortions and misunderstandings that are circulating in this country in the name of 'history'. It has also saddened me because it is this general attitude that possibly was the biggest single contribution to the inevitable explosion in 1952.

I was away from Kenya for four of the years immediately prior to this, but countless hours of talk over the flickering evening fires had given me the story of my people's struggle since the days of their former freedom. When first the British came with their missionaries, traders and administrators we felt they had some things to teach us which were good. Education, medicine, farming and industrial techniques, these we welcomed. As a tribe the Europeans had certain characteristics which were, perhaps, not pleasant. Quick to anger, inhospitable, aloof, boorish and insensitive, they often behaved as if God had created Kenya and us for their use. They accepted the dignity of man as long as his skin was white. I am giving you now some of the general impressions they left upon us, while realizing that there were many individual exceptions who belied them.

Little of this would perhaps have mattered had not the British Government been forced in the early 1900s, both by pressure groups in England and disobedient Governors in Kenya, into a policy of taking over our land and giving it to Europeans to farm. This was the source of all future troubles. Many of our people had not enough land even then. In the

14

succeeding decades, with an ever-increasing population, the shortage of land became chronic and our landless young men found themselves working at miserable wages on enormous farms which their fathers had owned and which were now bringing huge houses and Jaguar cars to European strangers.

The inherent dangers in this situation grew as the Europeans tried to entrench their power politically and to hold back the legitimate advance of our people on every possible pretext. They were never more than 60,000 in a population of 7,000,000, but none of those 7,000,000 had any say in the government of the country until the 1950s. The Africans of Kenya were controlled and directed with the prime objective of serving the needs of the European settlers' farm economy. Labour laws, taxes, education, everything was done in the way the Europeans wanted. At the same time certain honourable Europeans, both in Kenya and Europe, tried to remedy some of the more conspicuous evils and the British Government, which always tried to present the image of a model colonial power, was compelled to start giving us education. Education was vital because it gave us the chance to use the same weapons in the struggle as our opponents. Some leading Africans were equipped to lead us and in the early 1920s the long battle began. The road has many milestones upon it; the Devonshire White Paper declaration about the paramountcy of the interests of the majority in 1923; the fight against an imposed White-dominated East African Federation in the late 1920s and early 1930s: the Carter Land Commission and Jomo Kenyatta's various visits to Europe. Our early strategy was to delay by all means in our hands any step which might give the Whites the last crucial power of domination, while building up among ourselves an army of educated people who could take over the country as soon as possible.

After the 1939–45 War, with the quickening pace of Independence elsewhere in Asia and Africa, the Whites in Kenya began to put on the pressure. Between 1946 and 1951 they sought, sometimes with the methods of desperation, to consolidate and enlarge their power so that it could never, never be shaken. The Africans on their side began to see that the situation was working up to a climax where a supreme effort might well be called for. The crux was representation in the Legislative

Council, but when the most moderate demands made in 1951 were turned down by the British Socialist Government, a tougher attitude became apparent in the inner councils of the Africans. It was in this atmosphere, and with the full realization of the sacrifices that might be involved if their warnings continued to be disregarded by the British Government, that the Africans began to prepare for the ultimate last-ditch stand that might be necessary to prevent the light of freedom being snuffed out. The unity of numbers was our strongest, indeed almost our only, weapon and plans for cementing that unity with the Movement of the Oath were put in train. There is no doubt that reasonable concessions at any time, concessions that would have shown that the British genuinely wished Kenya to obtain its independence under an African Government within a foreseeable period, would have been sufficient to stop much that followed. No significant concessions, of the sort to restore our lost faith in Britain's sincerity, were ever made. This then was the background to my return to Kenya in October 1952.

It was at Eldoret railway station on my way from Uganda to Nyeri that I read in the Swahili newspaper *Baraza* the news of the declaration of the Emergency. Gakeri, a friend of mine who worked for the railways and was later detained, put me up for the night at Nakuru and it surprised me to find that many people there had still not heard about the Emergency. News of this importance would surely travel faster than a railway train. In the morning we met some people who had just come from Nyeri. They said that things were very bad there and that the Reserves at this time were no place for young men, who were being chased and arrested on the slightest pretext. Many of them in desperation had already run away into the forest to escape this harrying. Thinking it unwise in these circumstances even to try to rejoin my mother in Nyeri, I also decided not to stay in Nakuru but with Wangui, my mother's sister. She was living with her son-in-law who was working as a labourer for the Forest Department at Bahati where they were thinning tree plantations.

I stayed with Wangui for one month earning some money by digging up patches of land on piecework for the forest labourers, each of whom was given a *shamba* in a new tree plantation inside the forest boundaries. They held these for three years during which their cultivations helped the young trees to take root. After the three years was up they were given fresh land in another part due to be planted with trees and the whole process began all over again. They lived high and deep in the forest at Bafuni, so called because it protruded from the hill like the ribs from a body. It was a beautiful part of the Rift Valley and at night I would lie outside exploring the landscape, my eyes ranging from the dark swelling hills of Njoro across to the red, green and blue lights winking back at me from the valley so far below.

I went to Nakuru from time to time and soon decided to become a member of the local branch of the Kenya African Union (K.A.U.). The fire that had been lit within me when I first heard Kenyatta speak at Njoro in 1947 showed no signs of dying down and I now had a greater certainty than ever before that it was my duty to devote my life to my people's struggle for freedom. The chairman of the Nakuru Branch of K.A.U. was John Kamonjo, an outstanding Kikuyu trader who had been known casually to me for many years. When I begged him to let me join K.A.U. he smiled gently in reply and asked why someone scarcely weaned from his mother should wish to join a political party. At that time the Special Branch were using large sums of money in their efforts to penetrate the party and so he had to be particularly careful. I poured out to him all my yearnings and ambitions for our people. He was apparently satisfied with my sincerity because after paying the five shillings membership fee I received my party card—No. 745. I hurried back home and gave it to my aunt to look after for me. I was terrified lest it be mislaid. She emptied out a green mineral water bottle in which the salt was normally kept, put the card inside and buried the bottle in the soil far out among the maize plants in our garden.

I now began to recruit most actively for K.A.U. in the Bahati area and I had soon persuaded sixteen men and nineteen women there to become members. Several of them I learnt later had already taken the Oath of Unity. There has been considerable discussion in Britain and Kenya over the last ten years about the exact relationship between the Kikuyu Central Association, the Kenya African Union and the movement which became internationally known as 'Mau Mau'. Many of the dogmatic statements on the status and connection of these three groups have been misleading, including those in the document known as the *Corfield Report*.[1] Mr. Corfield nowhere states whether he took direct evidence from anyone who was a member of any of these groups. I want to state as clearly as is possible what the situation was as far as I knew it.

The Kikuyu Central Association (K.C.A.) was the direct successor of the Young Kikuyu Association begun in 1921 by Harry Thuku who was deported to Kismayu in March 1922, a decision which led to some rioting in Nairobi. (On his return from exile in 1930 Harry Thuku became a wealthy landowner, an advanced farmer and a moderate. He was one of the most prominent of the so-called 'loyalists' in the recent Emergency.) The new leaders, Joseph Kang'ethe and Jesse Kariuki, considered the name Young Kikuyu Association to be unnecessarily limiting. The 'Young' was dropped and the word 'Central' was introduced since the Association was now to be open to all Africans in Central Province, including the non-Kikuyu tribes —the Meru and Kamba. K.C.A. was a political movement, dedicated to the recovery of the lost lands, increased political representation, greater educational opportunities, the fight against exploitation of labour on European farms and the abolition of the hut tax. Jomo Kenyatta became its general secretary in 1928 and represented the Association before various bodies in England. It was proscribed by the Kenya Government on 30 May 1940 as it was alleged that it had established a treasonable relationship with Italian agents and many of its leaders were restricted in Kapenguria.

Some time in the nineteen-twenties, following the oath used by the Young Kikuyu Association, the K.C.A. had introduced a simple oath of allegiance to the Association and to the sanctity of our lands. This was known as *muma wa chuba*, the bottle oath, and was taken with a Bible in the left hand and a lump of soil in the right. Like most oaths of this type all over the world it was secret. We often discussed in the detention camps the oaths of Freemasons, which were also taken secretly at night, and wondered why people thought ours were so much worse.

After the 1939–45 War had ended, various prominent African

---

[1] *Historical Survey of the Origins and Growth of Mau Mau* by F. D. Corfield (1960). Cmnd. 1030.

politicians, including James Gichuru and Eliud Mathu, decided to start another political organization which would have the same general objective as K.C.A. They resolved against the resuscitation of K.C.A. itself for two reasons. First it would be much easier to get the Government to agree to the establishment of a new party than to obtain the cancellation of the ban on K.C.A., which was anyway a dog with a bad name as far as the Government was concerned. Secondly, the time had come for the starting of a Colony-wide organization embracing all tribes which was hardly practicable with the word 'Kikuyu' in the title. The K.C.A. had been all that was possible in the Dark Ages of Kenya's political evolution, but the time now seemed ripe for something altogether more ambitious. Eliud Mathu also needed an organization to tell him what to say in the Legislative Council to which he was nominated in 1944. When Kenyatta returned from England he was fully in accord with this policy. There have been various attempts to condemn Kenyatta as an out-and-out Kikuyu tribalist. On the contrary there is no man in Kenya today whose outlook has been more genuinely non-tribal and indeed Pan-African. In Kenyatta's trial great play was made by the prosecution on the discovery among his papers when he was arrested of a letter written in 1948 summoning all the K.C.A. leaders to a conference. Corfield in his Report states: '. . . Mau Mau, the direct offspring of K.C.A., which was the instrument with which Jomo Kenyatta and his associates intended to subvert the Kikuyu peoples to his will.'[1] The Government Prosecution at the trial, and Corfield in his Report, twist and exaggerate every possible statement that can assist this view, because it is vital for them somehow to justify the criminal folly of their deliberate decision to arrest Kenyatta and, by removing the only man capable of advising and restraining the extremists, thus to open the way to the self-generating excesses on both sides during the ensuing revolt. But the letter was never sent and, even if it had been, the wrong deductions were drawn from it. The meeting had been proposed in order that the new ideas could be explained to the former K.C.A. leaders. In Nyeri in December 1960 K.A.N.U. called a meeting of the former K.A.U. Committee members, K.C.A. leaders, ex-detainees and loyalists. This

[1] Op. cit., p. 267.

meeting was not held to revive all these organizations and groups but to explain to them the new organization and to unite and assimilate them. Nor is there any evidence in *Corfield* to justify his statement that 'Mau Mau' was the direct offspring of K.C.A. The fact that many former K.C.A. officials took an oath is not evidence that the two organizations were the same. Many more people who were not members of K.C.A. took an oath than those who were. Nor is the fact that some former K.C.A. officials became office bearers in K.A.U. evidence that K.A.U. and K.C.A. were the same thing. If it is evidence of anything it is that there were still all too few African politicians in Kenya and that these officials still retained the confidence of the people.

The Kenya African Union was therefore developed by Gichuru and Mathu out of the Kenya African Study Union started by them in 1945. In 1946 it was decided to drop the word 'Study' which implied educational rather than political objectives. K.A.U. was a Colony-wide African political party open to all tribes and with a programme of considerable moderation. Members of K.A.U. did not take any oath. During the crucial years from 1947 to 1952 K.A.U. received little hope or encouragement in its pursuit of a moderate programme. Jomo Kenyatta himself was told by the Governor to train himself in local Native Council politics and not to think he was worthy of a seat in the Legislative Council: a clear invitation to him to turn into an extremist. As the years rolled by with no apparent advance and no political concessions, extremists both inside and outside the party were gaining influence at the expense of those, like Kenyatta, who were trying to steer a middle course. Inevitably the moderates were themselves forced to take up more extreme positions in their desperate efforts to prevent a major explosion in the country. Our fair land was being sacrificed on the two irreconcilable horns of the basic dilemma of British policy in Kenya—the encouragement of European settlement and the entrenchment of European privilege on the one hand, and the superficial lip-service paid to the ideals of democracy and African advance on the other.

I must now explain the movement which was given the name of 'Mau Mau'. After the 1939–45 War things were changing. Our social and economic grievances were plainer to all and

there were many more educated Africans who were beginning
to understand that the social system was not immutable.
Thousands more had recently returned from service in the
King's African Rifles all over the world. The granting of
Independence to India and Pakistan, the developing struggle in
Ghana, and the increased publicity given to such things in
newspapers and radio programmes, all contributed to the steady
growth of political sensibility among the Africans in Kenya.
Most of all was this happening among my own tribe, the Kikuyu.

They had long been in the van of Kenya politics; they were
living in overcrowded and undeveloped Reserves, in many
places with a density of well over a thousand to the square mile;
they felt deep grievances over the land which had been taken
from them, land without which they could have no religious
or social security. When the Europeans first came to the
country the Kikuyu fought under Waiyaki Hinga to preserve
their lands. Many of them were killed but the witch-doctor
advising them told them to stop fighting or the whole tribe
would be eliminated. He used the Kikuyu saying *Mundu ti
mwahu wa irigu oragagwo oro umwe umwe* which means 'people
are not a bunch of bananas to be killed one by one'. Waiyaki,
with whom Lugard became blood brother, later died at Kib-
wezi on his way to the Coast to which he had been deported. It
is not enough to say that the Europeans have a title to the land
and had taken only uninhabited areas. The Kikuyu rightly felt
that their uneducated forefathers had not understood the nature
and implications of the requests forced on them by the early
administrators and settlers, nor had they the weapons or power
to refuse any demand that was pressed really hard. Had no
Europeans come to the country they would have slowly settled
in the forests and the White Highlands. When that land was
finished the tribe would have considered what to do next. But
as it was they had been tricked. At the same time they were
suffering the humiliations of the colour bar. Many Europeans
refused to talk to educated Africans in any language but their
deplorably bad Swahili; old men were addressed as boys and
monkeys; Africans were barred from hotels and clubs; Africans
with land near European farms were not allowed to plant
coffee; there was a wholesale disregard for human dignity and
little respect for anyone with a black skin.

Normal political methods through K.A.U. seemed to be getting nowhere. The young men of the tribe saw that a time of crisis was approaching when great suffering might be necessary to achieve what they believed in. It is easy enough for anyone who knows my people to understand that it was a spontaneous decision that they should be bound together in unity by a simple oath. From what I have heard this oath began in the Kikuyu districts, starting in Kiambu. There was no central direction or control. The oath was not sophisticated or elaborate and initially was wholly unobjectionable. It started slowly, indeed regretfully, and was an oath of unity and brotherhood in the struggle for our land and our independence. It eventually spread all over the country among a people desperate to retain their self-respect and to prevent their subjugation in a European-dominated State. Although the situation was dangerous, even in October 1952, it was not so dangerous that it could not have been put right by a few political concessions (which would today, ten years later, seem trivial) and a little understanding. The movement could always have been extinguished in this way but the Government chose to answer it with a series of the harshest and most brutal measures ever taken against a native people in the British Empire in the twentieth century, and so the movement developed by action and re-action into a full-scale rebellion involving the soul of my people.

Although quite naturally most ex-officials of K.C.A. took the new oath it had nothing to do with K.C.A. or the old K.C.A. oath. I must, too, emphasize here that in all the statements and confessions made in my hearing by thousands of detainees in fourteen camps the name of Kenyatta was never once mentioned as being involved in an oath. *Mzee* was still trying desperately to get the Kenya Government to see sense in other ways. (*Mzee* is a Swahili word which means 'an old man', and so we gave it to Kenyatta as a sign of respect.) I repeat that there was no central direction in this movement which grew from the grass roots upwards. In the years of crisis, 1952–54, it developed a system of sub-location and location committees in Nairobi, the Kikuyu Districts and the Rift Valley and these became the main instruments of the so-called Passive Wing whose job was to help and supply the fighters in the forests. In the early days the secrecy and lack of direction made it an ideal cover for the violent and criminal elements which are a menace to any state or society. Sometimes these elements would misuse the organization which had begun as a straightforward and spontaneous movement of unity among a people without hope. Had the Government given the people any prospect of justice it is possible that Kenyatta and the other constitutional fighters for freedom would have had some chance to control the Kikuyu. As it was, even Kenyatta himself became an object of suspicion to the thugs and there is strong evidence of plots to assassinate him both at a meeting in Kaloleni Hall, Nairobi, and also at the burial of Senior Chief Waruhiu, killed by a gunman on 7 October 1952.

Few people seem to know the origin of the name 'Mau Mau'. Kenyatta said time and time again that he did not know these words and nor did his people. In spite of the attempts to prove in the *Corfield Report* and at his trial that this was merely a very skilful piece of double-talk in Kikuyu, Kenyatta was speaking nothing more nor less than the truth.

This is the real origin of the name 'Mau Mau'. Kikuyu children when playing and talking together often make puns and anagrams with common words. When I was a child I would say to other children 'Ithi, Ithi', instead of 'Thii, Thii' (meaning, 'Go, Go'), and 'Mau, Mau' instead of 'Uma, Uma'.

One evening, people went to a house in Naivasha area where the oath was to be administered. It was always the duty of the oath administrator to see that there was a good guard to keep watch outside while the oath was being given. That evening, the guard was given instructions that, if he heard footsteps and suspected it was the police or an enemy, he should shout the anagram 'Mau Mau' so that those in the house could escape. It would be a clear sign only for those in the house, for the enemy would not understand what the words 'Mau Mau' meant.

That night the police did come to the house and the guard shouted out. The people left the house. When the police came they found no people but only the paraphernalia of oathing. When they reported back to the Police H.Q., they said that they heard the words 'Mau Mau' as they approached but, on arrival at the house, saw nobody, only the paraphernalia of oathing. From then on, the oath of unity was given the name 'Mau Mau'. But the members of the movement did not call the movement 'Mau Mau'.

I have been told that the name 'Mau Mau' was used soon after by a Rift Valley Kikuyu called Parmenas who was a strong Protestant Christian leader from the American-run Inland Mission at Kijabe. Parmenas Kiritu later became a leader of the Torch Bearers, a group of 'loyalist' Africans organized by prominent Europeans in the Naivasha District. When Parmenas began to hear about the new movement and the oath which it used, he considered that it was anti-Christian. He therefore began to speak out against it in his sermons. Parmenas knew how Kikuyu children sometimes shouted the anagram 'Mau Mau'. He made use of this traditional habit to pour scorn on the movement as a childish thing. Then many people who did not know about the Society started to use these words which soon spread over the country.

I must make it clear that it did not have any special name; the world knows it by a title of abuse and ridicule with which it was described by one of its bitterest opponents. Parmenas Kiritu was awarded the B.E.M. for his services to the Government. In the light of all this it is ironical indeed that Kenyatta should have been convicted in a court of law for managing the 'Mau Mau' Society.

CHAPTER III

The Oath

I HAVE myself taken the oath twice. On the evening of 20 December 1953 a friend of mine called Kanyoi Githenji, who had been my school mate at K.I.S.A. Kabati-ini School, came to see me at Wangui's hut. He invited me to come over to his house and drink a cup of tea with him. While we were drinking he went out several times and once I heard him asking someone outside if they had a *mukuha*. This is an instrument like a pin used for removing jiggers (an insect which bores into the feet) or mending broken calabashes. When it was dark he suggested we went for a walk together. After going about three hundred yards along a narrow path into the fields we suddenly came upon some men and women sitting down in the maize on our left and I saw immediately to the right an arch between six and seven feet high, made of two banana stems joined at the top and plaited with bean stalks and the leaves of the *mugere* bush.

I was very surprised to see banana stems as to the best of my knowledge there were no banana plantations in this part of the Rift Valley Province but Kanyoi told me that they had been cut in Kabatini Forest from the *shamba* of a man called Kaburu Chege who was known to me and who had lived there in the forest for many years. It was clear to me that this was where the oath would be given. Kanyoi had been behaving strangely throughout the evening and in some ways I think I had begun much earlier to guess what was about to happen. I was told to move over to a place where three other people who were all known to me were standing. We were to take the oath together. We were then ordered to remove our shoes and our watches and any other metal things we had with us. Kanyoi pointed at me and told the people that I was a student from school who seemed to have a sincere wish to help the country and had been very active in persuading people to join the Kenya African Union. He believed that I was, therefore, the right sort of person to be given the Oath of Unity, *Ndemwa Ithatu*, as I was

25

4

likely to be just as active in serving this movement as I had been in K.A.U. The other three who were in my group were hit about a little, but because of Kanyoi's remarks about me the people said: 'Do not beat the student', and I was left alone. We passed through the arch seven times in single file and then stood silently in a line facing the oath administrator, whose name was Biniathi, waiting for the next part of the ceremony.

Biniathi held the lungs of a goat in his right hand and another piece of goat's meat in his left. We bowed towards the ground as he circled our heads seven times with the meat, counting aloud in Kikuyu. He then gave each of us in turn the lungs and told us to bite them. Next he ordered us to repeat slowly after him the following sentence:

> I speak the truth and vow before God
> And before this movement,
> The movement of Unity,
> The Unity which is put to the test
> The Unity that is mocked with the name of 'Mau Mau',
> That I shall go forward to fight for the land,
> The lands of Kirinyaga that we cultivated,
> The lands which were taken by the Europeans
>> And if I fail to do this
>> May this oath kill me,
>> May this seven kill me,
>> May this meat kill me.

> I speak the truth that I shall be working together
> With the forces of the movement of Unity
> And I shall help it with any contribution for which I
>> am asked,
> I am going to pay sixty-two shillings and fifty cents
>> and a ram for the movement
> If I do not have them now I shall pay in the future.
>> And if I fail to do this
>> May this oath kill me,
>> May this seven kill me,
>> May this meat kill me.

I was given a box on the ears for failing to repeat one sentence correctly. It was delivered by the administrator's assistant, who was standing beside him holding a gourd full of the blood of the goat used for the ceremony. Biniathi anointed each of us on the forehead with the blood, saying that he did this to remind us that we were now fighting for our land and to warn us never to think of selling our country.

After this Biniathi came to each of us individually and made three tiny scratches on our left wrists. This was the meaning of *Ndemwa Ithatu* (the three cuts) and it also explained Kanyoi's earlier search for a *Mukuha*. He then brought the other piece of meat to our wrists so that a few drops of our blood went on to it. Next he gave us in turn the meat to bite and while we were doing this he said, 'The act of eating this meat with the blood of each one of you on it shows that you are now united one to the other and with us.' This was the end of the ceremony and all four of us then went over to sit down with Kanyoi who wrote out our names and asked us to give him the five shillings special oathing fee, which we all did. We then went to wait among the other people in the maize and our shoes and watches were returned to us.

My emotions during the ceremony had been a mixture of fear and elation. Afterwards in the maize I felt exalted with a new spirit of power and strength. All my previous life seemed empty and meaningless. Even my education, of which I was so proud, appeared trivial beside this splendid and terrible force that had been given me. I had been born again and I sensed once more the feeling of opportunity and adventure that I had had on the first day my mother started teaching me to read and write. The other three in the maize were all silent and were clearly undergoing the same spiritual rebirth as myself.

Biniathi was aged about forty and was of medium height and build. Four of his front teeth were missing. He wore a black coat and grey trousers, a black, yellow and grey check shirt and no tie. No one of our people at Bahati knew how to administer the oath and he had recently come from Kiambu District to help. After each ceremony he used to receive such money as the local committee (*athuri a kirira*) of which I was not a member, decided. He was an excellent oath administrator and a humble man who gave very good advice to people on their problems and difficulties.

I asked Kanyoi if it was right for me to continue recruiting for K.A.U. He told me that K.A.U. was a completely different

organization from this one but that some of those at the
ceremony were also members of it. There was no objection to
my carrying on with K.A.U. but I should be careful not to tell
any of the K.A.U. people about my membership of this other
movement, which must remain secret. Kanyoi, whom I now
looked upon as my teacher, also warned us not to sleep with a
woman for seven days after the ceremony. If we wanted to
know if someone we met had taken the oath we should ask
them 'Where were you circumcised?' If the person gives a
normal truthful answer to this question we would know that he
had not taken the oath. Should the answer, however, be 'I was
circumcised at Karimania's with Karimania' this would be
sufficient sign that the person had taken the oath. I had never
heard the word 'Karimania' used as a name before. It can be
translated 'to turn the soil over and over' as in cultivation and
it is the word used for this in the oath.

I had slept that night at Kanyoi's house. I did not talk much
as my head was still full of the promises I had made at the
ceremony. In the morning, after eating some porridge with
Kanyoi, I returned to my aunt's house. Some days later I
informed Kanyoi that the time had come for me to return to
Nakuru and he asked me to come and visit him on the Sunday
before I left. I met Biniathi there and another man called
Muthee, who later went to fight in the forest and was killed
by an ambush of the King's African Rifles when he was
searching for food. We spent the day quietly, discussing politics
and our land grievances, especially the barriers to African
ownership of land in the White Highlands. We had the sense of
frustration about this that the owner of a house would feel if he
were turned out by a guest he had innocently welcomed. In the
evening we all went to another house where some people had
been skinning a goat. We sat down and Biniathi then told us to
take all our clothes off except our trousers, and we stood
patiently waiting to be called by him. I was called second after
Kanyoi and there was no disobeying the summons.

I took off my trousers and squatted facing Biniathi. He told
me to take the thorax of the goat which had been skinned, to
put my penis through a hole that had been made in it and to
hold the rest of it in my left hand in front of me. Before me on
the ground there were two small wooden stakes between which

the thorax (*ngata*) of the goat was suspended and fastened. By my right hand on the floor of the hut were seven small sticks each about four inches long. Biniathi told me to take the sticks one at a time, to put them into the *ngata* and slowly rub them in it while repeating after him these seven vows, one for each stick. (After each promise I was to bite the meat and throw the stick on to the ground on my left side.)

1. I speak the truth and vow before our God
   And by this *Batuni* oath of our movement
   Which is called the movement of fighting
   That if I am called on to kill for our soil
   If I am called on to shed my blood for it
   I shall obey and I shall never surrender
   And if I fail to go
   > May this oath kill me,
   > May this he-goat kill me,
   > May this seven kill me,
   > May this meat kill me.

2. I speak the truth and vow before our God
   And before our people of Africa
   That I shall never betray our country
   That I shall never betray anybody of this movement to the
   enemy
   Whether the enemy be European or African
   And if I do this
   > May this oath kill me, etc.

3. I speak the truth and vow before our God
   That if I am called during the night or the day
   To go to burn the store of a European who is our enemy
   I shall go forth without fear and I shall never surrender
   And if I fail to do this
   > May this oath kill me, etc.

4. I speak the truth and vow before our God
   That if I am called to go to fight the enemy
   Or to kill the enemy—I shall go
   Even if the enemy be my father or mother, my brother or
   sister
   And if I refuse
   > May this oath kill me, etc.

5. I speak the truth and vow before our God
    That if the people of the movement come to me by day or
        night
    And if they ask me to hide them
    I shall do so and I shall help them
    And if I fail to do this
        May this oath kill me, etc.

6. I speak the truth and vow before our God
    That I shall never take away the woman of another man
    That I shall never walk with prostitutes
    That I shall never steal anything belonging to another
        person in the movement
    Nor shall I hate any other member for his actions
    And if I do any of these things
        May this oath kill me, etc.

7. I speak the truth and vow before our God
    And by this *Batuni* oath of our movement
    That I shall never sell my country for money or any other
        thing
    That I shall abide until my death by all the promises that
        I have made this day
    That I shall never disclose our secrets to our enemy
    Nor shall I disclose them to anybody who does not belong
        to the movement
    And if I transgress against any of the vows that I have thus
        consciously made
    I shall agree to any punishment that the movement shall
        decide to give me
    And if I fail to do these things
        May this oath kill me, etc.

When I had said all these things I removed the thorax and
laid it on the ground, put on my trousers and went to another
part of the hut where I paid to Kanyoi six shillings and fifty
cents, which was the oathing fee. Thus it was that I took the
second or *Batuni* oath. This word seems to be derived from the
English 'platoon' and the oath itself was taken by all those who
were likely to be called on to give active service to the movement.
    This second oath was much stronger than the first and left
my mind full of strange and excited feelings. My initiation was

now complete and I had become a true Kikuyu with no doubts
where I stood in the revolt of my tribe. Complete secrecy had
again been enjoined on us as even some of those administering
the first oath had not yet taken the *Batuni*. After the ceremony
I returned to my aunt's hut for the night. Three days later I
went to Nakuru to stay with Obadiah Mwaniki, the man who
had come to our house with a bicycle so many years before. He
was still a staunch Christian and President of the Nakuru
African Court and because he was a Christian, and because of
the promises I made in the oath, I did not tell him what had
been happening. Although there was no clause in the oath
which forbade me to go to church or to remain a Christian,
ever since the time of my first oath my belief in the God of
Christ had been fading and I no longer went to church services
without an ulterior reason. However, since Obadiah was so
militant a Christian, while staying with him I went to church
every Sunday lest he should become suspicious or angry.

The *Muma wa Thenge* (the he-goat oath) is a prominent
feature of our social life, an integral part of the ceremonies
uniting partners in marriages, in the exchange or sale of land
(before the Europeans came, when land was plentiful, the sale of
land was almost unknown), or in transactions involving cattle
or goats. The warriors also took an oath, known as *Muma wa
Aanake* (the oath of the warriors) to bind them before going on a
raid. The purpose of all these oaths was to give those partici-
pating a feeling of mutual respect, unity and shared love, to
strengthen their relationship, to keep away any bad feelings
and to prevent any disputes. Most important of all, groups
bound together by this ceremony would never invoke sorcery
against each other. The fear of being killed by sorcery was
prevalent among our people. The *muma* (oath) removed that
fear and created a new and special relationship between the
families and clans involved. Envy, hate and enmity would be
unknown between them.

The Oath of Unity (given the mysterious and sinister name
of 'Mau Mau' by a cunning propaganda machine) had the same
background. It was intended to unite not only the Kikuyu,
Embu and Meru but all the other Kenya tribes. These might
not give their oaths in the same way, but every tribe in Kenya
had an oath for bringing together and solemnizing certain

transactions. It is not really surprising that the movement should have started first among the Kikuyu. They more than any other tribe felt the despair brought by pressing economic poverty; they more than any other tribe by their proximity to the forcing house of Nairobi were subject to urban pressures and the great increase in understanding and frustration brought by education; they more than any other tribe daily saw the lands that had been taken from them producing rich fruits for Europeans.

There is no question that at times the oath was forced upon people who did not wish to take it, though these were nothing like so many as the Government spokesmen would have had us believe: it was important for them to conceal from the outside world the real springs and motives of the Movement. It is also true that by 1953 and 1954 severe punishment sometimes including death was meted out by the courts of the Movement to those whom it considered traitors or spies. This was not the first political organization, nor will it be the last, which has been driven to set up its own judicial system parallel to that of the state. We had rejected the authority of the Kenya Government. We had organized in its place another Government, accepted by the large majority of our people, which was compelled to undertake in its infancy a desperate battle for survival, with the odds weighted most heavily against it. It is not surprising that the leaders insisted on military discipline or that failure to join and obey were considered most serious crimes against our Government. Nothing but absolute unity, implicit obedience and a sublime faith in our cause could bring victory against the guns, the armies, the money and the brains of the Kenya Government. It was a war for our homes, our land and our country in which the price of failure was death.

Many false notions have spread round the world about these oaths. It is said that a book has been placed in the library of the House of Commons describing the unnatural and obscene practices supposedly indulged in during the ceremonies. Some people are alleged to have been given as many as fourteen oaths, each one more foul and disgusting than the last. The two oaths which I have described above were the only legitimate ones. Naturally, as there was no central control of the organization, there were minor variations in the different districts and oath administrators did not everywhere use exactly the same technique.

The stories of the widespread use of the menstrual blood of women, of bestial intercourse with animals, of the eating of the embryos of unborn children ripped from their mothers' wombs, all these are either fabrications or, if anyone can prove any truth in them (and they have not yet done so to my satisfaction) they must have been confined to a minute number of perverted individuals driven crazy by their isolation in the forests. To imply that these sorts of oaths were indulged in wholesale by most of the Kikuyu tribe is like saying that all Englishmen are child-rapers and murderers simply because a few Englishmen do this every year.

In our society the sacredness of the menstrual blood is impressed on our young men and women by their mentors (*Atiiri*) at the time of circumcision. Abuse of it was a sin (*thahu*) which led to barrenness and other disasters and could only be purified in a most solemn ceremony. No Kikuyu leader in his senses would make use of such an ominous substance in a movement which could in no way afford to flaunt the spirits of our ancestors.

The 'evidence' containing these stories was largely compiled from confessions made in statements given either immediately after physical torture or in the knowledge that such torture was possible and indeed imminent. It is doubtful whether any court of law in the world would accept such evidence. During all the time I was in detention never once did I tell the whole truth as I am setting it down now, although six times screeners laboriously wrote out my false confessions which had been forced out of me. There is a Kikuyu proverb, '*Njita murume*', which is to say that when you knock someone about even if you ask him to call you God, he will do so; but the truth is still that you are not God.

Before the declaration of the Emergency in October 1952 there was no *Batuni* Oath in existence in any part of the Rift Valley. It may have been operating in the Reserves before then; I do not know. But in detention I met many of the leaders arrested in 1952 in the first major pick-up operation, which was given the code name of 'Jock Scott'. Not one of them had taken the second *Batuni* Oath and some had not even taken the first one.

We have a proverb, *Mwana angiguikiria ruhiu nawe ndukoe umuikirie*, which is to say, 'If a child throws a panga at you, do not throw it back because you will then appear much more foolish than the child, who may injure you with it'. In the early days of the Emergency the young men in the forest were armed only with spears and *simis*. Instead of political talks the Kenya Government brought against them the Bren guns and grenades of the Lancashire Fusiliers, the Kenya Regiment and the King's African Rifles. They gave no hope to those in the forest in those early days that there would be any other choice save between fighting or being killed. So the forces in the forests organized raids for weapons and bound themselves together with the *Batuni* Oath in the face of the overwhelming strength against them. In the beginning a deep faith in the ultimate truth and justice of their cause was the only weapon they had with which to oppose the Security Forces of the Government.

The first vital task was to get arms and ammunition. Prostitutes in the garrison towns of Kenya willingly gave their bodies to the Government troops for two rounds of ammunition which were passed down the tenuous supply lines to the fighters in the forest. Some of the soldiers in the King's African Rifles were not beyond selling arms direct and this was arranged through Kikuyu sympathizers working in civilian capacities in the military barracks. Soon the search for guns led to the insecure armouries on the isolated European farms in the Highlands. The sporadic murders of Europeans in these early days were usually an incidental part of raids primarily aimed at getting weapons. The armies in the forest also began to make their own guns out of bicycle frames, water piping, door bolts and rubber. Bombs were made out of bottles and explosives stolen by the Passive Wing out of Government stores. At first these home-made weapons often misfired with disastrous effects on their makers.

The Passive Wing was the name used by the Government to describe the hundreds of thousands of most unpassive sympathizers who organized the arms and ammunition, food and medical supplies which kept our armies in the forests fighting. By the end of 1953 this secret organization had reached a standard which can seldom have been equalled. We had even penetrated into Government House and G.H.Q. and there was

little that went on in any District Commissioner's Office in
Central Province without our knowledge. Convalescent homes
were set up for our wounded within yards of Government
dispensaries. Nearly every Home Guard Post was packed with
our men.

As time went on, stronger and stronger forces, including
thousands of British troops and bombing aeroplanes, were
brought against our troops in the forests who slowly became
desperate men, whose souls were filled with the hatred born
on both sides in the travail of any war. They were being shown
no quarter and so they gave none. Out of dire necessity the
groups of largely illiterate peasants who went into the forests
became, under their great generals, experts at guerrilla warfare,
and they defied the might of Britain and Kenya for four years.
It is tragic to consider now how all this could have been avoided
by a few minor political concessions. At that time a statement,
even, that Britain would free Jomo Kenyatta and give the
Africans of Kenya their Independence in 1965 would have been
sufficient to stop the fighting and bring the young men out of
the forest.

I was never in the forest myself but I hope that the true story
of the glorious fight of the armies in the Aberdares and Mount
Kenya forests will be written soon by someone who was. It is a
calamity that Dedan Kimathi was executed and is not with us
now to tell it, but perhaps Waruhiu Itote, General China, one
day will do so. None of us can accept the bias and inaccuracies
in the life of Dedan Kimathi, the greatest hero of us all, given
in Ian Henderson's book, *The Hunt for Kimathi*.

One of the aspects of the Emergency that foreigners seemed
least able to understand was the behaviour of the Kikuyu
women. They would lovingly feed and care for the other needs
of the forest armies all night and in the morning flatly deny
that anyone had been there should a Government officer come
inquiring. Yet, later in the same day, they would go out,
apparently cheerful, and obey the Government orders to dig
the huge ditches filled with bamboo stakes and designed to
create an impenetrable barrier between the forest and the native
Reserves. They would also build the massively fortified posts on
which the loyalist Home Guard based themselves. Later, as time
went on, they turned out in their thousands to sweep through

patches of forest and arrest any of our soldiers they found there. Is there any explanation of these apparently contradictory attitudes?

First, there is no doubt that ninety per cent. of the women of the Kikuyu tribe supported the fight for Freedom and Independence with their minds, their bodies and their souls. It is false to think that this support was confined to a few educated leaders. Secondly, during the early days of the Emergency the large majority of the women came to support the Movement that was being ridiculed as 'Mau Mau'. With the arrest of Jomo Kenyatta they realized that peaceful means of achieving their aims had failed and they accepted the alternative of violence fully realizing the suffering it would bring on all of them. At the same time there were a few women who supported the Government—some, for example, but not all of the wives of the Home Guards, certain Christian women who (as was also true of some men) genuinely valued their love of God higher than their love of country, and others who had personal motives. Since unity was our strongest weapon, all such people became enemies of the Movement. It was not that we were anti-Christian, merely that the struggle on earth was so desperate that Christianity could not be allowed to interfere. We had also noted that our enemies, in their cunning, were using it as a weapon against us. We considered it should not be degraded in this way.

Now the first duty of the majority, who were on our side, was to help the people of the forest. In many cases this duty was strengthened by family obligations since most of them had husbands, fathers, brothers or sons in the Land Freedom Armies, and there is no greater social crime among the Kikuyu than refusing food to members of your family. At the same time they had to help the Government, which had by now become so tough in the Reserves that, if they failed to obey their Chief's orders, they would be severely punished. It is not true to say that the majority feared the Movement; they feared the Government represented by the Chiefs, the headmen and the Home Guards. They obeyed the orders given by the Government but with a heavy heart: sometimes in the interests of the Movement they would appear to be enjoying a task, which in reality they detested, such as a sweep or digging a ditch.

At the beginning of the Emergency there were hardly any Loyalists or Home Guards. Here and there a few individuals, chiefs, wealthy traders, owners of property, tribal police and anyone else who had a vested interest in British government remaining, stood out against the Movement. Many others who were frightened of the strength of the opposing forces sat on the fence and a few, but very few, had real misgivings of conscience about obtaining our Independence in this violent way and felt the British should be given a while longer to show their good faith. The Government quickly realized that the only chance of defeating the Land Freedom Armies in the forest was to divide the Kikuyu tribe. This it proceeded to do on political, religious and social levels until the Emergency rapidly turned into a civil war than which no kind of conflict creates deeper hatreds. Neither the land, the property nor the family of a revolutionary were spared and the less noble of our tribe soon found, as collaborators have throughout history, it was more comfortable for the body, if not the spirit, on the side of the big battalions. The Government turned on all the propaganda it could to persuade the people that those in the forest only wished to kill everyone else. They in their turn heard about all these reprisals and became correspondingly tougher and more uncompromising. Such a war could only end in the virtual extermination of one side or the other. The shoot-at-sight policy of the Security Forces is vividly reflected in the casualty figures given in the *Corfield Report* which show 11,503 'terrorists' killed in comparison with 2,044 in the security forces. These figures exclude those who were executed in prisons or died in detention camps.

The Home Guard were known throughout Central Province as the *Kamatimu*. In Kikuyu customs there were two grades of Elder. The senior grade was made up of all those who had paid the *mburi ya ihaki* ('the goat of the grade'), which was the ceremonial fee to mark your acceptance. The lower grade was known as *Kamatimu* and consisted of all those who had not yet proved acceptable to the higher grade and had thus not yet paid their goats. The fighters in the forest therefore gave them this insulting name as people of a lower rank, who cannot undergo the hardships of the struggle but have sought the shelter of the enemy and are not worthy of acceptance. As these Home Guards were usually armed with spears (although they were

eventually issued with thousands of rifles) and *Kamatimu* literally
means 'the little people who carry spears', the name was doubly
appropriate.

Great use has been made of the accusations that the 'Mau
Mau' killed thousands of civilians in Nairobi and the Reserves
and then pushed them down latrine pits. The events at Lari
in March 1953 have become widely described as a massacre.
Although no one denies that the 'Mau Mau' courts sentenced
some traitors and enemies to death this is not the first time in
the history of the world that a revolutionary movement has been
forced to behave in this way. I have heard many detainees in the
camps discussing how some people were also murdered by the
loyalists for personal reasons or because of land disputes. Others
were the victims of ordinary robbers. Such murders could very
easily be put down to 'Mau Mau' and consequently never be
properly investigated by the C.I.D. Even the events at Lari are
not as simple as the Government tried to make them appear.
A Dutch sociologist who made a study of the area came to some
surprising conclusions about this 'massacre'. Her report was
given a limited circulation and then withdrawn by the Christian
Council of Kenya for reasons which were never made public.

As through the years we were joined in detention by
thousands of Passive Wing members and fighters captured in
the forest, we learnt of one way in which the Home Guard
had done well. The 'Johnnies', British Army soldiers, naturally
found it impossible to tell the difference between a 'Mau Mau'
Kikuyu and any other since neither side had any special
identification marks. Fortunately the Home Guards used to
accompany the troops on their patrols and try to prevent them
killing ordinary civilians. Even so, many accidents happened
and hundreds of harmless people were killed ; we were especially
saddened in detention to hear that an Othaya lunatic called
Karoki had been shot dead because he did not understand that
a curfew meant that he could not walk at night near his home.
However, we decided, when the Emergency was over, that the
detainees would not allow any revenge on these Home Guards
because they had at least tried to save many people. Most
Home Guards had, anyway, taken the oath and several used
secretly to help as much as they could. We have a Kikuyu
proverb, *Tutikuhe hiti keeri*, which is to say, 'Let us not give a

hyaena two meals'. When a man was killed in olden times his body was given to the hyaenas. To kill his killer as well would help no one except the hyaenas and so we did not do this. This decision by all those who suffered during the Emergency is the reason why peace has now returned to the Kikuyu people. Two of the strongest leaders of the Home Guards were Senior Chief Muhoya, B.E.M., of Nyeri District, and Senior Chief Njiri, O.B.E., of Fort Hall. Muhoya has two sons who are both in Secondary Schools teaching the future leaders of our country; Njiri's son became one of the two Members for Legislative Council for Fort Hall District, later giving up his seat in December 1961 so that Kenyatta could enter Legislative Council. There can be no profit in harming such people by taking vengeance on their fathers, nor will the spirit of revenge help us to harvest the real fruits of Independence, which will only be gathered in a spirit of tolerance, restraint and co-operation.

When I visited Ghana in August 1961 one of the big men there asked me what would now be the reward of the true nationalists who had suffered so much in the forests and the detention camps. He also stressed how much we must hate those loyalists who had sided with the Europeans in the struggle. I answered him with one of our proverbs: *Ndurumi irima tiyo ndari kuo*, which literally means 'That which digs the hole does not spend the night there'. It is the ant-bear which digs the hole in search of white ants and when it has found them and eaten them it leaves the hole for porcupines and other wild animals to sleep in. It is only human for those who struggled hardest to expect to reap the first rewards of freedom, but there will be more than enough for all and the ant-bear and the porcupine will not fight or kill one another.

We do not expect or need any more bloodshed in Kenya with the achievement of Independence though we will have to remain on our guard against neo-colonialism and imperialism. When a wart-hog gives birth to its young it behaves in the following strange way. It charges furiously with all its force, using its tough head like a battering-ram against a *mukuyu* (fig tree). The fruits of the tree are thus knocked down and provide food for its newborn young while the poor mother lies for several hours unconscious in its travail, in some cases unable ever to

rise again. This is what the fighters for freedom did for our
people and the generation yet unborn. Perhaps we shall yet be
called on again for similar sacrifices before all our people in
Africa, especially South Africa, are finally free again.

After these digressions I must go back to my story. When I
had taken the second oath I returned to Nakuru and resumed
my work for K.A.U., frequently hiring a bicycle to visit nearby
farms and villages trying to get new recruits for the party. In
January 1953 John Kamonjo, the leader of K.A.U. in Nakuru,
was arrested near his father's house which had been used for an
oath ceremony at which one of those present had refused to be
initiated. Some of the young men acting as stewards had tried
to frighten him into agreeing by putting a strangling rope round
his neck. When the threat was not sufficient they released him
and he went straight to the police. John, although he had
nothing to do with this episode, was included in the subse-
quent pick-up. From that day there was no official chairman of
K.A.U. in the town, nor did the organization have any proper
office; in fact in Nakuru it virtually disappeared. On 8 June
1953 the Kenya Government legally proscribed K.A.U., thus
leaving the African people no alternative save secret activities
or capitulation.

I had no official position in the other movement, but Muthee,
who had taken the *Batuni* Oath with me, had by now gone to
fight in the forest and had spread the news that I was a reliable
person. So groups from the forest in need of help would visit
me from time to time. Once a party came from the Aberdares,
led by a Meru in a smart police inspector's uniform and I was
happy to be able to assist them with money, boots and safe
quarters for the night. Some sympathizers on the railway staff
provided me with a railway guard's uniform and I had no
difficulty in travelling freely in this way to Eldoret and Kisumu
in the guard's van. This enabled me to help in the development
of our communications system and to act as a liaison officer
between groups in these areas.

In June 1953 I began to run a hotel in Nakuru which was
very successful. By now the Government had set up screening
camps, one at Molo, one at Kampi ya Simba outside Thomson's Falls and one at Kwa Nyangwethu near Bahati. These
camps were run by Europeans assisted by Kikuyu screening

elders chosen from the Home Guards. Soon we heard rumours about the harsh methods used in them. It is no part of the purpose of this book to rake up all the old stories of brutality in these screening camps : court cases through the years have adequately substantiated the facts. Kwa Nyangwethu was, however, particularly bad and was notorious not for mere beatings, but for castration. I have seen with my own eyes that Kongo Chuma whom I first met in Nakuru before he was detained and who is now living at Kiangai in Embu District, has been castrated. He had not been like this when he was in Nakuru but when we met in the detention camp at Athi River he told me it had been done to him by the screeners at Kwa Nyangwethu. He also told me that bottles of soda water were opened and pushed into the uterus of some women to make them confess. Kongo said these things were done by the Africans but the European officers knew what was going on.

So horrible were the stories rife about this camp while I was in Nakuru that I decided it was my duty to save as many of our people as possible from being sent there. I would find out from a Tribal Policeman called Solomon who had been at school with me in the days at Keruguoya in Embu whether any arrests were due to be made. If he knew the name of anyone likely to be picked up he would tell me and, if I knew the man, I would go to bribe the chief of the screening elders. The price varied from four hundred to six hundred shillings. Normally the victims would repay quickly but some could not afford these amounts and I used about one thousand shillings of my own money in this way.

Early in 1953 the European settlers decided that they must induce the Government to organize the repatriation from the Rift Valley to their Reserves of the hundreds of thousands of Kikuyu squatter families, who would be replaced by labour from other tribes. In Kenya's history there can seldom have been another single decision that brought such immediate misery and that it was taken shows that the situation had developed into the desperation of open war. One camp was established near the abattoir at Nakuru and another near the jail at Thomson's Falls. Then the Europeans began arbitrarily and relentlessly to move their labour from the farms to these camps where they lived, waiting for Government lorries to carry

them to Nyeri, Kiambu and Fort Hall. Rather than wait and
face the evil conditions of these camps many Kikuyu spent their
savings on hiring lorries to take them back to the Reserves. The
majority of the squatters had been born on the farms from
which they were being removed. They had never been to the
Reserves before, they owned no land there, they had no means
of livelihood, they would have to find the money to build a hut
or cram into already overcrowded houses, and many of them
did not even know the name of the place in the Reserves from
which their ancestors had come.

They were not allowed to take their cattle or sheep and goats
with them, nor were they allowed to wait to harvest the maize
which they had planted. The Labour Department would sell
both stock and crops and forward the proceeds to their new
District Commissioners for distribution to them 'in due course'.
I think that this repatriation aggravated beyond measure the
embryo sense of hopelessness and insecurity in the souls of our
people.

Complaint about the ways in which the operation was being
handled came to me daily and so I decided to go to see for
myself what was happening at Leshau, which was a collecting
centre near a main road. I did not dare stay watching for long
lest I be arrested, but I saw the lorries and some labourers
loading them under the supervision of European settlers. These
labourers were throwing small children up on to the lorries as
if they were bundles of firewood and they often landed heavily
on the floorboards. The cries of the children that day seemed
like sounds out of hell and the air smelt of hatred. I was glad
to get back to Nakuru.

My aunt, Wangui, and my blind stepbrother, Obadiah
Mwangi, decided that things were getting so bad that they
would go back to stay with my mother and Gathoni at Chinga.
I hired a lorry for 399 shillings to take them there and the driver
reported to me that they had arrived safely. I was sad at having
to say good-bye to my aunt who had helped me so much. Later
they sent me letters which said that in Kikuyu country the
people were getting many troubles and the young men were
being beaten by the Government security forces so much that
they were running away into the forest in large numbers.

When the first 'sweep' was organized in Nakuru in January

1953 I was arrested but fortunately, when we were taken to the place for questioning, I met a Meru constable called Baiti who had long been a friend of mine. He took me to his tent to drink some water and I asked him to help me. Like many others in the Kenya Police he was sympathetic to our cause and he knew I was not a really bad man. He told me to lie on the bed and he covered me with blankets. What with the sun and the tent and the blankets the sweat streamed off me but I was safe and in the evening when the operation was over Baiti and I walked out arm in arm through the gates. We went to the cinema and saw *King Solomon's Mines* together, and after this I gave him a drink. I learnt later that many other people escaped from that operation, some by bribing the constables and others by hiding in the bucket latrines after tipping the ordure outside the door so that the police walked hurriedly past in disgust, holding their noses. One day I managed to get a pistol from a soldier in the King's African Rifles at Lanet for three hundred shillings. I passed it on to Gakeri with instructions to give it to Gathego Thuo and Kimani who were going into the forest to fight. Tragically they were arrested at Njoro shortly afterwards by a Home Guard and later sentenced to several years' imprisonment each.

There was another big operation in June 1953 but luckily some of my friends in the police warned me about it. In view of the importance of my activities it seemed wise to avoid getting arrested and so the night before it was due I went to Nakuru cemetery where my mother's friend, Zacharia Ndung'u, had a lean-to shack made of tins inside the walls. He worked as a gardener for an Asian called Farrah Mahomed. Tribally, Zacharia was a second father to me and he could not refuse to give me shelter. As I had expected, none of the police bothered to search the cemetery. After the operation was finished I returned to Nakuru and I heard that large numbers had been arrested; many of my friends I did not see again until we were reunited in detention camps.

Soon after starting my hotel I also bought two bicycles which were hired out at a shilling an hour or twelve shillings a day. The man who looked after this side of the business received sixty shillings a month. He chauffeured those who could not ride themselves. At the end of the month, when people received their wages, it was possible to get fifteen to eighteen shillings a day, but I allowed him to keep anything over twelve shillings.

At a quarter to one on 28 October 1953 an Inspector, an African, of the Special Branch of the Kenya Police came into my hotel. It was just over a year after the declaration of a State of Emergency and the arrest of Jomo Kenyatta. As was usual at this time the place was crowded with men and women who had come to hear the newspapers read. This job was now being done by Ngahu Mara, from Fort Hall, my assistant in the hotel. He had succeeded Gibson Gichuri who had read very well but had been sentenced to three years' imprisonment after the operation in June. The court which heard his case had been held in the screening camp near the abattoir and I had been told by some who had escaped from there that the justice was rough. The method of deciding whether three or six years was an adequate sentence seemed arbitrary and the prisoners were not allowed to defend themselves. Gibson was the proud possessor of a certificate signed by Kenyatta which showed that he had passed his examination at Githunguri College, Kenyatta's own school in Kiambu. This certificate he soon stopped showing to prospective employers. He was my close friend and used to stay in my hotel while looking for the work which he never got.

The Inspector had two constables with him and he told me quietly that I was wanted in Police Headquarters. This could only mean that I was going to be detained. I went with him. At the appearance of the police, the newspaper reading had stopped and the people were quiet and sad at my going. I told them they should not worry. At Nakuru Police Headquarters I was informed that I would now be detained indefinitely under the Emergency Regulations and that I would be sent to a camp called Kowop in the far north of Samburu District. After being fingerprinted I was asked a series of questions. Did I play golf? Did I drink or smoke? Did I go with prostitutes? Was I married? Did I go to horse-racing? I then went back under arrest to the hotel to collect my clothes and other belongings. I also decided to take with me £140 which was the profit I had got in the six months since I started running the hotel, and clothes, and about ten books on history, English, geography and politics.

My friends among the police at Nakuru saw that I was

comfortable in my cell there while we waited for transport to
Kowop. After two days the journey started and another two
weeks later, with further stops at Thomson's Falls and Maralal
police stations, we jerked and bumped our way into the camp
at Kowop. As the lorry stopped inside the wire we were surrounded by detainees eager to recognize us. With a great whoop
of joy John Kamonjo, the former Chairman of the Nakuru
Branch of the Kenya African Union, greeted me. I was again
among friends. Strange places do not matter if you are with old
companions.

CHAPTER IV

The Camp of the Three Dry Hills

KOWOP was a small tented camp in the valley between three rocky hills. It was twenty-five miles north of Baragoi and about sixty from Lake Rudolf. Near Ngiro Hill there is good grass on which the nomadic tribes of the Samburu and the Turkana seasonally pasture their herds and flocks. Sometimes from the desolate and stormy landscape a group of their living huts (*manyatta*) would emerge like upside-down birds' nests, so flat and shallow that no one could stand up in them. Although Kowop was in Samburu District, many Turkana also came there and the two tribes existed side by side amicably enough. The climate was dry and hot and very different from Kikuyuland or the Rift Valley. There was no water anywhere except in a borehole from which it came with a taste of sulphur. Skin washed in this water with soap looked afterwards as if it had been smeared with lime, and many of the detainees got severe diarrhoea after drinking. I stayed in this camp until 20 August 1954 when it was closed down.

In the beginning there were only thirty-six of us there. We were very proud of our status as detained persons as opposed to convicted prisoners. This meant that we did not have to work except on our own chores; we could wear our own clothes; we could keep our money and we were allowed to wander freely about the compound in the evening. There was only one barbed wire fence around the perimeter, and this was so loose that goats could easily hop in and out if the wire was held open for them. No one seemed to be in the least worried that we should escape. Later we learnt the reason why. The Turkana said that they had been told by the District Commissioner that we Kikuyu were very disgusting people whose custom it was to eat the breasts of our women and even the embryos of children in the womb. Any Turkana or Samburu who brought him the head of an escaped detainee would be rewarded with *posho*, sugar and tea. When the Gold Coast was fighting for its

46

Independence, Muturi and some other farmers used to tell
their labourers that Ghanaians were cannibals and ate their own
children. We became frightened in those days that *Ngorogothi*
(people from the Gold Coast) would come to eat us. It seems
that all Africans fighting for Independence ate their children
in the eyes of the Europeans in Kenya.[1] The people in Samburu
District are always hungry in their harsh and inhospitable
country and when they heard this many of them decided to
stay around in the three dry hills waiting for us to escape.

A small committee had already been established among the
first group of detainees under the leadership of Gad Kamau
Gathumbi, a Kiambu man who had a shop in Nakuru, and
Samuel Kiburi, a former police officer from Embu District.
(Gad is now a trader at Limuru and a strong K.A.N.U. leader
in the area.) A few rules had been made by the committee and
anyone who broke one of them was automatically fined a ram
(*ndurume*) which he had to buy from the Turkana and which
was then eaten by all the other detainees. Fighting in the compound was forbidden as was using insulting words to another
detainee. Orders issued by the committee for cleaning the camp
must be obeyed and anyone asked to help carry food from the
store must comply. Finally, no one was allowed to interfere
with Wanjiku, who was the only female detainee in the camp.
She was in a difficult position, especially as many of those
desiring her falsely promised they would marry her when they
were released. The committee were remarkably successful in
protecting her although a man called Thuo who went too far
had to pay a ram. We arranged ourselves to partition off a
separate place for her in the biggest tent so that she should not
have to sleep in the same place as the men.

The rations were excellent. We received six ounces of rice,
one pound of maize meal, half a pound of vegetables, half a
pound of beans, ten ounces of potatoes and two ounces of sugar
a day and every week two and a half pounds of meat and three
and a half ounces of tea. The medical treatment was poor. A
half-trained Turkana dresser was attached to the camp. He knew
how to prescribe some simple medicines like mist. Kaolin, mist.

---

[1] Cf. Kenneth Kaunda *Zambia shall be free*, p. 109. 'Villagers had been told that
these Zambia men were cannibals. They especially liked children since these
provided tender meat.'

culminative, and mist. soda sal., but that was all. Fortunately among the detainees there was a fully qualified hospital assistant called Timothy Mwangi from Fort Hall and under his instructions we arranged to buy for our own use in the compound supplies of any medicines needed from Baragoi. Timothy was taken back into the Medical Department after his release and has been working as a hospital assistant in his own district.

Kowop was the most pleasant of all the camps in which I was detained. Those of us who still had money found we lacked nothing, including the essential cigarettes and snuff. One of the police constables attached to the camp, a Luo called Joram, had been a great friend of mine in Nakuru. He was most upset at my detention and losing my business, and arranged for two newspapers, the *East African Standard* and *Baraza*, to be sent to the camp for me under his name. One of my jobs was to translate these into Kikuyu for the other detainees. Although the Government could not compel us to work, we were kept busy by the committee. Apart from running a course in English for Gad and a few of the others, I was also appointed the writer of official letters of complaint.

When I first reached Kowop the officer in charge was a European from the Kenya Police Reserve who was lame and so was given the Kikuyu nickname of 'Gathua'. He was a good and quiet man who spent most of his time in his house or his office. He did not like visiting us in the compounds. He never punished anyone nor did he quarrel with any of us. He was later shot by another European at Thomson's Falls in a drunken brawl and we were all very sad to hear this. Gathua had a Kenya-born European assistant who was not a good man and used to sleep with the Turkana women. One day we refused to eat some meat which had gone bad and this European assistant was frightened there might be a disturbance. He therefore informed the Thomson's Falls police and the next morning an Assistant Superintendent came out to see us. He was a hard man and spoke very toughly. He said that if we went on refusing to eat the meat we would be facing very bad trouble as sure as his name was Derby. He was frightened of nobody and nothing and he had been fighting and killing the 'Mau Mau' for a long time. We were only a little thing. He then called out Gad Kamau Gathumbi and told him to shave his beard. If Gad refused or

caused any more trouble he would take him out of the camp and
shoot him. He said that we grew beards because each of us was
pretending to be another Kenyatta. Well, Kenyatta and his
beard were now facing a very great trouble in a jail somewhere
else.

He may have been only threatening but some of the detainees
who had known him in Thomson's Falls thought he might well
shoot Gad. However, we remained absolutely silent and did
not give him any answer as we thought his speech extremely
stupid. The Camp Committee had ruled that Gad was our
spokesman on these occasions and if he remained silent everyone
else should. After Derby's departure Gathua came back and
spoke to us. He said that were Derby to return to the camp and
see us still with our beards, he would be in great trouble. He
appealed to us to shave them off. As the last thing anyone
wanted was to get Gathua into trouble we agreed to do so.
We grew beards because they help to make someone appear a
good politician and they enlarge one's personality before the
public. At Kowop we all tried to grow beards and it was a sad
day when they were taken off, especially for the old men.
Secretly I was highly amused, especially as for some reason or
another mine had refused to grow.

One day the committee decided that we should try to open
amicable relations with the Turkana and the Samburu. Twice
a week a lorry used to go out to collect firewood. So, filling our
pockets with *posho*, tea and sugar, we gave them away to any
Turkana we met. Slowly they began to trust us more and
became friendly. They soon told us why they had been so
reluctant to talk with us. The committee passed a regulation
forbidding anyone to sleep with the Turkana women and girls
and when their men heard about this they began to respect us.
It was difficult to talk politics with them and it was best done in
parables. We tried to show them that when the Africans ruled
Kenya the backward tribes would get much more help than the
British were giving them now.

I had one particular Turkana friend called Ashakala, who
was a rich and clever man and had once been in the army.
His Swahili was excellent. He had a wife and three grown-up
daughters and I became virtually a member of the family.
Whenever the lorry went out there was something on it for

them from me, either a cloth or some rice or sugar. Eventually
I decided that our relationship was so special that they should
be given the names of my mother and sisters in accordance
with the Kikuyu custom. So Ashakala's wife became Wanjiku
and the three daughters Nyakio, Njoki and Wangui. They were
overcome with happiness and pleasure and said that the new
names seemed as a blessing to them. I took some photographs
of them, which were confiscated at Manyani. On Christmas
Day 1953 we organized some traditional Kikuyu dances in the
camp and many Turkana came to see and enjoy them.

When the Turkana held big meetings it was surprising to me
that they did not skin the meat they were to eat, but, after
removing the head and the entrails, put it to roast on the fire
with its skin on like a potato in its jacket. They told me that
if they took the skin off all the fat would slide away and be lost
and so they did not strip it until it was cooked. Keeping my
counsel while we were actually eating the meat, afterwards I
approached some of them and tried to explain that the fat still
escaped just the same. They seemed to understand my explanation but I do not expect they are doing anything different now.
I also noticed that their women would take the meat from the
fire and place it on their goatskin cloaks which the husband
would then use as a table from which to eat. The Samburu
people, who circumcise, are more advanced than the Turkana,
who do not, and their customs resemble those of the Masai
with whom we Kikuyu have many features in common. The
Turkana were still capable of astonishment at our suits, at the
luminous dial of a watch and the fact that it ticks.

In December 1953 and January 1954 another one hundred
and ninety detainees were brought in relays to Kowop from
Nyeri and Embu and twenty-two small green tents came to
accommodate them. Half way through the move Gathua and
his assistant were transferred elsewhere and two new officers
came. The senior man was, I think, called Sampson (E). He
had been a member of the Metropolitan Police in London and
was a humble and friendly man, wholly lacking in malice. As
he did not know Swahili I used to interpret for him. His assistant
was another Kenya-born European. He was a large man called
Newbury and seemed slightly simple. His apparent lack of
brains led to his getting the nickname *Marebe* (Empty Tins). By

the middle of January all the new detainees had arrived and one day, when Sampson was away, Newbury told us that it was the Government's intention that they should dig the latrines which we had refused to dig because we were not convicted prisoners. We had now re-formed our committee to include representatives from the new intake and it consisted of Gad Gathumbi, Tiras Muchiri (from Kibutio, a village in South Tetu, Nyeri, and now a teacher and politician), Peterson Kariuki (who had been Chief of Location 14 in Fort Hall and is now a businessman), John Mwangi Gachuhi (formerly an African District Council clerk from Fort Hall, now a clerk with a business firm in Nairobi), John Kamonjo, Samuel Kiburi, and six other elders. This committee was unanimous that no one should agree to dig the latrines. I think Newbury had decided on this action off his own bat as Sampson would never have consented. We have a saying in Kikuyu, *Ndiri njega ndiringanaga na muthi mwega*, which is to say, 'A good pestle never has a good mortar', and certainly we never seemed to have two good officers at the same time.

Newbury had shovels, pickaxes and crowbars brought and ordered the new detainees to start work. Justus Kangethe Gachui, an old man who had been a teacher at Kagumo Secondary School, acted as the spokesman and said they were not going to work. Newbury kept them outside sitting in the burning sun all day until the return in the evening of Sampson, who was very angry with his assistant and ordered Justus and his group back into the camp, telling us that there was no law to compel them to work. He then employed some Turkana to dig the pits for wages. This was not the only time that we wondered at the difference between Europeans born in Kenya and those born in Europe: we began to think that some Kenya European parents must train their children to hate all Africans.

Sampson encouraged us to go hunting to supplement the meat ration and the lorry left for these expeditions loaded to capacity with policemen, Kikuyus and Turkanas. It was good sport and once we brought back the carcasses of two wildebeeste. The Turkana could run very fast and used to act as guides. On one occasion we went to Ashakala's house and joined in an unrestrained beer party, policemen, detainees and Turkana all together, and when we got back to the camp many of the group were drunk and behaved badly. As a result I proposed to the committee that they should proscribe beer-drinking. This was accepted by the elders and became a regulation.

Gad continued to be our leader. Although not educated he was honest, reasonable and a true patriot. He had rapidly proved himself a *muthamaki* in the meetings of detainees and he swiftly developed into a fine orator and an able arbitrator of the petty disputes brought up before him from time to time. (A *muthamaki* is the name given to someone who has proved himself a natural leader and a wise man by his contributions to public debates.) I had now been given the extra job of dividing up the rations and with the expansion of literacy classes I had little leisure time. Among the books brought by me from Nakuru was *Ten Africans* by Margery Perham and I used to translate the autobiographies in it to the detainees and this became the most popular leisure activity in the camp. I was very sad when the book was eventually confiscated from me by the authorities at Manyani Camp.

When the committee heard that two of the detainees in the camp had never actually taken the Oath of Unity, they asked Gitu Ngangu from Nakuru to give it to them. He agreed and chose as his assistant Ndemi Mukuria, a man from South Tetu in Nyeri, who was a strong patriot and had been a member of the Forty Group.[1] The Turkana sold us a sheep for the ceremony, which was the normal first Oath of Unity and contained no references to killing. The committee had found it necessary to appoint their own policemen to find out who was contravening the regulations and we were astonished one day at some documents which were found in the coat of one of the two given the oath. They were copies of letters written before his detention to the Special Branch in Thomson's Falls describing the hardening resistance to the Government in that area, and also a letter, not yet dispatched, containing full details of the oath ceremony in the camp. The committee decided to confiscate the documents and ostracize him. In a detention camp it is a very hard punishment if people refuse to speak to you. He was later removed to Thomson's Falls by the authorities. He must have been sent to spy on us.

[1] This was the group of young men circumcised in 1940, most of whom did their military service together in the 1939–45 War.

Some other Kikuyu women had joined Wanjiku at Kowop and they now had their own tent. The committee tightened the regulations but found that many devices were being used to evade them, including nocturnal assignments in the bathroom. We therefore sent a deputation to the Commandant and explained to him that the present arrangements were not good and suggesting that he should have a separate place constructed for them outside the wire. This improved the situation although some men continued trying unsuccessfully to find ways and means of meeting them until one day all the women were transferred from Kowop to Kamiti Prison in Kiambu District near Nairobi, where we heard that Nyamathira, their leader, later died.

On 14 February, when Sampson was again away, Newbury sent out an order that no one should leave his tent at night. If anyone wanted to go to the lavatory he should ask permission. We had always been allowed to wander around in the camp in the evenings and we had never abused this privilege and so we were angry. For some reason Newbury decided to go up the watch tower himself that night. The whole proceeding was childish and ignominious so we organized relays of people to stand outside their tents and the night was full of people shouting: 'Officer, I want permission'. 'To go where?' came the reply. 'To pass water', 'To Nairobi', 'To Kowop', 'For a drink', and many other less printable desires. It may all seem rather crude and childish, but then so was Newbury. At last he was so incensed that he fired his revolver twice, apparently into the air, and we returned to our tents. Next morning I told him he had done a bad thing and I wrote to the District Commissioner asking him to come and investigate the incident.

Once more Sampson was not pleased at Newbury's actions and sided with us when, as a result of my letter, the District Commissioner came to talk with us. The District Commissioner seemed to be a bitter man and he spoke very fiercely. But when he saw that we were not frightened of him he became much more human and answered quite politely the many questions we asked him. After his visit we were once again allowed to move freely about the camp. Sampson was a man in whom we had great faith. He used to inspect the camp every Saturday and we cleaned it for him thoroughly. While he was in the camp we had given him a detainee to cook for him. When he was transferred in April we were sad to see him go. Newbury went at the same time. The officer called Chester who took over was brutal and foolish. He hated speaking to any detainee and looked at us in wonder as if we were animals behind the wire in a zoo.

One day he came into the compound and told us that he was going to make us work. We refused. He then forcibly pulled one man, Ndung'u Njoroge, outside the camp. Ndung'u resisted violently and I went with others to help him. All the police blew their whistles and surrounded the camp. Chester came inside and spoke to us. He was very angry and said that if we did not work our rations would be reduced. We were still adamant and from that day our rations were reduced by more than half. We began to hate Chester. Soon about twenty of our weaker brethren agreed to work out of sheer hunger. The committee then called a meeting and it was decided that unity was more important in this instance than standing on principles and so we reached a compromise with the Commandant by agreeing to work on an airstrip but nothing else. The airstrip would be of use to us in the rains when the roads were impassable and a sick man had to be flown out or rations flown in.

I continued to write letters to the Governor, the Commissioner of Police and the Colonial Secretary, voicing our complaints. These were smuggled out through Joram, the police constable. I was very careful not to let Chester see me fraternizing with the police at any time. In one letter I accused Chester of brutality and a police officer came to the camp from Maralal. He called a meeting of all the detainees. 'Where is Josiah Mwangi?' he shouted. 'Here I am,' I replied. 'Say Sir,' he said. 'Sir,' I said. He stared at me silently for a very long time with more hatred in his eyes than I had seen in any man ever before. He told me that he knew I was writing letters to people outside and then let me go back to the others.

I also wrote several letters to Chester himself, and once he called me outside his office and tore up the letters in contempt and spoke some very bad words. I became angry and seized his belt and threw him to the floor three times. The constables then took me outside the office and a quarter of an hour later I learnt my fate, which was to stand still in the sun facing

Kowop Hill for six hours. My legs became very sti
head ached that day but the violence had purged m
thing that had been boiling up dangerously inside m
time.

It was our custom to skin, in the compound, the goats which
we were given as our meat ration. Kikuyu people think the
best part of a goat is the head, which makes excellent soup.
Chester ordered us to give these to the police constables, which
made us all very angry. A way occurred to me of dealing
diplomatically with this. I was friendly with the police and so
I went to see them and asked them if they realized that, when
they handed the goats' heads over, the detainees were going to
point them in a certain direction and utter a curse on whoever
ate them. I had arranged for the detainees to do this and when
the constables saw it they were aghast and sent their sergeant
to tell Chester that they did not want the heads. Both sides
were pleased with me, the police for my warning them of
the witchcraft they always suspected the Kikuyu would use,
and the detainees for the promise of many bowls of good
soup.

During all this time we heard little reliable information about
the progress of the struggle in the forest. We were downcast
by the news of 'Operation Anvil' in April 1954 in Nairobi, when
24,000 people were arrested and sent to Langata Camp for
screening. The Camp Committee concentrated on keeping our
spirit of patriotism strong and undaunted. We had seen the
shortsighted folly of the Government gradually enlarging the
conflict, but we still felt that detention camps would finish by
the end of the year and that the Government could not fail to
listen to African wishes and give us independence in 1956.

On August 19 six lorries arrived outside the camp and many
of us thought this must be the moment for our release. As we
climbed into the vehicles Chester pointed me out as a ringleader
to the officer who was to accompany us. This man then hit me
three times with his cane. I nearly retaliated but decided that he
might kill me on the journey if I did. At Maralal we heard that
we were going to Langata, near Nairobi. Between Maralal and
Rumuruti we stuck in the evening at a place called Suguta
Marmar, and we pushed and heaved and dug the lorries out.
We slept that night without blankets, huddled together for

warmth like animals caught far from their lairs in a violent storm.

Many were the songs sung at Kowop, but this is the one that was written there by Gad Gathumbi, Richard Murugi, the carpenter, who called himself 'Yesu', and myself on the theme of the following two lines brought to us from our brothers who were struggling at Thomson's Falls:

> *Ngai twari ngo twari itimu na ruhiu*
> *Riu ciothe nitwatunyirwo ni ageni.*

> O God, we who used to carry a shield, a spear and a
>   sword
> Are no longer allowed by the foreigners to have them.

(It was part of the essence of manhood among the Kikuyu to carry a shield, a spear and a *simi*. The Government had forbidden the Africans to carry them without a special permit under the African Arms Ordinance.)

Mararaga matari toro	Our enemies cannot sleep
Magiciria uria makahota	For thinking how they can kill
Kuuraga munene witu ti Kenyatta	Our great leader, Kenyatta.
Nagutiri undu makahota	But they will never succeed
Ngai twari ngo twari itimu na ruhiu	O God, we used to carry a shield,
Riu ciothe nitwatunyirwo ni ageni	a spear and a simi.
Haria ciaigirwo wee niui	Now the foreigners have taken
Ngai cioe umahure nacio	all these away
	You, God, know where they
	were kept
	O God, take them and beat our
	enemies with them
Aanake a gikuyu umai	Warriors of Kikuyu, awake,
Nuu utarona muthuri ni arakura	Ye who cannot see that the old
Mwakoma igina ithii na ageni	man grows older
Ciana cia mumbi ikagunwo niki?	If you sleep the foreigners will
	seize our wealth
	And then what will the children
	of Mumbi feed on?

Miaka mirongo itano na iri mithiru *Nuu utarona uria twikitwo ni ageni* *Nawe kirimu woya mbia* *Wendia ruriri rwaku mbia*	In the last fifty-two years All have seen what the foreigners have done And you, you foolish men, have taken money And you are selling your country for money.
Wee kirimu thii woe ngiri *Kai ciathira ukaheo ki?* *Njoke ngwire atiri wakini* *Wahitithio njira muthenya* *Ni mugeni ukuroka guthii*	You, foolish men, go and take a thousand shillings, And when you finish that, what will you get? And now I tell you, friend of my age group, You have been shown the wrong way in the daytime By a foreigner who will desert us tomorrow.
Kiamugeni kiruaga gwaka *Kiroitirirwo ndia ndiku ni Ngai* *Wathani wake naguo uthire* *Bururi uyu witu wa Kenya* *Twiyathe twi ithuiki andu airu*	You cannot build on the word of a foreigner His word should be drowned in the deep waters by God, His rule should also be brought to an end In this country of ours, Kenya, Let the black people govern themselves alone.

CHAPTER V

Langata and the first visit to Manyani

THE long convoy of lorries arrived at Langata in a light drizzle at eight o'clock on the night of 21 August 1954. Langata is, I am told, about three miles from the centre of Nairobi, near the National Game Park, but I have had no time since my release to revisit it and during the ten days we stayed there practical geography lessons were discouraged. We were soon left in no doubt that, comparatively, Kowop had been a holiday camp. While we were still in the lorries a Seychellois K.P.R. (Kenya Police Reserve) officer came across and, clambering up on a tyre, leant over the side of the vehicle and to our amazement started hitting us with a long stick. He shouted out '*Ma Ma Mba*', '*Ma Ma Mba*', and seemed half-demented. Self-preservation being clearly vital we all began wriggling desperately to get underneath our friends so that they could nobly shield us. There was also a scramble, in which I was in the van, to the relative safety of the other side of the lorry. The blows were so wild that the parts of the body normally hit were missed more often than not and blood was drawn from heads and arms in the indiscriminate onslaught. He had an ugly and cruel face and could not speak English or Swahili properly. Fortunately the European officer who had brought the convoy from Maralal came on the scene and saved us. He told the Seychellois that he should not beat us but should wait until he brought his own convoy when he could do what he pleased with them. We felt considerable advance sympathy for 'them'.

Our officer, who had brought about thirty Tribal Police and Home Guards with him, then told us to alight from the lorries and double to our compound, Number 21. We were rushed there in such haste that many of our belongings were left behind. However, all our things were brought to us the next morning. At about half past eight that night, when we reached the compound, we were told to squat in lines, each containing five

people, and to place our hands on the top of our
was to be the recognized formation in all the cam
counted. An officer would walk quickly down the
reckoning out loud, and dealing out a smart blow v
to each row as he passed. The middle places in th
consequently in great demand as their occupants were not in
the front line like those on the wings. There was no chivalry
involved and I usually achieved a centre seat.

But the counting was not the end of that night's events. The
Seychellois stood up in front of us and said that we should now
repeat various phrases after him. While we were being counted
the compound had mysteriously filled up with many more
Tribal Police and Europeans until they seemed almost as many
as we were. The Seychellois first ordered us to say *Ma Ma mba*:
now these are meaningless syllables in Swahili so we repeated
them exactly, although we knew perfectly well he was trying
to make us say the Swahili for 'Mau Mau is bad'—*Mau Mau
mbaya*. A Kikuyu Home Guard then told us to repeat after
him, 'We Englishmen will rule this country for ever'. As he
was a Kikuyu this seemed an odd statement and we found no
denial of our principles in repeating it. All through this performance the Europeans and the Tribal Police were prowling
up and down lashing out at anyone who seemed in poor voice.
As we had not eaten since Kowop it was not surprising that
some of us did not feel like shouting. We were then told to say
'Jomo Kenyatta is a dog'. We were silent and refused to repeat
these words in spite of the blows from their sticks. Then we
were ordered to lie on our backs in the rain-water puddles in
the compound. Someone had a brainwave and we passed the
word round: 'Say he is a Creator (Kikuyu—*mba*) not a dog
(*mbwa*—Swahili)'. 'Say it, say it,' said the Tribal Police,
continuing to hit out at us. We did, but unfortunately a Kikuyu
understood the pun and they were furious. They selected a man
from South Tetu called Gachahi and stood him out in front
where he was beaten until at last he pronounced the words they
wanted. Gachahi had, however, put up a noble resistance and
he was not disgraced in our eyes. We were then told to say
'Dedan Kimathi and Stanley Mathenge will be finished in the
forest'. These were the names of the two Land Freedom Army
leaders in the Aberdares, and we could certainly not agree to

say this. Fortunately the Swahili word for 'flourish' (*ishi*) is very similar to that for 'finish' (*isha*) so by mumbling in deep voices we managed to disguise this one easily enough. Next we had to say 'Dedan Kimathi and Stanley Mathenge are dung'. The Swahili for this is *mafi*, which can be easily turned into *maji* (water), meaningless, but this did not matter. At last this extraordinary performance came to an end. It seemed stupid because anyone with normal intelligence could see that it would strengthen rather than weaken our faith and because the perpetrators were made to appear so childish during it. We had no food that night and as we went to sleep we discussed what had happened. We looked back on the three dry hills of Kowop with nostalgia. Langata was not a good place.

In the morning we looked round and the land was full of tents and rolls of Dannert wire, many, many more of each than we had ever seen before. Langata was being used as a transit camp for the Kikuyu who were arrested in 'Operation Anvil'. This had started in April 1954 and was designed to break up all the 'Mau Mau' committees in Nairobi and to destroy the sources of medical and military supplies which were still finding their way up to the forests. It was also hoped to capture the members of the various gangs operating in the city. This was to be achieved by cordoning off the different sectors and arresting wholesale everyone in them at the time. All the prisoners were then brought in front of Special Branch agents who were dressed in huge hoods with eye-holes, and who became known as 'Little Sacks', or *Gakunia*. The agents were a mixed lot. Some were ordinary 'spivs' who became professional betrayers because this gave them a steadier income than they had known before: as the tempo of the Emergency increased so did the demand for such people and the supply never seemed in danger of drying up. But there were also those whom we called *Tai Tai* because they came from the class of the educated young men who wore ties. Many of these were unemployed and became agents to earn money, while others were simply cowards and did it to escape arrest. All these groups originally had the same ardent desire for freedom that we had but the essence had been diluted by their own personal needs and fears. It was the illiterate people who throughout remained strongest in the struggle. Everyone filed slowly past these ghostly figures who would suddenly say 'Take him'. Anyone so named was brought to our camp to wait for the next train to a detention camp.

The Little Sacks used occasionally to come out to Langata itself where they could classify the people detained there. 'Black' was the category for unrepentant hard-core 'Mau Mau'; 'Grey' X
for heavily infected but not unreclaimable 'Mau Mau'; 'White' for clear or rehabilitated people. I never found out whether the inventor of these labels realized the double symbolism inherent in them. The camp to which detainees were sent from Langata depended on the category in which they had been placed.

The Government undoubtedly succeeded in its immediate military objective. Nairobi was cleaned out. But it also arrested and detained thousands of harmless people. I remember one lunatic who was put into the category of Black and sent to Manyani; this created great misery both for him and for those in whose compound he was put. It is open to doubt whether anyone can really have accurate knowledge of the secret life of more than about fifty people and the 'Little Sacks' put away hundreds apiece. They had to produce results to get their money; they would, too, have been less than human had they not been malicious on occasion. 'Operation Anvil' doubled the numbers in detention at that time and left the Government with a headache and complications whose effects are still not fully worked out. At the time we reached Langata there were about four thousand people detained there and they were being moved to Manyani in batches of a thousand twice a week.

After two days without food or water we were very hungry but our throats were so dry that swallowing was difficult. On Timothy Mwangi's advice we first of all drank some lukewarm water with salt. It seemed to do some good or perhaps we just thought it helped and therefore it did. When at last we saw food again and were just settling down to some stiff porridge, we were called to be counted. This seemed unnecessarily officious and we refused to go. All was well for a few minutes until suddenly a red cloud of Tribal Police burst upon us and hit us from our half-eaten porridge to the place where we were to be counted. That was the last we saw of that meal. This was followed by T.A.B. injections and then an inspection. When a Tribal Policeman found a detainee with money he would give him a very hard blow which made him forget everything for a moment and by the time memory had returned the money had gone. It was the usual custom on arrival in a compound rapidly to bury any particularly precious belongings or money, since no detainee would steal it, but to our horror after the inspection we did not return to Compound 21 but to 10. The possession of money being one of the secrets of survival in a detention camp we were all upset at this, but living as we were under two sets of laws, ours and theirs, we could not expect anyone to help us when we broke theirs in obeying ours. I had begun to think seriously about the problem of my own money. I still had two thousand two hundred and forty-two shillings and there was a strong rumour going round Langata that we were going to Manyani and that no one was allowed to keep money there. I therefore decided to pack away two thousand shillings in the shoulder-pads and lapels of my coat and to keep the two hundred and forty-two with me. Many hours careful sewing produced a faultless result. Without this money it would have been difficult to make the various contacts and arrangements which later became so helpful at Manyani and elsewhere.

The officers at Langata did not have individual compounds in their charge. They used to wander in and out of them all. There was one quiet European officer, with moustaches, who seemed very clever and intelligent. He would come and tell us that he did not believe in beating people but that sooner or later, one by one, everyone would confess what he had done. He was a Scot and seemed to have an air of knowing what the future would bring forth. We knew his name was Maclachlan because the loudspeakers were always calling him to go somewhere. The Seychellois was a great contrast. He seemed unable to count properly and spent most of his time glowering or shouting at us. His favourite theme was 'You kill babies, you eat people'. Some of our people were goaded to ask him, 'Have we eaten your mother or your father?' He was an unhappy-looking man and by the time we left I felt sorry for him.

While I was there two people were punished by being given twenty-four hours' solitary confinement in *Shimo* (Swahili for 'hole'). This was a pit about ten feet deep and eight feet square with six inches of mud on the bottom and covered with a steel cover. It was very cold down inside and a friend of mine in

No. 9, the neighbouring compound, told me it was most unpleasant. No one could think what its original use was. I was given a number at Langata, 54505, which I remained with at Manyani. We were also forcibly taught here to use the word 'Effendi' when addressing any European. 'Effendi' was originally a Turkish title of respect, and presumably came down into the King's African Rifles in Uganda through Egypt and the Sudanese troops. It is only normally used today in Kenya by a private soldier addressing his officer. Since forgetting to say it involved painful reminders, it became such an instinctive reaction to a white face that whether it belonged to a clergyman or a Member of Parliament, a doctor or a lady, we greeted them all as 'Effendi'.

After we had been in Langata for three days the warders began to tell us that we were going to Manyani on 31 August. Manyani was the camp for category 'Black', which grade everyone from Kowop had automatically achieved. We did not suffer the indignity of confirmation from the Little Sacks, which we took as a great compliment. The warders also laid special emphasis on the fact that at Manyani we would only be allowed to keep one suit. To help us they would be prepared to buy any clothing surplus to this, although we would naturally realize that prices in the circumstances would be a little low. Many consequently sold their extra belongings for a song, hoping that they could somehow look after the money.

On 31 August 1954, 1,200 of us were moved by the special detainee train (*Gari ya Waya*), whose windows were covered in barbed wire. We were on our way to Manyani in Kenya's Coast Province. When we left the train again it was to see a broad road lined on each side with an avenue of prison warders standing a few feet apart. There were thousands of them armed with long batons. As it was three miles to the camp from the station these thousands were still not sufficient, so they were leapfrogged ahead of us as we went. The warders seized anything that was not tied in a bundle or packed in a box. If anyone stopped to argue he was hit until he moved on. We eventually reached the end of the avenue and found ourselves in Compound 26. A large tough-looking officer came in and standing with arms folded made a speech of welcome as follows: 'You have now arrived at Manyani. This is Manyani and you will soon understand about Manyani. If you have anything like money or letters, watches or penknives or any other muck, produce it. If anyone tries to hide anything he will get something bad. After handing things in here you will go to the kitchen where you will be inspected and your extra clothes will be put in store. You will remain with one set of clothes only. Do you understand?' We uttered an affirmative grunt and in spite of the lessons of Langata began busily scratching the earth to bury our treasures. One officer took the money in, another the personal articles. The rumour rapidly circulated that they were writing 2,000 shillings down as 200 shillings, 200 shillings as twenty shillings, twenty shillings remained twenty shillings. Now my 242 shillings was not sewn up and I had no intention of losing it. I therefore rolled up the two 100-shilling notes as tightly as possible and stuck them deep down in the curls of my hair. Curly hair has its advantages. I gave one of the warders the two shillings since one never knew when such a friend might come in useful. I handed in the two twenty-shilling notes and my watch, for neither of which did I get a receipt nor have I ever seen them again.

We then went to a place near the kitchens where we were to be inspected. Other detainees faced with handing in their money hid it in their mouths (where with care it can be concealed without affecting speech), between their toes and even in the rectum and the groin. We were ordered to remove our clothes and all parts of our anatomy were thoroughly examined. We were also made to jump up and down like Kamba dancers in the hope that the jigging might dislodge money or whatever else we had hidden. My clothes, my camera and my books were taken off me. The books were an inconsolable loss and that night I was very miserable. To our dismay after the inspection we were returned not to Compound 26 but to 21. All the articles which had been buried were now lost. It was, however, all the same since few detainees ever saw again the money and belongings that were handed in at Manyani. This was not solely due to pilfering by warders but also to the poor storage conditions and the system of labelling. To have preserved them all safely would have required a degree of organization and ability that was simply not available to the Prison Department at that time.

The next morning we met the 'screeners' for the first time. Their leader was a detainee called Henry. Henry had a strange habit of calling for one detainee to lie on the ground in front of him so that he could put his foot on him. From this position of authority he seemed to gain sufficient strength to be able to call out our names. Oddly enough, since the alternative was squatting motionless in a most uncomfortable position, there was almost a stampede for the honour of becoming his footstool. We considered all screeners to be traitors. Most of those who had been brought from the Reserves to do it had allowed their love of money to conquer their patriotism. Those who had been detainees had exchanged the life of suffering for one of relative liberty. There were a few, very few, of both categories who sincerely felt that the Society of the Oath was such a bad means of achieving our objectives that Independence itself would become compromised and tainted should it succeed. These men were genuine and honest and we respected them although we could not accept their views. In all the camps in which I was detained I knew of only three of whom this could be said. All screeners were insidiously affected by the abnormal atmosphere behind the wire and by the mental strain involved in what they were doing. Their attitude was distorted until they often felt they were living in a topsy-turvy world and 'good' and 'bad' became blurred concepts. Looking back it is not surprising to me that some of them occasionally behaved in such cruel and distressing ways. It was as if they had to do something violent to rid themselves of their self-contempt for double-crossing their own souls.

We were all quickly re-classified as Black and sent to Compound 9. There were about nine hundred of us in it and the young European officer in charge was careful to see no one beat us. The food had deteriorated and now consisted of eight ounces of maize flour and beans a day. We still did no work except cooking our food and dealing with the sanitary buckets. The hours passed in talking politics and playing draughts or *bau*, which is played with stones on a 'board' of holes in the ground. This game is very widespread in East Africa, especially among the pastoral tribes to whom each stone is a token 'cow' and each hole a cattle *boma* (enclosure). The end-game is most intricate and requires great concentration. The ultimate winner is the player who finishes up by taking the most stones from the *bomas* of his opponent.

Manyani had still not settled down and Compound 9 was being used as a transit area. Every two or three days the camp authorities would stir the pot vigorously and detainees would be sent all over the place on transfer to other compounds. There was no possibility of organizing ourselves in this fluid situation, although the Kowop group had not disintegrated much. However, on 5 October we were all moved to Compound 13 and after a month there things seemed to have settled sufficiently for us to begin regulating our lives again. The officer in charge of the camp had asked each compound to elect a Leader to represent them before him. In Compound 13 there were seventeen huts each containing about sixty detainees and I was surprised and honoured when they elected me. It was probably because I had a higher education than anyone else on the compound at that time. The illiterates had great faith in those of us who were educated, although we did not always merit it.

I decided to ask the detainees to elect a committee of six to advise and help me, and suggested that it should as far as possible be representative of each District. They were M'Ariuda M'Ikiao (Meru), Grishon Murage (Embu), Zakariah Kibuthu (Kiambu), Tiras Muchiri (Nyeri), Geoffrey Maimba (Embu), and John Waweru (Embu). All these have now been released and Grishon is a Government headman, Kibuthu has an allotment on the Mwea-Tebere Rice Irrigation Scheme, Tiras and Geoffrey are teachers in Intermediate Schools, and John Waweru is employed by the Government as a Community Development Assistant in North Tetu, Nyeri. First we organized the division of labour in a fair way. Each hut or 'club' had its own rota for cooks. Each hut took it in turn to provide people to transport the sanitary buckets and also supplied one man who was hut orderly every day, acting as my messenger. Later, in January, when we started working on the airfield, the committee also ensured that the workers were supplied in a just way so that no one person had to do more than another. I also looked after the two hundred yellow shorts that we were commanded to wear whenever we left the compound. At the end of November I requested an interview with the Camp

Commandant; this was granted. He seemed an intelligent man but I thought he had what we Kikuyu call *kanua monjore* (a hard mouth). First of all I said that we regarded ourselves in the same way as prisoners of war and I knew all about the Geneva Convention. He seemed surprised at my words. Then I asked him to arrange for a Visiting Committee to come to Manyani so that we could make to them any representations we wished. It was my turn to be surprised when he readily agreed and he kept his word.

During that month things became steadily worse in the camp. By now we were working on the airfield at Manyani and I was receiving many reports of bad treatment there. I was not pleased when I heard that they were made to cut the sticks with which they were later beaten. There had also been a toughening-up of the attitude of the warders in the compounds. At that time none of them were Kikuyu; there were Nandi, Kipsigis and Luo from Kenya and several from Tanganyika tribes. So when we were told that a Visiting Committee would be coming in January I decided to speak out on all our grievances. Jimmy Jeremiah and Wilfred Havelock were two of its members whom I recognized and I gave them all a frank statement of what had been happening and asked for their help. There were ten other compound Leaders present who tacitly supported me. I was left in little doubt that these criticisms were unwelcome to the camp officers for on the next morning, lying on a bench, naked save for my yellow shorts, I was given twenty-four strokes by a warder in the presence of Marlow, one of the camp officers who earned the nickname from us of *Mapiga*—'The Hitter'. Nevertheless, the beatings in the compounds and on the airfield diminished considerably. Many of the other compound Leaders decided against being outspoken after what had been done to me, but one of them, my great friend Robinson Mwangi, supported me to the end both before the committee and among the detainees.

He is the one man whose face always comes back to me as I write down the story of those times. He was the Leader of Compound 16. Robinson is a true nationalist and, even after Kenyatta's arrest, did all he could to help him. He had been educated up to Form II. At this time many of the educated young men were becoming screeners in the camp; we both

decided to stay with our own people, the illiterates, helping
them organize themselves and writing letters for them. Robinson is now a leader of the K.A.N.U. Party Organization in
Fort Hall District.

There was a Protestant missionary working at Manyani
called S. J. Cole. We called him *Matuini* (Kikuyu for 'Heaven')
because he told people about going to heaven. He used to
talk with me about our troubles and he had a great influence
for the good there. He asked the Commandant to allow
me to speak about Christianity in the other compounds
and I did this. I would read to them Chapter 13 of the First
Letter to the Corinthians with Paul's beautiful words describing
Charity and how it 'Beareth all things, believeth all things,
hopeth all things, endureth all things'. Then I would explain
how important it was that they should not provoke the camp
officials unnecessarily. This would give Robinson and myself
extra power with which to fight for their rights. We have a
custom that when a young Kikuyu becomes a man he must give
to the brother of his mother a goat with ears of a special colour
and we have a proverb *Gwita mundu mama tikuo kuruta mburi ya
matu*, which is to say, 'To call a man uncle is not to give him the
goat of the ears'. So I explained to the detainees that if they obey
the camp laws and call the officers Effendi this does not mean
they are denying Independence. I also emphasized again that
we would not get across the river to Freedom without Unity,
even as ants clamber on each other and baboons link tails to
make a living bridge over a stream. I used to speak in this way
because I was a Christian and nowhere in the oath I had
taken was Christianity forbidden. Many detainees attended the
religious meetings, including some who were converted in the
camp. I see nothing contradictory in both being a Christian
and also taking the Oath of Unity.

In February the Visiting Committee returned. One of the
members, a clergyman called Macpherson, who was Moderator
of the Church of Scotland in Kenya, spoke Kikuyu fluently;
so I reiterated to him all our grievances and explained about
the beatings. In Compound 26 there had recently been some
escapes and as a result 150 warders from the special Riot
Squads had been sent in to teach them a lesson. Subsequently
six detainees from that compound had died in the camp hospital.

The authorities had put out the explanation that they had all died of typhoid and I wanted Macpherson to have this story investigated. We also asked for an increase in the basic ration and more variety in the diet. As we were leaving the room, Marlow said quietly to me that he had noted that I had not been able to keep my mouth shut. The next morning I was given another twelve strokes and seven days' solitary confinement in a small cell with penal diet.

That week in the small cell was one of the worst experiences of my life. S. J. Cole came to visit me and seemed to me almost to be crying when he saw me. He looked ill and heavy of heart. He asked me if I had water. When I said I had none he took a bucket and went himself to bring water for me where some officers and warders could see him. They did not try to stop him. When he came back, he gave me some water to drink and we knelt and prayed together and he told me the story of Paul and Silas in jail at Philippi. When he went he left me a copy of the New Testament. During those seven days I never once excreted, possibly because I had nothing to eat.

The small cell was near Compound 16 and Robinson Mwangi would shout all the news across to me. This had to be a monologue since, although I could hear him, my replies were not audible. On my return to the compound I could not help myself and I felt very bitter against Marlow. So I wrote a memorandum direct to the Colonial Office about what was happening in the camp, by-passing the Kenya Government completely. Dipping into my precious funds I bribed a warder to get me writing materials and send the letters, paying out only when he brought me the receipt of posting. The letters were copied and sent to Barbara Castle, M.P., who later tried to have the situation investigated.

There was another good European called Dr. Kirren who was in charge of the hospital. Once I had a conversation with him for three hours and he said his job was to cure detainees who had typhoid, not those who were ill from beatings. He tried hard to improve our conditions and to restore sanity among the camp officers. Another good man was Humphrey of the Health Department, known as *Kihuga* because he was a man of action, who saved many of our lives with his work on hygiene and the camp water supply. He would fight anyone, even a European, who dared to touch any of the detainees working for him. In February the detainees were sent to work in the local quarries. After several hours sweating in the hot sun they returned to camp without washing. This seems to have been the immediate cause of an outbreak of pellagra, which was aggravated by shortage of food and vitamin deficiencies. At the March session of the Visiting Committee I insisted on the ration being increased especially as our people were now doing such hard labour. This was done and we were also given a vitamin pill daily.

Our relationship with the warders in the camp depended on how much money and goods we had. In the early days certain of them seemed to consider they had a right to take any food from us that they wanted. Robinson and I decided to have a showdown and when a corporal, a Mgogo from Tanganyika, came and took six pounds of meat from our compound I stopped him in front of all the detainees and removed the meat. I told him that if he needed the meat so badly he should become a detainee and eat it with us. As far as possible we maintained friendly relations with the warders themselves while we waged covert war with the N.C.O.s. Shortly after the meat episode a sergeant came to try and take some cooking fat. I refused to allow him to do so. A few minutes later he called me outside and took me to the guardroom where there were three N.C.O.s and five warders sitting. They had constituted themselves a court and they told me that I had done wrong and must be punished. They took me to a place where the detainees could see what was happening and they put me on the ground and a Mchagga tribesman gave me forty strokes. They did not take my clothes off and the strokes were given in rapid succession and so, although painful, it did not hurt as much as some of the more official punishments had. However, the detainees were furious and I was not very calm myself, so I decided to tell the new Compound Officer, R. M. Child. He had been wounded in the ankle at Kariaini in the Aberdare forest above the Othaya location and he was a good man. He said it would not be wise for me to accuse the warders before the Commandant but promised that he would deal with them. He stopped all beating in our compound and ordered the warders in our presence to throw away their sticks. The Riot Squad was never called into our compound and I dealt with any difficulties that arose. In other compounds the beating continued and I was very worried and uneasy that nothing we could do seemed to stop it.

The camp was surrounded by an electric fence and because of this the authorities felt that it was escape-proof in any normal sense. However, two terrorist generals, Mwangi Mambo and Kariuki Chotara, escaped from Compound 16 by putting planks on to the wire and walking over it. Few of us felt sufficient faith in the insulation, or our balancing ability, to wish to follow them but we greatly admired their courage. Later they were both arrested in Nairobi and Mwangi was executed and Kariuki sentenced to life imprisonment. While I was at Lodwar he came there and stayed with me before going to Lokitaung where Kenyatta was serving his sentence. Compound 16 was then hammered by the Riot Squad and thirty-five detainees were crippled, some permanently. I wrote to the Chief Secretary about this incident, 'posting' the letter in the usual way. A few days later when asked if I had written it I agreed and an officer ordered me to be given another twenty-four strokes. The punishment was carried out by a warder outside the big camp office in full view of Compounds 11 and 16. During these occurrences Robinson was transferred to Compound 6 and Daniel Mbarathi, who stood unsuccessfully as an Independent K.A.N.U. candidate for Fort Hall in the general election of February 1961, followed him as leader.

As a further result of this escape an order came from the Commandant that all detainees taking sanitary buckets to the sewage disposal area, which was about a half-mile walk, should carry them on their heads. It was nearly impossible in normal conditions, and absolutely impossible in the rain, to complete the journey without covering head and shoulders with urine and ordure. Shinda Kikombe, a well-known Kikuyu entertainer detained at Manyani, refers to this episode on one of his gramophone records. Robinson and I protested strongly to the Visiting Committee in April and this was stopped. We also asked if we could now be returned some of the property which had been taken off us since the clothes we had with us were beginning to wear out. They replied that this could not be permitted but we would be allowed to receive shirts sent to us

by our relatives. We also complained about the practice alarm
system. There was a regulation that if we heard the alarm siren
sound those detainees who were working far away from the
camp, in the quarry, the farm or the brickfield, should lie down
prone immediately without moving or they would be shot.
Those who were near the camp should run quickly to their
compounds for the inevitable 'Counting'. What actually happened was that, as soon as the siren went, the warders started
laying about whoever was nearest them and, even if someone
was moving like an Olympic sprinter he would get hit; the
cooks had to leave the food burning, which meant no food for
the compound that day; and if the alarm went during a meal
we had to leave our food and go to be counted. There were
considerable security problems at Manyani and we appreciated
this but we asked that just a little more consideration should be
shown. After the April Committee it seemed to us that the
situation improved.

While a smoker can exist behind barbed wire indefinitely
without women he can only survive a limited time nowadays
without *muthogoto*—cigarettes or snuff. We got our tobacco by
buying it from the warders, and we got money by selling camp
blankets to them. Two people would pool their four blankets,
sell one for five shillings, use one broadside-on to lie on and
have one each to wrap round themselves. When an officer came
to count the blankets, they would rapidly split one down the
middle and report with one and a half each. In most military
and prison stores one and a half equals two, fortunately. Others
would sell the shirts they were now receiving from their relatives.

It was equally important to be able to light cigarettes and we
had various means of doing this. With care one matchstick can
be split into four. It is also possible to twist a piece of cloth
like a rope and keep fire in it a long time and it could be lit
from the camp kitchens and carried away secretly to our 'clubs'.[1]
We sometimes used the methods of our ancestors who used to
twist a stick (*githegethi*) vigorously between their palms on to a
depression in another larger block of wood (*gika*) until a black
substance was created by the friction and became fire. If all
else failed it was possible to rub a razor-blade furiously on a
cement floor until fire came out. Such was the hunger for

[1] Each aluminium hut or tent in a camp was called a 'club'.

cigarettes that detainees would exchange them for meat or even smoke the dried leaves off trees. I had personally never felt this craving and I would look on in wonder as my friends sat, a dozen or so round in a circle, passing round the precious sweepings of the day, one puff each and on to the next man. Sometimes one fell down as a result of a strong puff which made him dizzy.

At one time some of the warders began collecting dried cattle and donkey dung, breaking it up and putting it in small packets which they then handed secretly to detainees through the wire, pretending that it was tobacco. The detainee hid it in his 'club' till evening when he found he had been tricked. When this problem was brought to me I decided we must teach them a lesson. The warders used to buy any fat we could spare at ten shillings a tin. We found some small tins, half filled them with human ordure, put ashes on top to stop the smell, covered this with diesel oil and then filled the last quarter with the cooking fat which they wanted to buy. They were very angry when they found out and I met their representatives and explained that we expected certain minimum standards of honour to be observed in these dealings. The word was passed round and no detainees had to smoke cattle dung from then on. Although there were the strictest regulations against smoking in every Kenya Special Detention Camp, they were successfully evaded on a grand scale in them all. I also arranged for an expensive but regular supply of newspapers through the warders.

It must seem strange to an outsider that while the warders would sell tobacco and newspapers today, tomorrow they would meticulously search our quarters on the orders of their superiors for the same tobacco and triumphantly haul us up for punishment if they discovered anything. None of us would need to have this explained but perhaps the following Kikuyu allegory will help others. We say that when a man takes a dog out hunting a jackal, the dog will run far ahead out of sight and start playing with the jackal in a hidden place because they are really of the same kind. When the man catches up with them the dog will straightaway begin barking fiercely and chasing the jackal again for a safe distance. This is because it is the man who gives the dog food which it will not get if it disobeys his orders.

In many ways the most important nourishment we had was

7

from the two news services that we operated. The *Manyani Times* was the news that was known to be true and which had been picked up from newspapers by those cleaning in the warders' lines or had been heard on a wireless by someone working near an officer's house. We were extremely cunning at obtaining news without being seen to do so. The *Waya Times* was the news that was largely speculation, rumour or light relief. In the evenings, after food, each 'club' in every compound would send a representative to the barbed wire partitions to get the news. We were extremely lucky in Compound 13 since we could converse with five other compounds. Anyone who had any news would stand up and say '*giteo*', which is Kikuyu for 'respect' and brought instant silence all round him. Then he would say, 'I now begin my words of *Manyani Times* [or *Waya Times*] which are that . . .' This immediately told his listeners how much credibility to place in what was coming. *Waya Times* news items might include the dismissal of the Governor, the date of Independence (never later than 1956), the revocation of unpleasant regulations by the Commissioner for Prisons, our imminent release, the transfer of an unpopular officer or an electoral victory by the British Labour Party in whom we still passionately believed. Most *Waya Times* headlines exhibited gross wishful thinking on the reporter's part. There were also more localized titbits such as 'Jeremiah (a screener) sent home to his mother for a shirt and she has sent him a baby-carrier (*ngoi*) instead' or 'Jonathan (another screener) sent home to his wife for a pair of pants and she has sent him knickers instead'. Possibly she did not know what pants look like but we changed this rumour to imply that his wife had done this because she did not approve of his surrendering. Crude humour but uproariously funny to men in our circumstances. The warders disliked our news service intensely and whenever they saw us eagerly listening to it someone would throw a few stones to break us up. The evening news hour was also used for throwing tobacco to friends in other compounds. Sometimes a poor shot would land in the lane between and there was then trouble for both compounds.

In early April we were first visited by some people whom we ridiculed as *Ogi a Njata* (Wise Men of the Star) because of the red star emblem they wore on their breast pockets. They were people who had been detained on Governor's Detention Orders and had agreed to support the Government after screening at Athi River Camp. There were many of them. They lived with the screeners but every morning they would go into whatever compound they liked and try to persuade some detainees to agree to confess as they had. They had a few converts here and there and it was unpleasant to see our former absolute unity being eroded in however small a way. We found that *Waya Times* rumours did not have as long a currency as before.

In late April there was a dock strike at Mombasa. It was suggested that 10,000 detainees should be sent to break it, and once more my hoard of money was depleted in order to send letters to the Colonial Secretary, the Governor, and various Members of Parliament, stressing that this would be against the Geneva Convention. I also complained of various brutalities. Marlow ('the Hitter') had been getting worse and in Compound 17 he threw a bowl of scalding hot porridge at a detainee who was badly burnt all over his body and subsequently spent a long time recovering in the camp hospital. One day Marlow came to our compound for an inspection. He had instructed that whenever he entered everyone should stand up and stay absolutely still. Kamau Nduyu from South Tetu started moving and Marlow gave him so strong a clout that it not only knocked down Kamau but also dislodged Marlow's own hat. The detainees rushed to pick up the hat, leaving Kamau where he was. Afterwards I was furious with them and spent a few minutes explaining the different levels of creation of a hat and a human being. However, I forgave them; Marlow on the war-path was a frightening sight. Finally in these letters I accused the authorities at Manyani of deliberately concealing brutalities under the cloak of a typhoid epidemic and I challenged them to show us one warder or camp officer who had died of typhoid. For one reason or another we were not sent to break the strike at Mombasa and the bread that had been ordered to go with us was eaten in the compounds instead.

When the Visiting Committee came in early May I brought all these allegations in front of them. On their departure Marlow summoned me and with another officer and a Mluhya lance-corporal marched me over to a spot near the small cell in the Headquarters sector and there ordered the lance-corporal to give me sixty strokes. My clothes were not removed, the beating was distributed over a wide area of my body and was delivered rapidly and so the pain was not as bad as it might have been, although my buttocks swelled considerably. Marlow often used personally to beat detainees in the compounds although the Camp Commandant probably knew nothing about any of these goings-on.

Next morning Marlow took me outside 'C' Camp to a place near the Forest and said that he would shoot me unless I wrote down on a piece of paper that I would not send any more letters to England, that I would co-operate with the Government and that I would help to type in the screeners' office. Although the thought of death was still not wholly desirable, I refused. He then took from his car a piece of three-ply wood about three feet by two feet and told me to hold it up above my head at arm's length. He walked five yards away and said that he was going to kill me if I did not agree to write the sentences. Still, not imagining he could be serious, I refused. To my horror he raised his gun and shot at me. I remember a tremendous noise and knowing that I was now dead and then nothing. He had, in fact, shot through the wood and I had fallen down with it. Out of the void I then heard the words '*Simama, simama*' (Swahili for 'Get up') and by a notable piece of deduction in the circumstances I decided that this was unlikely to be the language of heaven or hell and that I was therefore probably alive. As if hypnotized I stood up and faced him and we went through the rigmarole all over again. I refused and he shot again; again I fell into the abyss and knew emptiness and smelt death. Then distantly I heard '*Amka, amka*' (Swahili for 'Wake up, wake up') and the second time I rose from the dead. My body was now running with sweat and my mind was no longer able to grasp whereabouts we were or what was happening. 'For the third and last time,' he said, 'will you agree to write those sentences?' It was like a scene out of a film and without really knowing what I was being asked I repeated my 'No'. He fired again and this time I felt something sear through the base of the thumb on my right hand. Absolutely certain that I had at least been seriously wounded and was about to die I fell down again. When I saw the blood, which stained all my sweat so that wherever I felt was blood and still more blood,

I rushed at him and clasped him round the waist and said, 'Look at this blood, you have killed me, there is blood all over me.' Marlow laughed and said, 'You are very bad hard-core.' He then returned me to the camp and put me in solitary confinement in the small cell. I think now he probably did not mean to kill me, it was merely done to frighten me which it certainly succeeded in doing.

On 1 June I was taken by car from the cell to Compound 13 by Marlow and the Camp Commandant. The detainees had been formed up in a semicircle and those in other compounds were also watching: the crowd was about six thousand. They told me to remove a bench from the car and carry it out into the middle of the detainees. The detainees were all told to stand and the other officers and warders came in to watch. Quite an audience for the performance. The Commandant then shouted in Swahili, 'Here is your leader. He wants to show you he is God. You follow him because he writes letters to the Colonial Office. Do not follow him any more. If you do you will get into the same trouble as he is in today. Mwangi, take off your clothes and lie down on the bench.' I was then given twelve strokes by a Jaluo sergeant-major. He certainly knew how to cane and these were very hard ones. The Commandant then asked me if I would stop writing letters. I replied that I would no longer send out letters when I was convinced that the just complaints of the detainees had been answered. If beatings continued so would my letters. I would never co-operate with the Government or help the Special Branch. I was then taken to Compound 6 where there was a European who gave me another twenty-eight strokes which many detainees witnessed. Finally I was thrown inside Hut No. 1 in the compound and forbidden to mix with the other detainees. That evening the *Manyani Times* gave a full report of the episode. After this public exposure I regretfully sensed the birth of a new bitterness deep within me and it has not been easy to eradicate it.

No. 1 hut was surrounded with barbed wire and although I was supposed to have no contact with the others, Robinson Mwangi organized my feeding as I lay there weak and exhausted. Under his care I slowly regained my strength. At this time Compound 6 was the worst in the camp. All the most uncompromising detainees had been brought there and the treatment was tough. The Riot Squad was always coming in and they would make everyone take off their clothes and beat them all round the compound, young and old naked together, which is shameful to my people. But they did not disturb me in my isolation, although I could feel that the place was becoming like a mental home.

On 16 June a group of us were sent to Compound 8, where I was again elected compound Leader. There were eight hundred and eight of us there but we did not stay long. On 22 June we were transferred in a grand dispersal all over the Colony, five hundred to the Mwea Camps, one hundred and twenty to South Yatta, one hundred and fifty to Fort Hall, and thirty to Nyeri. Eight only were left behind. As we were going Marlow said to me: 'Never, never come back to Manyani.' I felt sad at leaving so many of our people behind in that camp where nobody could be happy or normal, whether detainee, warder or European officer.

CHAPTER VI

South Yatta and my second visit to Manyani

ALL Kenya's Detention Camps were sited in isolated, hot and barren areas and South Yatta Works Camp in desolate bush country about twenty-five miles from Thika was no exception to this rule. The prime reason for putting it in this particular place was to help in the construction of the Yatta furrow. This project, which had originally been planned in 1925, was designed to bring water from the Mbagathi River forty miles across the country of the Akamba tribe to the dry plains of Yatta. In South Yatta Camp everyone was expected to work, the young and able digging the furrow, the old and crippled removing the sanitary buckets and scrubbing them, while the sick cleaned out the camp and did any chores required. Those left behind had so much to do that they often preferred, in spite of their illness, to join the work gangs. The system certainly discouraged malingerers but it equally surely prevented many sick people from being cured in time. When we arrived from Manyani on 23 June 1955 the furrow had gone four and a half miles. During our two months there we dug out a further two miles.

The Kenya Government, conscious at last of the impossibility of keeping 80,000 people behind barbed wire for ever, had developed a policy for releasing the detainees to their homes. It was built upon the twin pillars of confession and hard work. First of all we were re-screened and put into the categories of Black, Grey or White; later, when the implications of these titles penetrated even the Government, the names were changed to Z (hard-core Black), Z2 (just ordinary Black), and Y1 (Grey) and Y2 (White). The camps themselves were then divided into Special Camps and Works Camps. The former consisted largely of Zs with a smattering of Y1s, while Y2s were sent to the Works Camps. The Works Camps were sited in places near some project on which the detainees could work out their 'sins' by the penance of hard labour. Because of various International Agreements they would, of course, be paid for the hours they toiled and the money so earned would be placed either in a Post Office Savings Book, which would be handed to a detainee on his final release, or given to the detainee as tokens which could be exchanged for luxuries in the Camp Centres. Works Camps were also established in all the Kikuyu districts and a detainee would steadily work and confess his way nearer home. At last he would come out of the 'pipeline', as it was called, to the camp set up in his own division where he would be subject to domestic pressures and the benign influence of the local elders and the Chiefs. Then the great day would come when, purged of his 'Mau Mau' oaths and beliefs and a fine example of all the virtues, he would appear before a committee of what one District Officer described as his 'Elders and Peers', who would then authorize his release and one fully 'rehabilitated' Kikuyu would return to his people. Even under this scheme it was at this time envisaged that 12,000 would remain in permanent exile from Kikuyuland, working on settlement schemes in remote areas of the Colony.

The ideas behind the setting up of the pipeline system showed how far the Kenya authorities were from understanding the nature of the 'Mau Mau' movement. The spirit of African nationalism, of which we were a part, is not something that can be removed by screening. Fundamentally it is a vital physical organ in our bodies, and in the 1950s no one could be a full African human being in Kenya without it. In some people it was damaged and crippled and even used for purposes other than those for which it was designed. In some instances a few Africans managed for short periods to exist without it but ultimately it could only be extinguished by death. The Kenya Government made two mistakes. At times it seemed to think that 'Mau Mau' and the motives inducing people to take the oath could be separated from the Kenya branch of African nationalism and that one could be dealt with in isolation from the other: it did not see that by this time the 'Mau Mau' movement was merely an extension of the deepest springs of African nationalism to which ordinary expression had been denied. Secondly, it hoped that with the confession of the oath the baby of nationalism would be swept away with the bath water. The Colonial Government could not be expected to see it our way. The authorities considered that by confessing we were gaining something. Those of us who resisted 'rehabilitation' to the end did so because we considered that by confession we would lose something essential without which we could not live. We considered that the 'rehabilitated' ex-detainee screeners had sold their souls for an easy time. They were weak people who could not stand the tough alternative existence and they could be forgiven for being weak, if not for other things. Most of those who confessed and surrendered have now found again what they temporarily gave up. Many of the official visitors to camps would leave after contrasting the happy faces and cheerfulness of the surrendered detainees with the bitter and inhuman look on our faces. And yet the 'hard-core' were happier and at greater peace with their souls than the 'surrenderers' who were forced into the false position of playing a double rôle and knowing in their hearts that we 'hard-core' alone were straight, honest and true to our people and Africa.

The detainees reacted in different ways to this system which seemed to take so simple a view of the human personality. A few achieved their release by telling the truth, many more by telling lies. Many of us decided that the best method of fighting for our people at this time was to refuse to yield to the screeners to the limit of our endurance, thus embarrassing the Government as much as possible. The 'pipeline' system in its original conception did not involve beating or hitting in any way. But because it was basically unsound it began to go slower and slower and it was at this stage that the Government officers employed the violence that in the end destroyed the use of confession as the foundation of the 'pipeline'. Few people anywhere feel bound by words uttered under torture. It is impossible for me to say at what level the orders for such treatment were given but it is obvious that some of the Government Ministers and senior officials of the Administration must have known what was going on. We used to tell each other that the Government had a pipeline through which it wanted us all to go to get home. Unfortunately it was the same size of pipe for all and some of us were much larger (or more hard-core) than others and we stuck in it very quickly. So they

had to take a hammer to hit us so that we could be forced to fit
into their pipeline. Some of us could see much more sensible
and easier ways of getting home than through a pipe that was
so small, but no one wanted to listen to them.

South Yatta was the first Works Camp in which I had been.
My new number was S.Y.W.C. 1880. It was a small camp with
a capacity for about one thousand and we lived in aluminium,
tent-shaped huts which were built much closer together than
those at Manyani had been. We had been very relieved when
none of the prison warders beat us on arrival. We had a daily
ration of eighteen ounces of maize meal and six ounces of beans,
and general living conditions were poor. There was no medical
dresser, but fortunately we managed to find one of the detainees
to do the job, Muriithi Kihara, who had been working in the
King George VI Hospital, Nairobi, before his arrest. He did all
he could to help us but could not prevent a fresh outbreak of
pellagra, from which one detainee died in the camp hospital.
Cigarettes and snuff were permitted in the camp and tokens
could be exchanged for them.

The day was hard: we woke at 5 a.m., took some maize
gruel and by six we were at the Main Gate for division into
labour gangs. We then had to walk between five and seven
miles to the furrow, returning again in the evening. We were
doing piecework in the furrow which was ten feet wide and
between sixteen and eighteen feet high. The old men, and even
some of the young men, did not find it easy to finish the two-foot
stint in the hard rocky soil, which had first to be loosened and
then shovelled up out of the trench. Those who failed to complete their *futi* would not have the day marked off on their
work-cards, which meant no pay for it at the end of the month.
Some people did not even achieve one month's pay for two
months' work before we left.

The warders who accompanied us to the furrow were from
the Akamba tribe. They were good and humble people who
never beat us and sometimes, when we were working, they
would take a few of us to the nearest huts and we would eat
and perhaps drink some gruel with the Akamba people living
there. Before our arrival the camp had been used for the
reception of Kikuyu repatriated from the Northern Province of
Tanganyika where they had been working. Most of them had

not taken the Oath of Unity: had they done so the following incident which occurred before we reached there could never have happened. When they went to work on the furrow they met some of the local Kamba girls, whom they then let in through the loose wire during the evenings. The Camp Commandant at that time, who was called Chichester, was more interested in the cleanliness of the camp than in the human beings detained there, but he did at that time officially allow the Kamba girls to enter the camp on Sundays, so that they might sell food to the inmates. As a by-product of the trading transactions some of the young Kikuyu repatriates made arrangements for the more beautiful Kamba girls to remain overnight in their huts within the compound as their guests. This went on for four months until one of the girls was, not surprisingly, found to be pregnant. By Kamba custom, since the detainee did not intend to marry her, he or his father had to be fined two goats and a ram. But he could not produce these animals and, since someone had to, the elders decided that Chichester was acting *in loco parentis* and should find the beasts. His protests were not over-vigorous as he did not wish the incident brought to the notice of his superiors, and the local elders greatly enjoyed the meat which they shared with some of the Kamba warders. Chichester's 'grandchild' turned out to be twins. The girls were no longer allowed to hold their Sunday markets but little was done to prevent them meeting the repatriates when they were out on work gangs.

This could never have happened among those who had taken the oath. No one who was in the hard-core group was allowed to meet with a woman, to drink alcohol or take the Indian hemp drug (*bhangi*). Anyone who was found even talking words of love to a girl was sentenced by us as if his intentions had been carried out. People were punished by being compelled to walk on their knees many times up and down on the concrete floor of a hut: this could be most painful. But the worst punishment was to be ostracized, which was reserved for bad offences, and seemed like dying alive. Under these sanctions we were well-disciplined and when our group arrived at South Yatta, we were friendly and polite to the Kamba but nobody considered talking love to their women; consequently they respected and trusted us.

I met several old friends in this camp and I was especially pleased to meet again Gad Kamau Gathumbi, who had been brought there earlier from Manyani. We saw that our people were suffering from bad food, hard labour and poor medical facilities and at their urging I wrote a letter to the usual list of addresses (Colonial Secretary, M.P.s, Governor, Commissioner of Prisons and Provincial Commissioner) asking for lorries to take us to work and for proper medical arrangements, a qualified medical assistant, a sick bay, and recreational facilities. I also requested that our diet should be brought up to what was laid down in the regulations, six ounces of rice, twelve ounces of beans, eight ounces of potatoes, eight ounces of vegetables, twenty-one ounces of maize flour and eight ounces of meat. Paper and stamps were obtainable in the canteen and I gave a warder money to post the letter for me. Gad and I were angry with the other educated men in the camp who seemed to be scared of the consequences of writing such a letter, but it was the same old story of the literates being weaker in resistance than the illiterates.

The letter had a surprising effect. Within two weeks of its being sent all the grievances were put right. Chichester had been transferred before we reached the camp and in the evening of 28 July 1955 the new Commandant summoned me to his office. I admitted writing the letter and he sent me to solitary confinement in the small cell, where I spent the next month on a penal diet. Once more my policy of making friends with the warders, as opposed to the N.C.O.s, paid off and they brought me extra food. When the Commandant discovered this the cell was surrounded with an additional barbed wire fence. By now the authorities were fed up with me and on 30 August I was sent by train with forty-two other Zs to Manyani, back down the pipeline.

Manyani looked the same; hundreds of uniform aluminium huts gleaming on a plain, thousands of warders rustling to and fro in their khaki and more than fifteen thousand human beings seething inside an electric fence, black skins dressed in white prison clothes, waiting for freedom. There were some changes. Marlow had gone, for which I humbly thanked God; the food had improved and now included *njahi* (black gram), which is a food especially beloved by Kikuyu. We ourselves at home give it to *athoni*, our relatives by marriage, and to the elders. After my final release the first things I sent to Jomo Kenyatta were supplies of *njahi*, as a mark of my deep respect for him. The *njahi* were soon finished, for we were many, and then they gave us *njugu* (groundnuts) which is another favourite Kikuyu food.

Before we were allowed to enter the camp we were taken to the dip. This was the same as those designed for cattle and was about twenty feet long, six feet deep and four feet wide. It was filled with water strongly impregnated with Jeyes Fluid. The officers told us that we would have to be dipped in this as those coming into the camp from outside were thought to be bringing infectious diseases with them. So we were sent down the ramp in single file, dressed but carrying all our spare clothes and other belongings. Everything had to go under the water and every part of every one of us had to be immersed. The officers and warders standing on the top hit our heads as we came through, forcing us to submerge ourselves completely. Tears were streaming out of my stinging eyes when I came out of the dip. All of us felt that this was an unnecessary operation aimed more at degrading our humanity than removing any possible infections.

We were taken to Compound 9 where I was again elected leader. The officer in charge was a half-caste whom we named Muru-wa-Wachuka (son of Wachuka). Some detainees knew that his mother had been a prostitute and that his father was an Englishman. He was badly educated and spoke very little English and so he asked me to help him with the letters he had to write to the Camp Commandant. One evening at lock-up time he came into Compound 9 after he had been drinking and began an unprovoked and indiscriminate assault on the nearest detainees. I was furious and seized the stick he was using, broke it in small pieces and threw it away. I told him that if he carried on in that way I would have to see whether he was stronger than me or not. This open challenge to a fight nettled him and he summoned me to the compound office, where he threatened to beat me. By this time I was raging with fury and to his surprise I retaliated by seizing his throat and throttling him. He was a tall man but weak and seemed powerless to resist me. After a few seconds I threw him down to the ground at my feet and told him to behave himself. Slowly he got up and then called Sergeant Okello, a Jaluo who was a good man and used to behave well and treat us like human beings, to take me to be locked up by myself in the guardroom in the compound. In July 1961 I met Muruwa in Nairobi, and when I started speaking to him, he turned away and went swiftly in another direction.

He appointed George Kibocha as compound Leader in my place (no more elections) and they called in two of the screeners to talk with the other detainees; the first was Saul, later prominent in political life, and the other was Samuel, who claimed to be of the same clan as Kenyatta. The detainees told me that they were contemptuous of these two and said to Samuel, 'You have tried to destroy the name of our leader who is in Lokitaung and you have sold the soul of Africa to eat the rich white maize porridge and left us resisting alone on thin millet gruel. We cannot listen to your words since you are no longer one of us.' Lokitaung was the dreary outpost in the Northern Frontier District where Kenyatta was imprisoned. The screeners at Manyani ate good meals with porridge made of maize meal, while the diet of hard-core detainees was weak millet gruel. Samuel is now a trader and although he had not the strength to resist the pressures at Manyani, his heart is in the right place.

When I had been three days in the guardroom the detainees won my battle and I was set free. From then on Muruwa avoided me and stopped hitting people in my presence, but we remained scornful of him. He could not even count without using his fingers like a small boy in Standard II. It seemed absurd to put so ignorant a man in charge of anything. Shortly afterwards several of us were transferred to Compound 13, where I met again many friends whom we had left behind when we were sent to South Yatta and we were given a rousing welcome by them. The compound Leader was now a man from Fort Hall called Adam who was assisted by Daniel.

I suggested that we should start to teach literacy to those who had not been educated, especially as now that the airfield was finished we were not doing any manual labour. So we organized a group of young men who could read and write and started daily morning lessons. It was not possible to hold them in the evening as no lamps were provided in the compounds from the beginning to the end of my detention at Manyani. We could collect handfuls of very fine sand, sieve and heap it in one place and then flatten and smooth it out to the size of a slate. We used sharp-pointed sticks which worked excellently provided the sand was dry and the grain particles were minute enough. We divided the students into their different standards and I took the advanced classes for those who had completed Standards VI, VII and VIII. At the same time I taught the ideas and techniques of politics and current affairs to larger groups of anyone interested. There is no doubt that this all created a firm feeling of unity among us and encouraged our natural resistance to the blandishments of the screeners. Daniel, who later joined the 'surrenders', was frightened of the increasing influence that I was having and reported what we were doing to the authorities. So I was removed to Compound 6 and I later heard that the classes had been discontinued by the orders of the screeners.

Compound 6 must have been just about the most horrible place not only in Kenya but in the whole world at this time. The only other people in it were eight detainees who had been brought from Compound 9 accused of taking an oath. This was a completely false allegation. The compound Leader there, who had succeeded George Kibocha and whose name I cannot remember, was one of those who tried to curry favour with the authorities in order to hasten his release. In our Kikuyu country the old men use the fat off the meat as an ointment for the skin, and after washing they rub it on themselves and there is a general opinion that it is most beneficial. Some of my friends who have done science tell me that this is likely to be true. These detainees used to preserve the fat off the meat whenever it was in the rations and do exactly the same. In view of the heavy incidence of pellagra this seemed a wise precaution. The compound Leader found some of these pieces of fat and reported them to the authorities who were by then so oath-conscious that they jumped almost with joy to the obvious conclusion. All these people from Compound 9 were old friends of mine.

The officer in charge was a European called Wells. I do not like using strong words but he was nothing more nor less than a cruel and vicious sadist. Under him there was an African sergeant, a Mnyakyusa from Tanganyika, whom we gave two names, 'Wagithundia' and 'Wakaranja'. When he approached the compound we used to say *Giguthundia*, which is the ordinary Kikuyu word for 'he appears'. He asked us why we said it so we told him that it was a good name, a praise word for extolling a kind and noble person like him. He purred with happiness and asked us to call him this for ever. He was also called Wakaranja because Karanja was the name of the first Kikuyu he had met in Manyani and he seemed to assume as a result that all Kikuyu were called Karanja. He was not an intelligent man; even if an officer swore at him he would reply seriously, 'Thank you, *effendi*'. When John O'Washika dared to speak to an officer in English rather than Swahili he seized him and said, '*Kimbelembele chako kirefu kama tereni*', which means, 'You are pushing yourself forward like a train', and hit him hard. John unsuccessfully contested the North Nyanza constituency in the general election of February 1961 and is a leading member of the K.A.N.U. branch there. We used to discuss this extraordinary fellow in the evenings and we decided that if there were anywhere established a University of Fools he would inevitably become Chancellor of it.

After a few days batches of the hard-cores from all the other compounds were drafted into No. 6, including such gentlemen as Stephen Aloo (a former Police Inspector and now working with Brooke Bond) and David Oluoch Okello (former Chairman of K.A.U., Central Nyanza, who has returned to politics), all of whom were true nationalists and none of whom were Kikuyu. John O'Washika, a Mluhya, was also sent there. It is another false impression that has been spread abroad that there were no tribes other than Kikuyu represented in these camps. While the vast majority were Kikuyu there were also many from such different tribes as Jaluo, Abaluhya, Kitosh, Akamba and Masai, who provided some of the strongest resistance of all.

Compound 6 had its own regimen. Wells seemed to have been given a free hand by the Commandant to try out his own methods, assisted by Wagithundia and a Mkamba corporal. The ordinary warders, with whom we had so many secret arrangements and relationships, took no part in what I must now describe. At 6 a.m. we were woken up and taken outside where we were made to run very fast; at 7.30 a.m. we took some thin gruel. At 8 a.m. the real business of the day began. Our tormentors, Wells, the sergeant and the corporal, took it in turns to supervise us. Until 1 p.m. we did a series of violent exercises. These included running fast with the hands above the head, hundreds of press-ups, jumping like frogs at the knees-bend position for long distances with our hands clasped behind our knees, and many other exercises, all in the burning heat of the sun. The orders were that wherever we went we had to run and whatever we did must be done quickly. Anyone who slacked, and many who did not, were beaten with the sticks or the length of hose pipe which the overseers carried. They would increase the speed of press-ups until it was impossible to obey and we must have looked like Charlie Chaplin does when one of his silent films is speeded up. Many people when doing the frog jump would fall forward on their faces in exhaustion, badly damaging their teeth.

Once when I relaxed during a press-up the corporal came and gave me several almighty blows on my ears. To my dismay when he had finished I found I could hear nothing and for two days I remained like this, trying to lip-read what was going on. Then I put water in my ears and tried by filling my mouth with air to break through my ear-drums. This worked with one ear and then Wells sent a dresser who cleaned the other one with hydrogen-peroxide. At Lodwar, because it was discharging, I was given sixteen injections by a doctor but it is still bad and I sometimes have severe earaches today and I remain rather deaf in the one ear. Those whom Wells particularly disliked he would force to remove their trousers and piggy-back another naked person. This was the most shameful thing of all. Once when a young man called Kimani was in a press-ups position Wells came and poured a bucket of water over his naked buttocks, laughing as he did it.

At 1 p.m. we would play 'Do this' and 'Do that'. This was a most welcome respite for us and Wagithundia would become so happy if he was able to catch us out that we went out of our way to do it wrong both to prolong the interval of relief and also to try to keep him as good-humoured as possible. At 5 p.m. we were returned to our compounds and the long agony of the day was over. The evening and the night were like a holiday from pain. People do not realize how wonderful ordinary life is, how much pleasure there is just in being rid of beatings and

8

barbed wire and in not being organized and breathing in free
air and talking to free people. To the minds on both sides in this
struggle strange things were happening and our personalities
were changing in odd ways.

One day Paul Muchemi, son of Johanna Kunyiha, M.B.E.,[1]
of Nyeri, was beaten so badly by the Kamba corporal that blood
came out of his head. I decided that I must take the risk of
sending another letter out, although my previous experiences
as an author were scarcely very encouraging. It was impossible
to suborn any of the warders in Compound 6 but after some time
I thought of a way and I wrote the letter on lavatory paper and
then hid it under a sanitary bucket. We were not allowed out of
our compound and so our buckets were emptied by detainees
from Compound 7. Kamau Githirwa found it and smuggled it
out of the camp in the usual way. It was addressed to the Chief
Secretary and Commissioner of Prisons. I had written on it a
note to whoever found it suggesting that they should rewrite it
on good paper before sending it; it is not known to me whether
they did so.

A few days later the Commandant called me before him and
asked me if the letter was mine. I still did not know whether he
was told by higher authorities to investigate my charges or not.
I agreed and he told me I would be punished. There was an
order that no one should write a letter outside unless it first
went through 'the proper channels' for censoring. My kind of
letter would be censored to obliteration and so it was not
possible to obey this regulation. All the detainees available,
about four thousand, were assembled near Compound 6 and
the Commandant said to them, 'This is your leader, Mwangi.
He is a most dangerous man and he spends his time writing
letters outside the camp, an action which is against the law.
We sent him to South Yatta down the pipeline on his way home
and he wrote another letter there and so he was brought back to
Manyani, where he has now written another letter. He is now
going to learn his lesson in your presence and I advise none of
you to try writing letters yourselves.' I was stripped and given
twelve strokes by a Mkamba sergeant. These were just about
the most painful ones I ever received and they drew much blood
from my buttocks. When the detainees saw my body, which was

[1] See also p. 6.

thin and bruised with the treatment we were receiving in Compound 6, they buzzed with anger like a swarm of bees. I was given strength to endure all these things because I knew that I was right and that all the other detainees thought I was doing right. This is the sort of strength that no amount of beating can weaken. When will people realize that such beatings only stiffen the resolve of the victim? A beating may do some good when the person beaten knows he has done wrong, although I do not personally think so. But when he thinks that he has done right (whether he has or has not) beating immeasurably toughens his determination. Finally the authorities by their treatment were rapidly building me up as a martyr which was again contrary to their real objectives. They were no longer governed by reasonable thinking but by their emotions, like the instinctive and useless lashing out of a large animal goaded by a small one.

Afterwards the Commandant told me to stand up and say to the detainees that I would never again write any more letters. He could hardly have chosen a more psychologically inept moment and I made my usual reply that if they would cease beating and maltreating my people I would stop writing letters. But, I said bitterly, even if you kill me, my people will know that I have died for truth and their rights. This made him yet angrier and he ordered that I should be kept in solitary confinement in the small cell for seven days. But first they told me to go to the hospital because of the blood coming out of my buttocks and the detainee dressers there told me to take courage because all the detainees were rejoicing in my struggle for them. Then they took me to the cells near Headquarters Company.

The 'small cell' is a corrugated iron structure with a cement floor about six feet by four feet. There were thirty-two in all at Manyani, built in blocks of four. They gave me no food or water but fortunately someone had thrown a bucket of water on to the floor to make it uncomfortable for me to sleep on. So for the first three days until it dried up I was able to lick wetness off the cement and during that time I could think straight and speak out loud to myself. On the fourth and fifth days cold water started coming out of my skin in a sort of sweat. Still no food or water, no one came to look at me, silence and sweat. On the sixth and seventh days my eyes became heavy stones and the nightmares began. Turbaned Indians passed by all wearing red beards; different coloured stars shot in and out of my eyes; old Kikuyu women were dancing and always there were people moving to and fro. They never seemed to have faces I knew but the scenes were all vaguely familiar and appeared like a distorted reflection of events which I dimly remembered happening. On the eighth day I no longer realized where I was, nor did my body seem to be part of me. I felt like a human wheel turning round and round and then like a man falling through thousands of feet from a high mountain into a thick forest. My mouth would not open and there was only left the awful business of falling into the deep blue valley which I could see quite clearly. This would be the end; I could do nothing to prevent it and yet some bit of me did not start the falling, something stopped me sinking down into the relief and peace of the blueness.

On the sixth day, although I did not realize it, Gad Kamau Gathumbi and three others had been put into small cells near mine because they were alleged to have assaulted Adam, the Leader in Compound 13. Gad knew I was there and was very surprised not to see me on the roll-call on the seventh day. He suffered much thinking about me all through that day and on the eighth he insisted on the corporal opening my cell. They gently carried me out into the sun and Gad thought I had gone. The doctor was called and gave me an injection and then took me to the hospital. I spent one day in hospital and then I was returned to the small cell. However, Gad became my nurse and I slowly began to recover on a diet of milk and boveast. There is no doubt that I owe my life on this occasion to Gad Kamau Gathumbi.

Robinson Mwangi was the Leader of Compound 1 at this time and he had seen what had been done to me and he never ceased complaining and demanding better treatment for the detainees. Most of the other educated people considered we were mad not to desert the illiterates and seek the easy comfort of the 'surrenders'. But it was they who were wrong and this is one of the reasons why Daniel, who turned his heart away from us, failed in his election campaign. The people thought it was better to vote for someone who, even though he had never been detained, had also never betrayed true nationalism than to be led by someone who had been tested in the fire of the camps and found wanting.

Because of his intransigence Robinson was moved to Compound 6, where he became the Leader and where I rejoined him after my release from the small cells. When the Visiting Committee came he did not hesitate to tell them about the maltreatment we were receiving and, as usual, this had some effect because the people in Compound 6 were transferred to Compound 21. At this time several thousand detainees were brought to Manyani from the Special Camp at Mackinnon Road which could hold 6,000 in all and which was now being closed down. They told us many stories which we had no reason to disbelieve and which showed that their treatment there was as bad as ours. They slept in the old covered hangars which had been built during the war and were now divided up into cages. One thousand two hundred detainees were in each hangar. They never went out into the sun and they could never tell if it was day or night when they woke up. Because of the murmuring of innumerable voices it sounded like a huge market-place. There were several brutal officers there, including a German. The detainees were very dissatisfied with the general conditions in the hangars.

Robinson and I soon felt the itch to write another letter and we composed a joint one to the Colonial Secretary enumerating all the grievances in the camp and also extending our sights to the situation in the Reserves. We had recently had a special edition of the *Waya Times* on this subject from General Kibera Gatu, who had been captured while on a mission to Othaya from the Aberdare Forests. (He is now a hotel-keeper in Othaya.) He told us about the savage twenty-three-hour curfew orders and the children starving to death in the villages. Terrible as all this was we also came to learn in the camps of the fight against malnutrition among our children and old people by the International and British Red Cross Societies; some Roman Catholic missionaries had also been active in bringing food and succour to the needy. The detainees appreciated very much all this assistance without which many more would certainly have died. We also wanted an investigation into the death of Maina Matawa (from Othaya in Nyeri), who had run away from Mackinnon Road because of the violence meted out to him there and had been shot dead near Manyani.

We sent the letter through the usual channels but unfortunately a copy was found during an inspection which had been mounted to try and find any other letters about; it had been hidden inside a clothing bag shared by Wambugu Mangua and Ngunjiri Githiomi (both from Nyeri District; one is now working as a clerk in a Nairobi firm and the other as a clerk in the Ministry of Works, Nyeri). When the officers asked who had written it, I told them I had. I had forced Robinson to agree with this plan because it was vital to prevent them taking both of us and leaving the illiterates like orphans with no one to look after them. The 'C' Company Commandant, Romney, interrogated me about it. He knew Robinson's handwriting and was suspicious of my motives for facing the music alone. He wanted to get us both away. He asked me why I had written it and he was angry at my reply that the reasons were obvious and contained within the letter. When he asked me how I had smuggled it out I answered that I had given it to a small bird to take for me. I was determined not to divulge the name of any of the warders involved lest they refuse to take any more letters out for us. He was furious with me and I was taken immediately to the small cell where I stayed from the middle of March to 8 June 1956. Gad Kamau Gathumbi was still there and we stayed together all this time.

We were on half rations but the other detainees managed to pilfer meat for us from the stores and they would wrap it in some sacking and send it swooshing with a broom along the drains to us under the wire when they were supposed to be cleaning them out with water. We were so hungry that we did not mind the dirt that sometimes came with it. At this time there was an allegation that an oath called 'Manyani 25 *Thenge*' had been taken in Compound 25 whose leader was Daniel Mathenge, who in 1960 was elected chairman of K.A.N.U. in the North Tetu Division of Nyeri. There was no truth in this allegation and indeed, to the best of my knowledge, the only oath taken in any camp was that given to two people in Kowop. Looking for the evidence gave the authorities another excuse to hurt a few more detainees and the fact that so many of them confessed to taking this oath in the 'rehabilitation' statements is further proof of the general uselessness of the whole system at this time. Brutality had so distorted the meaning of truth that it now meant 'saying what those people want to hear with as few lies as possible'.

In general at this time conditions in Manyani had improved slightly. We protested vigorously when an order came for the hair to be shaved off our heads. Not only is this shameful in our custom, where it is only done by old men or old women, but it also caused great hardships to those working without any hair in the hot sun.

While in Compound 21 I met several of those who had been fighting in the forest and among them one who had also been a pseudo-gangster and was from Location 12 in Fort Hall. These pseudo-gangs were formed from people who had been in the forest but, according to the Government, volunteered almost immediately after capture to go back in again and act as gangsters so as to decoy those they had left behind only a few hours before. I was curious to know what were the reasons that made them act in this way. To understand their motives it is necessary to know that there were two distinct fighting groups engaged in this war. The first group were *Njamba cia ita* (literally 'Cock of the Army'), the true warriors and soldiers, whom we used to give the praise name of *Ihii* (uncircumcised). It was their job to fight the British troops and the Security Forces and anyone else hunting them in the forest. They were the Land Freedom Army, and they were organized in battalions and sections like any other military unit. In the forest their camps, which were numbered, were known as 'Bush 12' or 'Bush 4' and were neatly laid out like any army's bivouac. When they came out to fight in the Reserves they blew their trumpets or their whistles when surrounding a post in efforts to bring the Security Forces to battle. It was not their job to kill civilians; they fought those fighting against them and they were responsible for many daring raids and hard-fought battles, such as the attack on Naivasha Police Station and assaults on Home Guard Posts and Administrative Headquarters. In so far as any war is ever fought cleanly, they fought this one cleanly.

One of the most important people in this army was the *Mundu Mugo wa Ita* or 'Prophet of the Army', who would advise when and where to attack. Wang'ombe Ruga, who was

descended from a long line of *arathi* (dreamers) in Nyeri, had
this job in Kimathi's Army on Nyandarua (the Aberdare
Mountains) and he was with me at Manyani, Aguthi and Showground Camps. He told me that they had their own very strict
laws in the forest just as we had in detention. These laws were
passed at annual meetings of the 'Kenya Parliament' which
were held three times in a huge cave deep in the forested mountains. One other general told me that the Government wasted
much money in its attempts to bomb them out of the forest.
Although a few were killed accidentally, it was only too easy to
make the pilots drop their bombs uselessly by lighting a decoy
fire which quickly attracted them, the warriors being by then
far away. In some ways the Government gravely underestimated
not only the motives but also the intelligence of the forest armies.
The aeroplanes were called *Nyagikonyo* because the bomb-racks
look like navels (*gikonyo*) on their bellies.

The second distinct group of fighters were the *Komerera*. The
word means those who are awake when they are thought to be
asleep and these people used to hide either in the Reserves or
on the forest edge and would fight and kill even their own
people in the search for food and guns. They fought everyone,
including civilians, and they did not have the skill to make their
own guns nor could they fight a pure battle. This group was
composed of weaker characters and lacked discipline and
control, nor was it responsible to any higher authority, to the
Laws of the 'Kenya Parliament' nor even to the instructions of
the *mundu mugo*, and the *Komerera* did very much as they
pleased. Although the number of atrocities committed by our
fighters has been exaggerated and played up, there is no doubt
that some bad things were done. Someone killed by a panga
looks in worse shape than someone killed by a rifle, because a
panga will not kill cleanly, but even so some inexcusable things
occurred. I wish to make it plain that these were condemned
both by the 'Kenya Parliament' in the forest and also by
ourselves in the detention camps. We were not happy to hear
of a European woman or child killed on a farm, or to hear of
cattle being maimed. But we paid tribute to the great courage
and brains of those who were fighting the real battle with the
real enemy, fearlessly and nobly from their forest strongholds.

There were three reasons why the pseudo-gangsters went

back into the forest. First the situation was changing every year. By 1954 the resistance of those who had gone in the forest in 1952 had already forced upon the Kenya Government major modifications in its attitude to the African case. No longer was there much glib talk of dealing with the rebellion in three or six months. So, over the years, the slammed door that had driven my people into active resistance had been opened. Some pseudo-gangsters genuinely wished to tell their comrades this and to get them to come out. Progress by politics was becoming possible again. Secondly, some of the pseudo-gangsters were dealt with in a rough manner and it was inferred that they could only save their lives by doing what they were asked. In these circumstances, which are against the usual conventions of war, they were forced to go back. Thirdly, many of the pseudo-gangsters wished to let their comrades in the forests know that there was no longer the simple alternative of 'fight or be killed'. Another course was now possible, to surrender and live. Few of those in the forest believed this even as late as 1956 and there had been many reports of prisoners being shot that were by no means without a basis of fact. At one time in Chinga Location the Security Forces simply did not take prisoners. By 1957, with the announcement of the general election and African elected members for the Legislative Council, the battle had really been won. This is why there are many ex-Generals and ex-fighters in the country today going peacefully and quietly about their business as hotel-keepers, stock-traders or farmers. We have got it all, there is now nothing left to justify violence, secret movements or war, and those that still indulge in such things do not do so in our name.

On 8 June, 205 of the alleged ringleaders from all over the camp were called to Compound 30 where our legs were fettered to prepare us for the journey to the island of Saiyusi. Robinson, Gad and I were very happy to be reunited again. We decided to make a joke of the fetters and so we arranged that everyone should run with a smiling face to collect his from the officers. They must not be allowed to see they had scored over us at any time. Saiyusi is an island three square miles in area in the middle of Lake Victoria, near Kisumu. We heard that the Kenya Government called it 'The island of No Return'.

CHAPTER VII

Fetters, Island and Dust

I DO not know who makes fetters, but Kenya must have taken up a large part of his annual production in 1956. Since few people today have much experience of wearing them, and most of the rest seem to be under the impression that they went out with the Inquisition, perhaps I could here give a few tips about them. When fettered it is important to walk as little as possible, because they are specifically designed to prevent movement. It took us four and a half hours, from 5 a.m. to 9.30 a.m., to walk the three miles from the camp to the railway station. Large fetters are less constricting than the small type, but with the small ones it is possible to keep the feet together and jump as in a sack race. Some of the young men could move very swiftly for short distances by jumping. The metal inevitably chafes the skin whatever happens. Some fetters have a wider link between each shackle than others. It is not possible to take up the slack by walking with the feet wider apart, this soon becomes too great a strain on the legs. So the extra width falls to the ground, drags in the earth and dust and piles up an ever-increasing load behind it. This makes progress difficult and we used to pass some string under the link and attach it round the waist in a girdle. This could be tightened to raise the link right off the ground if required.

Then there was the debagging difficulty. We had only one pair of trousers each and periodically these had to be removed for washing. It took us some time to find the way and Kenyatta once told me that even his group at Lokitaung were originally baffled by the problem. I would not like to think of anyone else in a similar position perplexed by this, so here is the answer. The secret is one leg at a time. Lower the trousers and push one trouser-leg down inside the shackle, between it and the leg, until you have stuffed through as much as will go, including some of the crutch. Then pull the shackle as high up the leg as it will go and remove your foot from the trouser-leg which should

now all be below the shackle. Next feed back all the loose cloth
of the trouser-leg back through the shackle. One leg is now free.
Repeat the process on the other leg and the trousers can now
be washed. Putting them on again merely involves reversing
the operation.

In Nairobi the train took on three more detainees, among
them General Kahinga, and in Nakuru it halted for three hours.
Many people whom I had known before came to see us when
they heard we were there and they brought food and tobacco
which at first the warders refused to allow us to keep. When
the women at the station saw the fetters on the legs of Gathogo
Mwitumi, as he hobbled off the train to report to a warder
who called him, they wept bitter tears. We told them not to
be unhappy because wearing such things was now a hobby of
ours and we did not feel uncomfortable in them. Fetters are
most unpleasant really but we said this so that the women of
Kikuyu should know that we were still strong and not down-
hearted and also because we did not in any circumstances wish
our tormentors to think that they had at last done something
that distressed us. Then one of the women called Kabura
courageously went and asked the officer in charge to allow
them to give us food and he overruled the warders. When we
reached Saiyusi we composed a song of praise and thanks to her
and the other women.

We arrived at Kisumu on 11 June 1956 and we were
straightway taken to H.M. Prison, Odiaga, Kisumu. Next
morning we were divided into two groups, one hundred remaining at Odiaga and one hundred and eight destined for Saiyusi
Island. I was among those going to Saiyusi, while Robinson
Mwangi remained at Odiaga. Although I deeply regretted my
separation from him, it might have been worse to have been
together since one educated leader was still with each group.
On the morning of 12 June, still fettered, we were put into
lorries and when we were settled, thirty-five to each lorry, to
our disgust we saw warders fasten large nets over the tops of the
lorries, as if we were fishes or birds. The meshes were about the
same size as those used on goal posts and the nets were made in
Odiaga Prison. We took this as yet another attempt to destroy
our spirits and as usual it had the opposite effect of reviving
us as we realized how much of a symbol we were becoming.

If some of us had not held out, it would have been so much
easier to have explained away 'Mau Mau' as a primitive and
atavistic throw-back movement of a people misled by a foolish
leader. From under the net things looked strange and the warders
seemed full of cracks and nothing was clear. Thus we passed
through Bondo and Sakwa up to the banks of Lake Victoria
where the fetters were at last removed and we were handcuffed
instead. The boats took fifty people each and I was in the first
group to cross over to the island. The motion was new to me
and several of us were sick.

The camp and officers' houses at Saiyusi had been built by
the 'Mau Mau' convicts who were sent there in 1954. At the end
of 1955 the convicts were gradually completing their sentences
and detainees were drafted in place of them. About eight
hundred detainees from Manyani were already in the Island
when we arrived and I was very surprised and touched at the
shout of welcome they gave me. To my utter astonishment they
chaired me from the gate to one of the huts where they had
prepared a splendid meal of welcome, comprising tea and real
bread and butter. It was four years since I had last eaten bread
and butter which had always been one of my favourite foods
in normal days and it tasted wonderful. Many of the people
there had been with me in Compound 13 at Manyani and we
talked many hours together before I went off to join my group
in another hut, happier than I had been for many a long
day.

The following morning we were ordered to go out to work,
as the other detainees had been doing up to that time, but we
refused to obey this order, which was illegal. The detainees
elected a delegation to interview the Commandant, consisting
of Harry Kamanda Njoroge (now a salesman in Nairobi),
Gathogo Mwitumi (now a trader and K.A.N.U. Vice-Chairman
in Nakuru), Wambugu Kamuiru and myself. We quietly explained to the officer that we were not going to work because we
were not convicted prisoners and also that we were covered in
our refusal under Section 18B of the International Convention.
We did not propose to fight or use violence or be unreasonable
but we were not going to work. Our protest was accepted and
we were told to remain in our huts all day except when going to
eat or when we were taken to wash. The huts were very large

and each one could sleep a hundred people; we called them 'barracks'. We used to spend our time talking politics and teaching ourselves. To my relief it was possible to buy books again in the camp canteen and we obtained some English Readers and Michael West's *Dictionary*. Most of the instruction was done by John Gakuha, who is now a schoolmaster in Nyeri. He was a marvellous teacher and managed to help many of our people. As the leader of the group I found that I had little time for teaching. I was busy filling in the letter-forms for the illiterates to send to their homes, writing letters of complaint, preparing for interviews with the Commandant and administering the day-to-day affairs in the 'barrack'.

I also had to arrange for the editing of the daily news bulletin, gathered from the usual sources, and known at Saiyusi as *The Kamongo Times*. *Kamongo* is the Luo name for a very large fish found in Lake Victoria, sometimes as much as five feet long and eighteen inches wide. It makes very good eating and excellent soup and the detainees used to catch it when clearing the grass near the lake shore for vegetable plots. The Kamongo comes in from the lake and burrows under the sandy soil about ten feet, creating a small inlet for the water. It then pushes up into the grasses and makes a minute pool, which seems to be a trap for insects and other animals. The Kamongo then retires into its subterranean inlet, occasionally returning to flick its powerful tail to and fro with the result that the water in the trap is very clear. When a detainee came on this hole and possibly even saw the flicking tail, he would call some others and they would stand ready with their pangas, one where he could see the tail, the other where he thought the head might be under the sand. On a word of command they would simultaneously plunge their pangas down and usually kill the fish. Sometimes we were left with a piece of tail and the Kamongo threshed its way violently down the inlet to safety; at other times there was a tough struggle before it was finally caught. Very heavy, it took at least two people to carry it in.

It was strange for us Kikuyu to wake up in the morning and find ourselves on a small island encircled with green and grim water, full of hungry crocodiles. There was no question of escape and we began at times to despair of ever seeing our blue hills, red soil and crumpled valleys again. The Camp

Commandant was a Canadian called Kendal, whom we nicknamed *Karimanjaga*—'Cultivating naked'—because he never
wore a vest or shirt when he was on the island. He did not beat
us but relations were not friendly because of our refusal to work.
Before we reached Saiyusi the detainees already there had been
working on the extensive farms on the island, producing paw-
paws, cassava, maize, beans and many vegetables, all of which
grew in profusion. Shortly after this, lest our uncompromising
attitude should contaminate them, the authorities transferred
all the other detainees, except thirty, who were also classified
as irreconcilable 'hard-cores'. To my delight among these was
my old friend from Kihuri in Othaya, James Thuku Mangothi,
who had come to Tryon's farm all those years ago and who had
spoken English to him and helped to inspire my yearning to
educate myself.

The Commandant told us that as we would not work it would
be necessary to reduce our diet. When this was carried out we
all went on hunger strike and the detainees asked me to go to
see the Commandant. I asked him under what authority he had
ordered a reduction in our diet and I requested that he quote
the regulation to me. He could not and was astonished when I
repeated to him from memory the paragraph which laid down
the minimum diet for detainees. While in Manyani for the
second time I had arranged to buy for twenty shillings an eight-
page copy of the Detention Camp Regulations from a Mkamba
working as a warder clerk in the Headquarters Office. Exorbi-
tant as the price was, I had to have it and I concealed this
priceless document with my money in my coat lapels. I also
explained to Kendal that we did not intend to make trouble for
him but that we would appreciate an immediate return to the
statutory minimum diet and also better medical facilities, since
the island was teeming with flies and mosquitoes. Both these
requests were granted.

However, the Commissioner of Prisons authorized the Commandant to place me in the small cell for sixteen days with
penal diet. This was apparently because I had been the ringleader in organizing the refusal to work and the hunger strike.
But this time my stay there was relatively pleasant since the Luo
warders, being friendly and sympathetic to us, were happy to
bring me extra food given them by the detainee cooks in the

kitchen and I even put on weight. The only trouble was that there was nothing to do and nothing to read, only plenty to think about. During my sojourn in the small cell the remaining group of one hundred, who had been left in Odiaga, arrived, and Robinson Mwangi was among them. He told me that conditions there were not too bad but they were getting the rations of convicted prisoners rather than those laid down for detainees: they had all been looking forward to rejoining us on Saiyusi.

The Commandant had given orders that we should be kept locked inside our huts both day and night since we would not work. We protested vigorously against this but to no avail, and so one day when we returned to the huts after taking food we refused to go inside them. The warders started to crowd us, hustling and beating us to force us back into the huts. We had previously agreed among ourselves that if this happened we would resist and, if necessary, fight them. We rapidly armed ourselves with plates and stones and, using one plate as a shield and others as boomerangs, we bombarded the warders. We also seized some of the wooden posts which made up the inner fence. When Robinson and his group heard this battle going on they broke down the door of the hut in which they had been confined and burst out to reinforce us. The flying plates and hurtling stones caused many injuries on both sides but we slowly drove the warders away out of range. Gad Kamau was among those injured, but he soon recovered. At this stage we heard four shots fired into the air by Kendal and saw him slowly approaching the battlefield alone. He quietly asked us to sit down and counted us, and then told us to go back into the 'barrack'. He agreed to meet a delegation the next morning to discuss our complaints and told us that he wanted no more fighting.

I went to see him as arranged and after that we were allowed out of the huts into the compound several hours every day. We both knew that forced incarceration inside huts was not in the regulations. I then wrote a letter to the Chief Secretary about the incident, with copies to E. W. Mathu and W. W. W. Awori, who were the nominated African Members of Legislative Council at this time. Although relations with the warders had become strained since the fight, there were still some friendly individuals among them and I arranged for the letters

to be carried by the wife of a Luo going on leave. She concealed
them under her knickers and I have no reason to doubt their
safe posting.

There was also trouble of the same kind going on in Mageta
Island which we heard about from the warders transferred to
Saiyusi from there. This did not surprise us since, before leaving
Manyani, we had all agreed that wherever we were sent we
would refuse to work whatever the consequences. This seemed
to be our most effective way of embarrassing the Government
and helping our friends still fighting in the forests.

The authorities decided to send a team of European Special
Branch officers to investigate the troubles. They started at
Mageta and then came to Saiyusi where they called forty-two
of us to the office. We were then questioned and scientifically
beaten up with sticks and punches. Since there were five of
them, none of us had any chance although I tried to defend
myself as vigorously as possible. Five of our number agreed
to co-operate with the Government after this treatment, but
thirty-seven refused. Thirty-five of these were isolated in a
special hut, while Robinson Mwangi and myself were thrown
into a small cell together. Our shirts had been torn to shreds
and our bodies were badly bruised. That was a memorable
night: we had no blankets and it was very cold and so we slept
on the cement floor huddled up together trying to keep warm
with what was left of our shirts covering up our eyes. The
mosquitoes seemed particularly active and the final anguish
was restraining the need to urinate since no bucket had been
provided. We saw the sun's light creeping in under the door
with relief.

Next day we were taken back to Odiaga Prison where we
rejoined many others from Mageta Island, making about four
hundred in all. The fetters were replaced and as we shuffled
off to our food they clinked and tinkled like the bells used in
church, bells of tears, sobbing for the afflictions of our people.
At Odiaga I met for the first time Joseph Kirira Karechu who
has been my friend and fellow-worker ever since. He is intelligent and able and a man of fine character. We were now a trio
with Robinson and we decided to devote ourselves to helping
the other detainees to preserve their nationalism and their
faith. The warders were helpful and we wrote a letter to the

Commissioner of Prisons complaining about our food—we had been put on half rations—and a warder posted it for us for five shillings.

The Government did not seem to know where to take us next, but one day a Special Branch officer told me that 'the Government are going to send you to a very hot place called Lodwar so that you can die there'. We laughed at them and their hopes that they could bruise our spirit in this way. Some of us felt that we had already been through so much that anything else would be small stuff. After one month at Odiaga we were taken to Kisumu Airport on 11 August 1956, handcuffed in pairs. My companion was Kirori Motoku, a splendid old man aged about sixty. Kirori had been a thorn in the flesh of the Administration in Nyeri for many years: he was a true nationalist, an energetic trader, and a leader of his people. In 1961 he became a leader of K.A.N.U. in his area of Nyeri District.

We were going in a special flight by East African Airways to Lodwar, thirty-five of us in each plane, handcuffed in pairs except for an old man called Gathekya who was handcuffed to himself. Gathekya passed the whole journey curled up, clutching his stomach tightly and shivering as if with fever. He told us later that when he looked out of the window he saw oil dripping out of the engine. He debated with himself what to do about it and decided that he could not go and tell the pilot because if the pilot came to have a look he would leave the steering wheel and the plane would crash. So he held his peace, prepared for an imminent explosion, and prayed.

After a short while a red light went on in the front and a voice came out of an amplifier, speaking in English like the crack of doom, 'Gentlemen, we are about to fly over Lake Victoria. You will find your life-jackets under your seats.' Few of us knew English but those of us that did spread the word around and the handcuffed passengers tried desperately to get out their life-jackets, pulling in different directions. Gathekya remained curled up, looking at his oil, oblivious of the life-jacket which anyway he could not reach. The rest of us wondered if anyone would have time to unlock us if we did descend hurriedly. A spirit of fatalism sank down on us all for the rest of the journey.

Those who were in our aeroplane were lucky: we landed at

dusk and thus missed the reception party arranged for previous flights. Joseph Kirira told me they had been forced to run about carrying *karais* (basins) filled with stones, completely purposelessly, and had been so badly beaten by the Turkana policemen that one detainee, called Ngugi Mwarari, had collapsed and had to be carried off to the camp dispensary. That very evening we three, Robinson, Joseph and myself, composed a letter to the Camp Commandant, Buxton, asking him to come and discuss this affair with us next morning. He came and called all the detainees together and addressed us in Swahili as follows:

'You are all very evil hard-core "Mau Mau" from the Saiyusi and Mageta Island Camps where you refused to work. Here you must work and whether you like it or not you are going to work and this is an order which it is my job to see obeyed. If you refuse, you will see what will happen.' He then sat down and Gathogo Mwitumi stood up and asked him to call the local District Commissioner so that we could discuss this matter together. Buxton jumped up quickly and answered fiercely, 'You people—I want you to realize once and for all that I am the Camp Officer and the Rehabilitation Officer. I am the Governor and District Commissioner of Lodwar. I am the God of Lodwar. I am absolutely ready to deal with you all in any way I think fit until you obey orders.' Gathogo then asked him whether he would tell us which was the law he was using which could compel us to work. Buxton immediately replied, 'Forget all the laws you have been using as weapons in Saiyusi and Mageta. The Government is not stupid. My word is the Law of Lodwar and you must work. That is all.' Suddenly turning his back he left us. I was impressed by this man whose tough and uncompromising words were those of a straight and honest man doing his duty. We liked this kind of man, who says what he means and does what he says, which is why most African politicians perversely prefer Briggs and Cavendish-Bentinck to Blundell and Havelock. I suppose this may be because it is easier to cut a stiff piece of paper than a pillow.

We returned to our compound wondering exactly why such a man had felt able to speak so harshly. Many people came to my hut, No. 13, and we debated far into the night what we should do. At this time there were some detainees who had come from Athi River Camp and they were working. (Among them was Jeremiah Kirumwa Keiru, who has been working with me in business since his release.) They threw their weight on the side of our agreeing to work. Many others from our group maintained strongly that we should continue to refuse to do any work other than the usual basic camp chores. During this discussion my mind had been chewing over the Camp Commandant's speech and I felt that he was not a man to say things he could not carry out. I also had sensed that something had happened to give him the power to take the line he had. It is the custom of our people for the leaders to make the final speeches on such occasions and it is their duty to discuss all the points which have been brought up and then put forward their own views. So when all others had spoken I addressed them as follows: 'My people, I have been your leader now for many years and during all this time it has been my object to use every means possible to keep you all out of danger. We have now reached a crisis in our affairs. This is a real battle and unless we are very sensible we are going to fail.' I then told them the story of Napoleon Bonaparte, who conquered all Europe and then sent his armies into Russia where the enemy retreated before him, entangling him in a net woven by General Winter until very many of them died from hunger, intense cold and exposure. I then recalled to them the Commandant's remark about our use of the laws as a weapon at Saiyusi and Mageta and his comment that the Government was not stupid. 'This means to me that the law has been changed either in Kenya or the Colonial Office so that now detainees can be compelled to work. As you know, we have always in the past sheltered under our rights in the laws. We have tried as hard as we could to do no illegal action and it is this that has been our strength and power. It is my duty to tell you that I believe this weapon has now been removed from us and that we will destroy ourselves if we fight on this bad ground and with no arms. So let us agree now to work and let us use all our brains to find other ways to continue the struggle for our rights and for Independence.'

After a further short discussion of my views we all decided to start working on Monday, 13 August 1956. Very early that morning the Camp Commandant, not knowing whether we

had agreed to work or not, was busy organizing the warders
and issuing them with rifles, shotguns and clubs. We discovered
later that the District Officer in Lodwar had also concealed a
heavily armed force of 120 Kenya Police and forty Turkana
Tribal Police who were ready, should we refuse, to rush in and
compel us to obey. When they saw us go out quietly they
rejoiced, thinking they had won a great victory. But all they had
done was to make us change our weapons, and my mind had
already begun to think of using 'Go-slow' tactics, moving at
what we call 'chameleon's pace', and other devices within the
law. Our people were very pleased that they had accepted my
advice.

Lodwar is forty miles from Lake Rudolf in the thorn and
dusty desert of Kenya's Northern Frontier Province. Two
hundred miles from Kitale, it is four hundred and fifty miles
from Nairobi. As at Kowop, dry and rocky hills surround its
site near the banks of the Turkwell River, which evaporates
completely in the hot season but briefly becomes a heaving,
raging torrent during the rains. The sun starts roasting the
land soon after 6 a.m. and the night scarcely gives the scorched
earth time to cool down before the next dawn. No one can bear
to wrap a blanket round himself in the heat of the night. The
people who live there are the Turkana and their existence with
their herds is hard indeed. Many of them walk round naked
and they eat the meat and drink the milk of their cattle. They
also make great use of a tree called *mukoma*, which grows fifteen
to twenty feet tall and looks similar to a pawpaw. The Turkana
eat its fruits, which are the size of apples and which they beat
into a mash and mix with the blood of cattle and goats, drawn
from their throats through a hole made with a miniature bow
and arrow. They also make a fermented beer out of the fruit
and use the young leaves to make baskets, boxes and mats.
We used to roof our huts with it, but the Turkana did not do
this. I rapidly learnt how to make these things and I used to
augment my financial resources by selling mats to the warders
at prices varying from five to twenty shillings, according to
size and quality. We arranged to send Jomo Kenyatta, our
beloved leader, a box and I also made a large hat for him which
appears in some of the earliest photographs taken of him at
Maralal. He was by now in Lokitaung and we were in regular

contact with him through the warders going on transfers between the two camps.

The camp itself was a prison which had been built to house the 'Mau Mau' convicts sent there to construct the airfield. It was a square compound surrounded by a double barbed-wire fence, and split down the middle by a corridor four feet wide. The area on each side of this corridor was divided into three cages, also surrounded by barbed wire. In each of these there was a stone-built blockhouse with a corrugated iron roof. These blocks were divided into four compartments. We made our own dispositions for accommodation and friends naturally tended to be in the same rooms. I was in Number 13 and we were usually thirteen in there. Outside the compound wire were the kitchens and the place where clothes were repaired on a sewing-machine and where Kirori Motoku tended the lamps. Lodwar was the only camp where we were given these. A short distance from the kitchens was another block of two rooms used as an isolation area or 'small cells'.

Joseph Kirira and I shared the same bed together for the fourteen months that we were in Lodwar. There is a saying in Swahili, *Usimuamini mtu ikiwa hamjamaliza gunia la chumvi pamoja*, which is to say, 'Never trust somebody until you have finished a bag of salt together'. Joseph and I have now started our second bag and he is now my trusted political companion and business partner.

In Lodwar we created the best organization among the detainees of any camp I was in. Robinson Mwangi was elected camp leader, while Joseph Kirira became the chairman of the camp committee.

Each room chose its own leader who was then responsible to the camp leader for the carrying out of executive decisions. The camp committee consisted of one member elected from every room, making twenty-two in all plus the camp leader, his assistant and myself as educational member and political adviser. This committee met once a week, but special urgent meetings could be called at any time by the chairman or the secretary (Maina Muhiki, from Fort Hall, one of the twenty-two members, and now a clerk of works to an international construction company in Nairobi), in consultation with the camp leader. It was not necessary for the rooms to have their own committees as they were sufficiently few to hold full meetings for such things as electing their representative and their cook. We kept minutes of all our committee meetings and we destroyed the book when we left the camp. The camp leader was the executive officer of the camp committee, and he was ultimately responsible to them for all his decisions and actions. However, between meetings of the committee his authority was paramount. During his time at Lodwar, Robinson never did any action which the committee questioned, and he was a fine leader. Robinson's assistant was John Giathi of Kiambu, now working as a clerk for East African Breweries. My work was the usual one of writing letters to the authorities and Socialist M.P.s in England, and also teaching my people to read and write. Each room had to provide one cook, which was an extremely popular profession because of its perks and opportunities. However, we did not allow anyone who wanted to go, we insisted on one person being democratically selected from each room. Number 13 chose Wambugu Wachira and he served us very well.

We had a library at Lodwar, supplied by the Ministry of Community Development. It was a poor selection, all the books passing a most rigorous censorship before being approved, and nothing being included which was remotely connected with politics. Still, it was good to see print again and we once found a history book that must have slipped in accidentally as it contained an account of the Slave Trade and the struggle against it. The library was kept in our room and the librarian was Wachira Kariga who was good at suggesting the right type of reading for each of his varied customers. The absence of political books was annoying but since we knew that everyone could not become a politician we decided to organize classes from Standard I to Standard IX so that anyone, even if completely illiterate, could start his education there. We had not enough qualified teachers to execute this plan so we arranged that those learning in Standards III, IV and V should spend part of their time on a rota, teaching Standards I and II. The students in Standards VI and VII taught in Standards II, III and IV. I was myself responsible for Standards VIII and IX, which were for those who had already completed an Intermediate Course. Our students worked extremely hard and it makes me very proud today to see that some of our 'old boys' have become qualified in book-keeping and accounts, while others are now teachers in schools, instructing the future leaders and citizens of our country. I shall never forget the determination with which an old man called Kimana Wachuku from Fort Hall, who is seventy-five years old, would regularly attend Standard I and strive to learn reading and writing. His ability was such that he quickly earned promotion to Standard II. Sometimes we would gather round him and he would quietly tell us the history of our country from his own knowledge, and, since he had been born before the white man came, we learnt much about the Government's mistakes over the years which had led us to our present situation. Many of our detainees were inspired by these classes and are even now, after their release, continuing to study. At Lodwar we organized one of the first free educational schools in East Africa.

The camp committee laid down the following regulations, which governed our behaviour far more directly than any of the Government rules.

1. Nobody should fight any other detainee, inside or outside the compound.
2. Nobody should have sexual intercourse with any of the Turkana women or with the wives of any of the staff of the camp.
3. Nobody should threaten, insult or show hate to any of the other detainees.
4. Nobody should spit or urinate in the compound or in any other way intentionally spoil it.
5. Nobody should drink alcoholic liquor inside or outside the camp. Nobody should smoke Indian hemp, *bhangi*, inside or outside the camp.
6. Nobody should steal anything belonging to another detainee or a warder. Nobody should take away a library book for ever.
7. Nobody should disobey the order of a hut leader to dispose of the sanitary buckets, even on Sundays and any other holidays.
8. No one could choose for himself to do work which he feels is light and will give him rest. All the other detainees must consent.
9. When other detainees are working, no one may malinger.

10. No one may abuse or be insolent to the Camp Commandant, the warders or visitors from outside, without good reason or the permission of the camp leader.
11. No one may tell lies to other detainees.
12. No one may jump the queue when taking food.

These were the twelve Laws of Lodwar and they were confirmed by all the people in a public meeting. Any breach of them was tried before the camp judge, who was a man called Wakamore from Kiambu. He was assisted by a jury of five elders, one from each District in the Central Province, except Kiambu and Meru, plus a single representative from Nyanza Province. The public prosecutor was usually Paul Muchemi, whose father (Johanna Kunyiha) was President of one of the Government's Divisional Courts in Nyeri District, and I do not recall one case brought by him which failed. The Committee appointed Nguru Ndirangu as the camp policeman. It was his job to keep his eyes open and report any offences to the camp leader, and he did an excellent job. He is now released and is a farmer and leader of K.A.N.U. in his sub-location. The system worked well and all the people respected the laws and each other. The court was empowered to pass sentences which were carried out immediately, unless there was an appeal. There was a separate Appeal Court consisting of five different elders, drawn from Embu, Fort Hall, Kiambu and Nyeri Districts, and one again from Nyanza Province. There were very few appeals. The court used to sit in the afternoons in one of the huts. The court was open to the public, but since the huts were small and we were all very busy at this time, few in fact attended. The maximum penalties varied for each offence and were as follows:

Laws 1 and 2. To draw thirty-two buckets of water for filling up the hut water tanks or to be ostracized. This last was only once inflicted, on a young man from Embu who was found talking and laughing with the lover of a warder.

(The reader may not consider drawing thirty-two buckets of water a hard task, but the only time available for this was in the comparative cool of the evening between four and six o'clock. The water tank was outside the compound about four hundred yards away and it came in a pipe from the Turkwell River.

It ran out into the buckets very slowly and a 'convict' was lucky if he managed to bring more than four in one evening. I remember well the look of misery on the face of one poor man who slipped and knocked one of the two buckets he was carrying and then the disequilibrium upset the other as well. Only buckets in the tank were assessed, buckets 'in the bush' did not count.)

Law 3. To fill the kitchen water tanks for two days. (This was a hard punishment.)

Laws 4 and 7. To empty and clean the sanitary buckets for four days.

Laws 5 and 6. To draw twenty-six buckets of water.

Law 8. To draw twenty-eight buckets and complete eight circuits of a hut walking on the knees. (This was most painful.)

Law 9. To complete ten circuits on the knees and to resume work immediately unless proved sick to the satisfaction of the court.

Law 10. To complete ten circuits and draw twenty-eight buckets of water or to be ostracized.

Law 11. To draw twelve buckets of water and complete eight circuits.

Law 12. A summary sentence by the kitchen leader who told the offender to wait till everyone else had received their food. The court which sat later could then sentence him to ten circuits and to draw fourteen buckets. The kitchen leader was appointed by the camp committee, of which he was not a member although he might occasionally be invited to attend for special reasons.

The sentence of the court was publicly broadcast in every hut so that all might know the offence, the offender and what he was to do. There were relatively few cases because the detainees honoured the law and behaved very well.

It has been alleged in many quarters that the detainees used to pray to the Devil in an evil and primitive manner. It is time that the truth was known and as one of my duties in Lodwar was to lead the prayers every morning in my hut, I will tell how the ceremony was conducted. We usually prayed sitting, although on certain days (such as the anniversary of Kenyatta's arrest, 20 October, or when a political trial was taking place) we would stand. Some of those in the hut were Christians and others were not: we all prayed together. We would face towards Mount Kenya and spit on the palms of our hand. In our country we always spit on our hands before greeting someone who should be particularly respected. We would then raise our hands, with the palms open, to the level of our heads and the conductor would sing:

> O God, Only Creator and Destroyer of all the children of Adam;
> O God, who gave us this land of Africa;
> We who have sinned we pray before thee, humbly and earnestly,
> That thou wilt hearken to these the lamentations of thy children,
> Who are now suffering in the wilderness of the hot sun,
> Those whom thou hast given this land of Kirinyaga [Mt. Kenya],
> This land which is being tormented by the tribe of the White Men.
> O God, may thou never allow this inheritance which thou gavest us
> To be seized by the strangers;
> Our God, we have faith that thou wilt support us.
> For in the same way thou gavest the White Man the land of Europe
> As his inheritance,
> So thou puttest the waters for a boundary between us.
> As we do not in jealousy covet their land or their goods,
> O Lord, who dwells in the most high hills of Kirinyaga,
> So help them to understand these things and to leave us to our inheritance.
>
> Help our leader, Kenyatta, and help all the other leaders of the Africans,
> Who are striving to free us from the chains of slavery,
> In the East and the West, from the North to the South.
>
> Help all those who are sick in hospitals and those others wounded in the forest
> And who cannot get medicines.
> Help the orphans and the widows, help the injured wherever they may be.
>
> O Lord, hasten the end of this time of blood, flowing like a river through our land,
> And bring back peace and concord to our country.
>
> O Lord, let all our hearts remember thee always
> And let our souls be linked like the passages in a mole hole,
> And let all Africans speak with one voice,
> And take away from us all foul pestilences.

Turn, O Lord, all those that hate us so that they may become our
    friends.
Hasten Freedom for all Africans.
Save us from our present bondage.

O God, we do not presume to command thee to do these things
But we entreat and most earnestly do beseech thee,
Almighty, more wonderful than any earthly power,
O Lord who abideth and liveth for ever
We pray to thee thus, remembering our ancestors,
Gikuyu and Mumbi, whom thou placest under the mountain of
    Kirinyaga
To reap the fruits of this land.
We put our trust in thee, O Lord
Who abideth for ever and ever,
Praise be to God.
Praise be to God.
Praise be to God.

The work that we did there was to break and carry stones to
build the hospital at Lodwar, while some of us were taken by
the Hydraulic Department to help them clear the bush where
they were searching for water supplies. Although at the time
we found the job hard and unrewarding, we were overjoyed
later when we heard that many Turkana and our leader, Jomo
Kenyatta, were treated in our hospital. One day three of those
working on bush clearing, Cornelius Gathungu, Kibocho and
Kibaki, decided to escape. Normally anyone wishing to escape
was expected to ask permission from the camp committee so that
we could prepare for the inevitable retaliation, but these three
did not. I personally never once considered escaping since I felt
my place was with the illiterates in the camps, who were fighting
for freedom as strongly as many of those outside.

In Manyani an escape had always been the signal for several
days' concentrated beastliness on the part of all concerned.
However, to our surprise, Buxton came to see us in the camp
and he was actually smiling as he said, 'There are three of you
who have escaped. You are going to see that the Government
has a long hand. I will guarantee that they will never cross into
another District before they are either killed or arrested and
brought back here.' I had begun to suspect the truth and, sure
enough, it was the story of Kowop all over again : maize meal

and tea in exchange for the head of a detainee. Buxton was right and all three were re-arrested and returned to the camp before midnight the same day. Their heads only would have been brought back had it not been for the intervention of the local Turkana chief who advised his warriors to bring in their booty alive, and with the legs on, as this might earn them even more rations than the head would fetch alone. The reward given to them was deducted from our rations, although they were given rice as well, which must have come from somewhere else as we did not have it. The three erstwhile escapers were sentenced to six months' imprisonment, which was a mild substitute to their expectations in the hands of the Turkana. The whole episode proved distinctly encouraging to others of the same mind. Cornelius was later imprisoned for seven years in 1961 as a member of the Land Freedom Army, Kibocho serves in a shop in Nairobi, while Kibaki is a political worker in Fort Hall.

When we agreed to work because we suspected that the law had been changed, we decided that we would not accept any money for the days worked. This may sound petty but it was not and the reason for it was fundamental to our position. We wished to obey the Government laws where possible. The law had now been altered and we could be compelled to work. The law also stated that we should be given money in exchange for our labour. It did not say that we must accept this money. Now we were detainees and we had not been convicted before any court, we were political prisoners. We did not consider that political prisoners should be forced to work and any Government that did so was contravening the natural Rights of Man and was, in our eyes, performing the act of slavery. To accept money would make it look to the outsider as if we also accepted the principle which informed this new law. So we told the Commandant that while we would obey the law to work we would not agree to receive wages for it. We would work as slaves. We did not expect him to understand our position and nor did he. Letters showing a similar lack of understanding passed up and down the usual channels.

There was another advantage in our position. If we refused to accept money it would be very difficult for the authorities to compel us to work very hard. I then proposed to the camp committee that we should write a memorandum to the Governor and the Commissioner of Prisons setting out our views and that all those who wished to work as slaves should sign the letter. This was agreed and out of four hundred and twenty-six people in the camp over four hundred signed. A few abstained for reasons which I do not know, but only five were actually accepting money. We smuggled one copy out but decided to send the other one up to the Government through the Commandant. We waited for results, working slowly and not being beaten by the warders. At this time we also extracted some improvements in the food. A state of balance had been reached and there was a peaceful and almost pleasant lull in our lives.

The Commissioner of Prisons, Lewis, visited the camp and explained about the new law compelling us to work. We asked some questions and he told us that whether we liked it or not the money would be paid to us on our release. We still maintained our position. Shortly after this Buxton went on leave. His successor was a very different person. He insisted on everyone working, even the sick and the cripples, and he used to come round inspecting our huts, which Buxton never did, and whenever he spoke to us it was in a mood of anger, and hate was in all his words. We disliked him so much that we decided to send a secret letter of complaint to his superiors, a thing we would never have done with his predecessor. When he discovered this he became still more bitter and the camp was in a state of unhappiness and unrest until we were visited by a committee of the International Red Cross from Geneva, led by Philippe Junod. We selected a delegation of five members of the camp committee to meet them. I was the spokesman and I felt much better after I had poured out to them all the unpleasantness and difficulties with which we had to contend. Junod was a very intelligent and quiet man, and listened to all our troubles with close attention. We gave him the Kikuyu name *Muthuri wa Itathi*. This is a title of great respect given to an old man (*muthuri*) who judges actions peacefully, calmly and justly without favouring either side; *Itathi* is a tree whose leaves are carried in a bunch by old men to flick flies away and from which is cut the sticks used for guiding and herding the cattle of the homestead. He was a truly good man. After their visit our conditions became much better for the next three months. It was strange how quickly things would slide back after the immediate improvements resulting from any committee's visit. Perhaps the only solution is to have permanent resident committees, though I think that in the Kenya Emergency they would have been hard put to it to stay uncontaminated themselves: this sort of evil is most infectious.

In our case the decline was accelerated by the arrival of an Assistant Camp Commandant called Mansfield who was as bad as his superior and so we now had a poor pestle and a poor mortar and the resulting mixture was likely to taste bitter. We nicknamed him *Kamao*, which is the word for a small tin prison mug, as he was about four feet eight inches tall with a body as broad as an elephant's. He began to maltreat us, beating us as we worked and he also reduced our food by half. So one day we refused to go to work until he restored the rations and agreed to stop manhandling us. He became enraged at this and told us we had five minutes to go outside: if we did not, he would call the alarm and send the warders in to shift us by force. After three minutes he came in and said solemnly, 'Two [pause] minutes [pause] more.' He looked so lugubrious and foolish that we could not help pitying him: it is not pleasant to have one's bluff called. Many of us said, 'We don't want even one second more. Carry on.'

He waited two more solid minutes, arms folded, peering absurdly at us through the wire and then he ran to the alarm and gave it one turn, looked at us defiantly, gave it another, looked desperately again and then gave it a final twirl. The warders came running towards our compound and Mansfield told them to go in and beat us out of the place. Unfortunately for him they did absolutely nothing. Their R.S.M., a Jaluo, warned them that they should be careful because sooner or later all the detainees were going to be released and they might remember what had been done to them. The warders, anyway, found the order uncongenial even without this warning since they had stayed in peaceful co-existence with us for many months. Several of them were my students and I used to correct their exercises and set them work. I was also giving private tuition to the R.S.M. in his house and we had become great friends. I wanted to help him but I wanted even more to hear

his wireless so that I could bring back the news of the world
to the others: so it was that our lessons always coincided with
the news broadcasts. The warders were human beings like
ourselves and they were often reasonable people. We were dogs
and jackals together.

The Camp Commandant was called to resolve the impasse.
He did not say anything to Mansfield but he agreed to restore
the rations and stop the beating and we agreed to go out and
work again. After another month we heard that our rate of
work did not satisfy the local District Commissioner. He was
alleged to have ordered that we should be made to cover much
more quickly the two miles between the quarry and the hospital
to which we were carrying the building stones. They did not
seem to have any lorries up there. The *Mukoma Times*, as the
Lodwar News Service was called, did not miss many points
and rapidly compared our task with the construction of the
Pyramids by the children of Israel under the Pharaohs. When
the detainees first heard about this order they were very stubborn and said that we must refuse completely to do any work at
all, whatever the consequences or at least until one person dies.
Then I reasoned with them. 'What is the point of resisting until
someone dies and then going to do the action which you first
rejected? Is there any profit in that man's death? Either we
must resist to the end and until we all die or if we think we are
not strong enough to undergo all this long pain, then we should
submit before it is inflicted upon us. But there remains a third
course to follow. We should go to work, we should wear our
lightest clothes and we should take these stones and run as
quickly to and from the hospital, we must burst ourselves to
carry them faster and faster, and when you have done this
several times you will see. You will see the warders themselves
who have to accompany us and they are wearing a pair of heavy
boots, a hot and stuffy starched khaki uniform, puttees and they
are carrying a long baton and a rifle weighing nine pounds.
They will not be able to keep up with us in our light clothes.'

That day the detainees did as I suggested and the results
were most satisfactory. Lodwar is a very hot place and although
the detainees had a tough trip one way with the stones, on the
return journey we were unloaded and running like rabbits.
The warders became harassed and dishevelled, they took their

rifles off their shoulders and trailed them bumping behind them
on the way. The sweat on the puttees made their legs sore and
painful; they unbuttoned their tunics, they puffed and panted,
they begged us to go more slowly. We replied that we must
obey the orders of the District Commissioner and we cantered
on. That evening the road to the hospital was littered with
blistered and limping warders. Next morning they told the
Commandant that they would not work in these conditions and
the R.S.M. informed us that we should resume our former
walking pace and if the District Commissioner asked any questions they would support us. We say in Kikuyu, *Ng'enda thi
ndiagaga mutegi*, which is to say, 'Even the thing which goes
under the ground [like a mole eating plant roots] can be
trapped.' Even a D.C. can be outwitted.

Work at Lodwar finished at 1 p.m. and, after cooking and
eating our food, we crept out of the scorching sun into our huts
where we studied until the cool of the evening. Between 5 p.m.
and 6.30 p.m. the more energetic played tenniquoits and football
while the more sensible amused themselves with draughts and
chess. I myself played centre-forward and captained the football
team which usually beat the Warders XI satisfactorily.

We were very sad one day when a warder, by whom we had
sent some presents to Kenyatta and the others at Lokitaung,
returned with the news that the old man, *Mzee*, was suffering
from a bad leg. The camp committee asked each hut to hold
special prayers every evening for his recovery. This was done
and we were very pleased when we heard he had recovered and
also to hear that he was educating his colleagues there. Waruhiu
Itote, General China, has never forgotten the lessons given to
him by Kenyatta and when I met Waruhiu at Gathigiriri
Special Camp he was full of praises for his kindness and patience
as a teacher.

One morning just as we were starting out to work at our
chameleon's pace we were called back by the Commandant,
who seemed very happy and said to us: 'Your hero, Field-
Marshal Sir Dedan Kimathi, was captured and wounded
yesterday by the Tribal Police at Nyeri. All the remaining
generals will be arrested in the same way. I hope that you can
now see clearly that the Government is going to win. Go to
work now.'

We were extremely worried to hear this news and at first
few of us believed it could be true. But shortly after I heard it
confirmed on the wireless. None of us felt like working and the
warders did not force us to either. Many of them looked as sad
as we were and it was obvious where their sympathies lay. That
day we did not have any literacy classes, the football match was
cancelled, and no one ate any luxuries. The court did not sit
in the afternoon. All the detainees mourned in silence, and those
who could find a piece of black cloth from old puttees, wore it
on their shoulders in their grief. In the evening we prayed in
our huts and sang his song. This was composed in the forest
and is very well known in our country.

THE SONG OF KIMATHI[1]

1. When our Kimathi ascended
   Into the mountains alone
   He asked for strength and
   courage
   To defeat the White Men

2. He said that we should tread
   The paths that he had trod
   That we should follow his
   steps
   And drink from his cup.

3. If you drink from the cup of
   courage
   The cup I have drunk from
   myself
   It is a cup of pain and of
   sorrow
   A cup of tears and of death

4. We are tormented because we
   are black
   We are not like the White
   Men
   We have not received their
   advantages
   But yet is our God in front.

RWIMBO RWA KIMATHI

1. Riria Kimathi witu ambatire
   Kirimaini ari wiki
   Nietirie hinya na umiriru
   Wakuhota nyakeru

2. Nioigire makinya makwa mothe
   Maria nii ndagereire,
   Nomo na inyui mukagerera mo,
   Namunyuire ikombe icio

3. Mwanyuira ikombe cia umiriru
   Iria nii ndanyuiriire
   Ni cia ruo ningi ni cia kieha
   Na maithori na gikuo

4. Tukurira tondu turi andu airu
   Natutiri nyakeru
   Natutiri a kirathimo kiao
   Ngai witu ari mbere

[1] Dedan Kimathi was the leader of the forces in the Aberdare Forests from 1952
until his capture and execution in 1957.

10

5. Do not wonder to be exiled
   Or to be imprisoned in camps
   Or to lose all your belongings
   Still is our God in front

5. *Mutikamakio niguthamanio*
   Kana ni guikio ciugu,
   Kana gutunywo indo na kuragwo
   Ngai witu ari mbere

6. Even when our hearts are
      troubled
   Jomo will never desert us
   Even as he was never aban-
      doned,
   O God, at Kapenguria[1] by
   thee.

6. *Ngoro ciitu ona cianyarirwo*
   Jomo ndagatutiga
   Tondu we ndatiganiirio kuu
   Kapenguria ni Ngai.

7. You must put on his endur-
      ance
   To face tribulation or death
   Knowing that you belong to
   The Kingdom of Gikuyu and
   Mumbi.

7. *Mwihumbei ukiririria wake,*
   Kunyarirwo kana gukua
   Mukimenyaga muri a uthamaki
   Wa Gikuyu na Mumbi

8. We pray thee, O God, to per-
      mit
   The White Men to return to
      their homes
   Because a tree without fruits
   Is never planted in a garden.

8. *Tukuhoya Ngai Atwitikirie*
   Nyakeru acoke kwao
   Niamu muti utari na maciaro
   Nduhandagwo mugunda.

Dedan Kimathi was a brave and valiant fighter for freedom and a great leader of his people in the forest. During the Second World War he served in the military forces fighting for Great Britain. After the war he was also employed by the Tetu Dairymen's Association in Nyeri and by the Shell Company at Thomson's Falls. I have been told by a student who was once taught by him that he was at that time a very gentle, kindly man. In the forest his courage was legendary and my people are already talking of putting up a statue to him in Nairobi. Some of them refuse to believe even today that the Kenya Government hanged him: they still think he is alive. His wife, Mukami, and their children, suffered greatly in Nyeri after his execution, and I have done all I can to help the family since my release. The new Government must assist such people and all the others orphaned in the struggle.

[1] The place where Kenyatta was tried and convicted in 1953.

When Ghana became independent on ... great rejoicing among the detainees and ... bration, including some Kikuyu traditio... *Wathi* (these are their famous jumpin... warders and their wives and lovers ca... with us when they heard what it was ... were said for the success of the new ... Wachuku, the oldest man in the camp. Kiman... us from the long shadow of his seventy-five years that ... for freedom in Kenya had started many years ago, and tha... we should not grow tired of it because of some temporary set-backs. The old men would soon be handing over to us younger men who should educate ourselves as much as we could while we had the chance. Joseph Kirira and I composed a special song for this occasion, which we called the Song of Africa.

SONG OF AFRICA

1. God gave to the black people
   This land of Africa
   Praise the God who dwells in
     the high places
   For his blessings

   Chorus
   We will continue in our
     praises
   Of the land of Africa
   From East to West
   From North to South

2. After much suffering
   The country of Egypt
   Was delivered from bondage
   And received Freedom

   Chorus

3. Abyssinia saw the light
   Shining down from the North
   Her people struggled mightily
   And rescued themselves from
     the mire

   Chorus

RWIMBO RWA AFRICA

1. *Ngai aheire Andu airu*
   Thi-ino ya Afirika
   Gocagai mwene Nyaga
   Tondu wa wendo wake

   Chorus
   Tugutura tugocaga
   Bururi wa Afirika
   Kuuma irathiro ithuiro
   Ruguru na itherero

2. *Thutha wa mathina maingi*
   Bururi wa Misiri
   Niwoimire ukomboini
   Ukiheo wiyathi

   Chorus

3. *Abyssinia yona utheri*
   Umite na rugongo
   Ikirutaniria muno
   Ikiuma mutondo-ini

   Chorus

do we loudly rejoice
hear the story of Ghana
the flag of Great Britain
Has been lowered for all time
there

Chorus

5. If you look round the whole
   of Kenya
   It is only a river of blood
   For we have our one single
   purpose
   To lay hold of Kenya's Freedom

Chorus

6. Listen to the sobbing
   Of our brothers in South
   Africa
   Where they are being tor-
   mented
   By the tribe of the Boers

Finale

We shall greatly rejoice
In the unity of all the black
people
Let us create in our unity
A United States of All Africa

4. *Nitwakenire makiria*
   Twaigua uhoro wa Ghana
   Bendere iria ya Ngeretha
   Nimamiharurukia

Chorus

5. *Ungirora Kenya yothe*
   No rui rwa thakame
   Tondu mworoto no umwe
   Wakunyita wiyathi

Chorus

6. *Thikiririai kiriro*
   Afirika ya muhuro
   Tondu nimaranyarirwo
   Ni mbari ya Nyakaburu

Finale

Tugakena muno muno
Andu airu twi hamwe
Tuthondeke ngwataniro
Uthamaki wa andu airu

Whenever a camp was peaceful the authorities would send
'rehabilitation' staff in to disturb it, and since we had settled
down in the co-operation of non-co-operation, they posted a
European officer and two African assistants, James and Walter,
to us. The camp committee then passed the thirteenth Lodwar
Law that forbade anyone to speak to these people. After a few
days during which they came into the huts and tried to talk
with us in vain, they abandoned this approach altogether, and
in August 1957 they called us in groups to a special hut outside the compound. There they questioned us individually and
placed us in various categories according to their ideas. We
produced many questions for them which they could not answer

satisfactorily to our minds and we rapidly placed them both in the category of traitors.

At Lodwar we used to read the newspapers brought to us by our friends among the warders and we kept well up with political events in the country. We were full of praise for Oginga Odinga, Member for Central Nyanza, when he first mentioned the name of Kenyatta in Legislative Council as our leader, and we noted the reservations of some of the other politicians. When Kenyatta was asked in March 1961 how he found Lodwar he described it as *Uhuru na Vumbi*, 'Freedom and Dust'. Many false interpretations were placed on his words but he meant simply what he said. Lodwar at certain times of the year has dust-storms which cover everything and every person all over and life at these times is very unpleasant there with this dust and the hot sun. Ben Gachahi and another detainee had short spells of insanity, brought on by the heat and conditions, but after treatment in hospital they returned to us.

By the end of our stay in Lodwar we had established friendly relations with the local Turkana and they no longer looked upon us as potential heads to be exchanged for food. We were shocked to see the terrible environment in which they struggled to live and we all felt that the Government should give them more help even if it was at the expense of development in our own areas of Kikuyu and Nyanza. We soon learnt some words in their language and began giving them food. Our rations were certainly enough at this time but they were very unvaried and monotonous. There being a limit to the amount of stiff maize meal porridge that one can consume, we often found we had some surplus. The camp committee decided that nothing should be thrown away but any excess should be carefully kept and passed on to the Turkana at the earliest opportunity.

On 25 October 1957 a group of sixty of us were told that we were going to be pushed back into the 'pipeline' and that we would start at Athi River Rehabilitation Centre. Stories of what was done at this place were already circulating: James and Walter were not averse to contrasting the treatment there with the soft time that could be so easily bought by a 'confession'. As the sun was rising we boarded the lorries, sadly said farewell to our brothers, and headed south towards Kitale, leaving the heat and the dust, and a new hospital, behind us.

CHAPTER VIII

The Pipeline, 'Rehabilitation' and Home

I LIKE travelling and seeing new places and it was good to be journeying through the sandy scrub, the large black rocks and the deceptively frail-looking thorn trees to Kitale. There is a steep hill called 'Royal' on the way, and the road zigzags up its flanks in a series of giddy-making hairpin bends. Looking over the side of the lorry into the deep straight drop below was terrifying and few of us spoke a word till we safely reached the top. We spent that night in Kitale Prison and resumed our journey next morning by train, reaching Athi River two days later, on 28 October 1957, the fourth anniversary of my arrest.

At Athi River we met some old acquaintances, Buxton of Lodwar days and Mansfield (who was nicknamed 'tin mug'). The former was friendly and cheerful, Mansfield looked churlish and had clearly not forgotten our last showdown with him. The camp was divided into six compounds, each capable of holding three hundred people, but they were no longer filled to capacity, each one having about one hundred and sixty to two hundred detainees. Our party of sixty was split up into six groups of ten and dispersed into different compounds. I went into Number 6, where I met many Manyani friends, which was pleasing, since I had left Robinson Mwangi, Gad Kamau, Joseph Kirira and David Oluoch Okello at Lodwar and I was not to see any of them again until after my release in 1960.

Athi River Camp was not finished when the Emergency was declared but as soon as it was completed all those detained under the Jock Scott operation and placed on Governor's Detention Orders (G.D.O.s) were transferred there from their original jail at Kajiado in Masai country. These first detainees included many highly educated people. The first Detention Orders had all required the individual approval and signature of the Governor. As the Emergency went on and the hundreds became thousands, the power of detention was delegated by the Governor first to Provincial Commissioners, and then to District Commissioners. The majority of us were detained under these Delegated Detention Orders (D.D.O.s). The theory was that the increase in the numbers involved made it impossible for the Governor to continue to satisfy himself as to the justice of each Order and that P.C.s and D.C.s would have more time to give to particular cases. What really happened was that even less care was taken over the preparation of requests for detention orders: a District Commissioner's signature is much easier to obtain than a Governor's.

When the Government decided to start 'rehabilitating' detainees, the camp was handed over to the Moral Rearmament (M.R.A.) organization. At this time Joseph Kirira was in Athi River and he told me that the camp was very well run and reasonably pleasant to live in. But soon the bogy of 'confession' appeared. The officials in charge there did not beat people but they used many other means, some more subtle than others. Rations were reduced and this forced the weakest to surrender. Joseph told me that prostitutes were brought into the camp to speak words of love and to dangle their legs before the detainees to remind them of some of the things they were missing. They were not allowed to taste these joys, though, merely to recall them, before the ladies were taken out. Some three or four people were 'rehabilitated' in this way but such devices could never move the true nationalist. We say that the love of a woman cannot be compared with the love for one's country: they are as different as earth and heaven. Since few people succumbed to these methods the Government moved all the hard-cores to Manda Island and Mackinnon Road and shortly afterwards took over the camp, in which only soft-cores were now left, from M.R.A. Some of the Manda Island people 'confessed' down there and were brought back to Athi River to help the screeners. In most cases their 'confessions' had been prompted more by homesickness than anything else and the Government told them that, even though they had confessed, they would first have to prove their loyalty at Athi River, and, clearly, the more people they converted, the greater would their loyalty (and their prospects of getting home) seem to be. Those

who 'confessed' but were bad converters were taken to the
Mokowe Settlement Scheme in the Coast Province, where they
were given houses and work. Most of these later came back into
the pipeline.

In 1957, an ex-Army officer, Rochester, and his wife were in
charge of the rehabilitation in the camp. By now there had been
a definite change in Government policy. It was assumed that
everyone would ultimately confess and noted that those who
were being slow about getting it out of their system were costing
considerable sums of public money. Physical persuasion to force
the rate of confessions was now allowed, although no one was
foolish enough to put this permission anywhere in writing.
Buxton called John Giathi and myself to his office on the day
after our arrival and told us that if we hardened our hearts as
we had at Lodwar we would not easily fit into the pipeline. We
must be soft to go through and he now wished us to co-operate
with the camp authorities and then when the time came for us
to be rehabilitated this would occur peacefully and without
trouble. 'O.K.?' 'Yes, sir,' we replied. He told John Giathi to
go to one of the offices where he would check the token money
totals on the pay sheets of the detainees, while I was taken to
the field to show the other young men how to play football and
to teach them athletics. No one in the camp had any qualms
about doing these kind of things as it was one of our Lodwar
Laws that we should obey the camp regulations, provided they
were legal and reasonable.

Two days later Rochester told me that he wished me to join
the staff of *Atiriri*, the Camp Magazine, which was edited by
Benjamin, who after his release resumed his printing and pub-
lishing interests, and distributed free to all detainees. My job
was to translate Kikuyu into English. Before I did this, I told
them that they should realize that I would only do this work
in the spirit of a prisoner doing, under orders, a job which he
dislikes. I would merely translate exactly what was written,
and if I saw a mistake, such as five shillings plus five shillings
equals twenty shillings, I would not alter it but put it down
just as it was, mistake and all. This was agreed. The others
working on the paper were Linus M. Mugi, Zakaria Kinja
Kibachia and Matthew Kimani.

Benjamin was a very clever and able man and an expert at

writing booklets in Kikuyu. He was a co-operator, but a most subtle one. He never beat anyone and he always treated the other detainees well. He composed a skilful pamphlet on 'confession' which was given to us all. He also produced sketches and plays in which the man who had confessed was always richer or surpassed in some way the man who remained hardcore. The warders and the soft-core liked these very much. We condemned them as The *Wamarebe* Plays (the same Empty Tins motif as Marebe of Kowop).

After a while Rochester and Buxton realized that I was not going to confess voluntarily, and, more dangerous still, that I had begun to collect a following which was like-minded. So they decided to use their ultimate weapon—force. One day they called me and told me they now wished me to confess. As usual I refused and I also told them clearly that they could only rehabilitate someone when he decided to be rehabilitated, and that any confessions extracted under force were not binding. At this point I was given a strong blow by Rochester which knocked me down.

Slowly I rose to my feet and I was then taken to another open place near the ration stores where three other men were called to come and help screen me. They were Jonah and Elijah, both from Nyeri, and a clerk from Kiambu. Four Europeans were also present, Rochester, Buxton and two prison officers. They said that this was my last chance to confess. I gave the same reply as before. Slowly and significantly they started on me. Europeans only; the African screeners took no part in what happened: people said that the Europeans thought they could do it without going too far and that they were frightened the Africans would deliver a fatal blow. Many of the detainees working nearby could see what was happening and after what seemed a long while, just before I mercifully fell unconscious, I saw Kiragu Wamugure, a great friend from Lodwar, standing among a group with tears streaming down their cheeks at my extreme suffering. My face was puffed up and split open, my right knee was fractured just below the kneecap by a club, and my chest was pierced by a strange instrument like a black truncheon with nails in it. I failed to die but the scars on my knees and chest will always be with me and I still suffer from severe attacks of pain in my abdomen and thorax. I was shaved completely, the blood flowing from that operation too. The screeners eventually carted me away, my clothes splotched red with blood, and paraded me in triumph past the barbed-wire compounds, telling my friends to come and see what their leader looked like now. I was thrown into a small cell and for two days no food was brought near me; even if it had been I should not have been able to open my mouth to put it in. The evening of my beating-up a detainee hanged himself in Compound 4. His sleeping companion, Jimmy from Embu, told me that he had seen my treatment and had said that he could not stand living in this hell any longer. He had used the rope which was issued by the Government to tie up our shorts.

The third day some detainees brought gruel to me. They said that the people in the camp were very worried that I would be beaten to death and they had been sent by the others to beg me to go and make a confession of some sort, remembering that it was forced and could therefore be retracted later. They also felt that this would then give me a chance of writing a letter to the authorities telling them what was going on. They did not want me to die, they wanted me to stay with them, even if I was now going to be a cripple for life.

So I confessed a whole pack of lies, embroidered with pieces of truth, and afterwards I was returned to the compound. On the next day I wrote a lengthy memorandum to everyone I could think of: Colonial Secretary, Barbara Castle, John Stonehouse, Tom Mboya, Argwings-Kodhek, the Commissioner of Prisons, and the Attorney-General. I gave the letters to Kaguongo and Nyota Githenji, who were detainees working on the bore-hole outside the compound, and who bribed some warders to post them. My finances were excellent at this time and I had about 2,400 shillings, much of it earned at Lodwar by making *mukoma*—baskets and mats.

A Commission of Inquiry from Nairobi came as a result of the letter. I was asked if I had written the letter and I said Yes, but I would now stop writing any more. However, I did not mean it for inside myself I now considered that the beating-up had freed me from the obligation of telling the truth to any of them.

Athi River was a confession centre. Although there was other work going on in the camp, the most important job was screen-

ing and being screened. Confessions had to be got somehow,
preferably voluntarily, but if necessary by force. The screeners
were old men from the Reserves and it was then that I again
met Noah who was once in charge of Kwa Nyangwethu screening camp at Nakuru. I asked him why people had been
castrated at Kwa Nyangwethu and he said there were two
reasons. First, they wanted to deal with those hard-core who
would not confess, and I was lucky the same thing had not
happened to me. Secondly, they wanted to experiment and see
if a human being so treated will grow fat like a castrated bull.
He was a coarse-fibred, stupid man.

In the morning we were screened or worked. In the afternoon
the authorities tried to fill our time so full of 'rehabilitation'
that we would not have a moment to organize ourselves. They
certainly succeeded and there was no detainee committee at
Athi River. A typical afternoon's programme might be:

Compound No. 1. Attend education classes in their compound. These
consisted mainly of the history of Kenya, with especial emphasis
on the terrible state of tribal conflict before the arrival of the
white man, followed by the story of the arrival of the white man
and how he has saved us from barbarism, and finally an explanation of the great benefits he has brought to our country, especially
in recent years. (I must say not all of us saw things in quite the
same way as the lecturers.)

Compound No. 2. Attend for lectures from the screening elders. How
to confess, what to confess, and how to help the Government by
telling them in what way the remaining terrorists can be captured.

Compounds Nos. 3 and 4. Football, tenniquoits, basketball and volley-
ball supervised by the screening elders.

Compound No. 5. Traditional Dances. Mucungwa, Mugoiyo, Mu-
thuo, Kumunda Mburi, Mukuogo, Kamano. The old men used
to sit singing the Marobo dance. We used to invent our own
anti-Government words where possible, but we were closely
watched.

Compound No. 6. Go out to the Cinema.

Each compound did a different item on the programme every
day.

There was a loudspeaker fixed in every hut, apparently with
two functions. It poured out all the time streams of pro-
Government propaganda, praising the loyalists, the British and

the West. At times this became so sickly that we could stand it
no longer and would smother the box with blankets until the
noise became a comical gurgle. Sooner or later a ubiquitous
'surrender' would denounce us and our crime would be published over the system and the blankets would have to be
removed. But we had gained a few minutes of peace. The
second use was to call the people who were to attend the
screening next day. Whenever we heard it start we would shout
'Keep silent and listen to whose neck will have a rope put round
it tomorrow.' *Kirai tuigue aria magathii gwikirwo rurigi ngingo
ruciu.* We all immediately fell silent because screening here was
the severest test yet and it was hard to sleep well if your name
had been called. I was especially grieved at the way in which
they dealt with the older people, such as Kirori Motoku, Wambugu Kamuiru (now treasurer of K.A.N.U. Nyeri branch) and
the Lodwar librarian, Wachira Karige. I shall never forget the
strength and courage which Kirori showed in the face of all
the indignities and outrages that were done to him there. He
never wavered and his advice and wisdom were most welcome
to us. He heard at this time that in his absence in detention the
Government had approved of the application of the 'stooge'
African District Council of Nyeri to confiscate twenty-eight
acres of his land and pay him fifteen pounds an acre compensa-
tion. The land, which was situated just outside the developing
township of Nyeri, is worth ten times that.

After Rochester had left, a District Officer was posted to the
camp. He was called Denis Lakin and he never beat me, but
at all times spoke in a reasonable and friendly manner. His
plan was to send everyone to their respective divisions in the
Reserves, where their Chiefs would be able to come to some
decision about them. As we were very few in Athi River then,
I think he also felt it unwise to bring any fresh people into the
camp while we were still there to contaminate them. He therefore recommended that I should be sent down to the divisional
camp at Othaya to await my release.

Late in February 1958, after a few days in transit at the
Karatina Works Camp, which was built for the people of
Mathira Division, I arrived at Othaya. Fate had decreed that
the Commandant was the very man who had relieved Buxton
at Lodwar and we were therefore old enemies. After the inspec-

tion we were all forcibly shaved with razor blades and were told that this would be done once a week. We were then given a set of old clothes while everything else we had was stored, including sandals, watches, money and so forth. No one in that camp was allowed to stay with even a handkerchief or pin of his own. Next we were told to double round the compound while a corporal flicked indiscriminately at us with a cane. Finally we were ordered to go to Compound 6 with our white shorts and white shirt: no vest or pants were issued. This compound was reserved for new intakes. There were six compounds in all and we were due to spend at least one month in each, coming out at best in six months' time. That evening I slept badly, considering in my mind what a childish and degrading place this was.

There were some people in our compound who had come from the special camps in the Mwea, down in the plains of Embu. They told us of the harsh treatment there and especially of the new intake procedure, whose acceptance ultimately led to the Hola tragedy. When a new intake of hard-cores arrived at the Mwea Camps they were given certain simple orders which they would normally refuse to obey. These orders were strictly legal but they were not ones which ordinary convicts would have to carry out in normal circumstances. The Government had concocted and issued a circular which said that if a detainee disobeyed a lawful order, 'compelling' force could be used to make him obey it. A large force of warders and Europeans would be waiting to greet the new intake and they then supplied the compelling force. Horrible things were done in the name of 'compelling', things unmentionable even in a book like this. After the shock treatment the detainees were forced to confess their oaths and these were written down on a piece of paper in the middle of the shambles. The experts in rehabilitation said that this was the medicine needed to jolt the hard-cores out of the rigid mental state into which they had gradually fallen. Where it all fell down was in its assessments of the motives behind our resistance. We had never been what they thought we were, depraved human beings, we were hard-core nationalists and only death could prevent us being this, however many oaths we confessed under torture.

After this intake had been satisfactorily dealt with their

re-education continued in the Mwea Camps where the screeners
were under the control of a Kikuyu District Assistant. They
were learning new refinements to help them, such as carrying
buckets full of small stones on the head at the double or doing
a knee-walk along a 'track' liberally strewn with small stones.
One man, Akulino, threw himself into the Thiba River to
escape this treatment. He was rescued but later hanged himself
in his hut.

The work at the Divisional Works Camp in Othaya was
hard. We used to leave very early, immediately after the counting, carrying crowbars and shovels: sometimes we dug bench
terraces, at other times we had to cut the new boundary lines
for the Land Consolidation Scheme, and this sometimes involved a six-mile journey on foot each way. Whatever job we
were doing we worked through the day until 4 p.m., without
lunch. There is no doubt that the detainees in this camp were
driven harder than at any other I knew and this was reflected
in their poor physical condition.

Land Consolidation[1] was a scheme excellent in conception
but badly carried out. Because of our system of land tenure
many people had numerous small fragments of land scattered
over the country. The Government's scheme was to measure
and total all these fragments, cut off an agreed percentage for
public purposes such as schools, hospitals, youth clubs, tea
nurseries and coffee factories, and delineate the amount remaining all in one place on a map. The boundaries were then taken
from the maps and cut in on the ground. The owner signified
his assent in writing to the new plot and when he paid the fees
(roughly ten shillings an acre) for the operation, he was issued
with a Land Title on which he could borrow money. Admirable
in conception the scheme as executed rarely carried with it the
support of the people. The committees tended to consist of
loyalists, the clerical staff were patently open to bribes, and the
detainees were not consulted about their land but were told
that their relatives would represent them. Again, there was
great scope for favouritism deciding whether to allocate a plot
on good or bad ground. The Government decided that the
Emergency had produced a situation in which the measure

[1] For a more detailed description of the Land Consolidation Scheme, see
Appendix, p. 183.

could be forced through; this would create the right conditions for an economic surge forward in agricultural production and it would also enable farmers to offer the land titles as security for loans from banks. There is no doubt that many detainees lost their share in their land at this time and the compulsion used has created considerable bitterness among others. It will be difficult for our politicians to keep the scheme unchanged when they take over the Government, unless more land is provided free elsewhere for those who were deprived of their rights.

On the third day at Othaya I told the other detainees, many of whom had been under my leadership at Manyani, South Yatta and Athi River, that they should not let anyone, even the warders, know that I was educated. I was going to play the part of a very slow and stupid man so that I could try to find out more about what was going on. The local District Officer was called Salisbury, we named him *Karuahu* because he was weak and also a bully, and I was beginning to hear stories about some of his actions. I made myself a complete clown. I would address warders as corporals, corporals as sergeants and sergeants as sergeant-majors or captain or any other important official title that came into my mind. Having arranged to get into the gang that swept out the D.O.'s offices I began to find things out. It seemed to me that he was selling the barbed wire which the Government had bought in huge quantities to fence in camps and Home Guard posts during the fighting Emergency, and that he was not giving the money to the Government but using it for other purposes. I was also suspicious about some other financial transactions going on, involving the Othaya Health Centre and detainees' money. Another letter was called for and my friend from Manyani, Domenico Kihoro, obtained the necessary paper from the store. One Sunday I wrote the letter in a corner of the compound concealed in a tent made of blankets and guarded by the detainees I could trust. The power of a letter, especially if copied to politicians in England, never ceased to surprise me and this one had the usual explosive effect.

A committee from Nairobi came to inquire at the camp. The C.I.D. spent months taking statements from people in Othaya and, although we heard that a good case was built up, as so

often, the Administration managed to prevent it coming to
court. This is another side of the Kenya story revealed first to
those who knew the reasons behind Colonel Young's resignation
as Commissioner of Police in 1955.[1] Whether as a result of all
this or from some other cause, Salisbury was transferred to North
Tetu, another division in Nyeri. In fact, he never reached there
but was sent to take charge of the Rehabilitation Camps in the
Mwea. Another officer who had been posted to Mwea and,
having seen what was going on there, had refused to do the job,
was sent in his place to North Tetu. Salisbury was a small and
short man, quick and incisive but not open to reasoning. He
was, like many District Officers, a bundle of energy and fire
and clearly enjoyed the great power the Emergency had given
to men in his position. But he lacked sympathy, had little
imagination and did not seem to realize that his 'subjects' often
did not get as much pleasure out of his ideas and projects as
he did.

A few days before he left he came to the camp and summoned all of us, warders included, and made an abusive speech,
in which he referred to the letter that had been written. He
then called me out to stand in front of everyone and said, 'Look
at him—he is a danger to the Government. All of you, return to
your huts and you will see tomorrow.' We certainly did see,
we were taken to dig out a steep road at Nduyi in Mahiga, and
no one stood still that day; we dug until the sweat dripped
down the shovels and mingled with the red earth. The warders
were tough and beat any slackers. They did not beat me,
however, and they seemed to have been shaken at my ability,
fool as I had appeared, to write such a letter. Truth to tell, few
of them approved of Salisbury's activities and they told me they
were not averse to my getting him into trouble, especially as
it was the truth. The digging of this road went on for a week
until I was sent back down the pipeline to the District Camp at
Aguthi. With my removal the work on the road stopped.
Salisbury's intention had been to make me very unpopular
with the other detainees and, had they all been 'rehabilitated'
as the Government thought they were, this could have suc-

[1] The full story of Colonel Young's resignation has never been revealed. But it
naturally gave rise to much heated speculation. For the official statement see
Parliamentary Debates, 2 February 1955, V. 536. 118–120. and 4 July 1956, V. 555.
112–113.

ceeded. But instead they liked me all the more and begged me to carry on writing letters.

Othaya was not a good camp. If anyone was found with snuff he was beaten mercilessly. The warders there were largely recruited from former Home Guards and, although they hit us so badly, we did not quarrel with them when we were released. We decided that they must be forgiven, for they did not know what they were doing. There will be no spirit of revenge to destroy our new Kenya. On Saturdays we would go down to wash our bodies and our only set of clothes in the Thuti River. This was a real mountain stream, clear water jumping hopefully along the rocks, a stream of my country, a far cry from the dirty, sluggish Turkwell disappearing into the sand or from the ominous heaving sea at Saiyusi. All around the camp were the closely cultivated fields of our Kikuyu people, and it was good to see again the waving sugar-cane, the green maize and the squat arrowroots nestling among the banana stems. The landscape was only marred by the huge conglomeration of huts on every ridge, the villages into which the people had been moved early in the Emergency. This was not how we liked to live, cramped up against each other, with no freedom, and with the life of the family open to the peeping eyes of the world. As I sat by the river wrapped in the coarse and prickly prison blankets, waiting for my clothes to dry, I mused on all these things and the changes that must quickly be made.

On Sundays we were allowed to go out of the big gate to an open place where, surrounded by warders, we were permitted to talk to our relatives without any interference. That first Sunday my family came in strength. My aunt Wangui, with whom I stayed at Bafuni when I came back from Uganda; her daughter Nyakinyua; my sister Njoki, who had now married, and her husband, John Kimondo; my sister Wangui who had married Gatiyu Wambura, detained with me in South Yatta; my cousins Simon Gachiengu and Godfrey Mugweru, and my daughter, Wangari, who is married to a Nairobi man—she is my daughter in Kikuyu tradition, being really the daughter of Nyakinyua, the daughter of my aunt Wangui. They all wept bitterly when they saw me, but I had lost the way of tears, and I told them that they should not cry for me as detention was something that all those fighting for our country had to undergo. They had brought me bananas, *njahi*, arrowroots and milk, and we ate and drank all this there together in that open place.

I had missed my mother, who was not with the others, and I asked Wangui whether she was sick. Wangui then gently told me that Mary Wanjiku, my mother, had died in January 1958 while I was at Athi River. I was stunned for a while and asked her again what she had said. She repeated the words once more. I sat there silent for about five minutes and suddenly I wanted to sob my heart out, but I could not do it in this public place in front of seven hundred other detainees and their families. My saliva tasted sour and bitter, my head was aching and I could not see out of my eyes. After a while I came to myself and smiled at my family and said to them, 'Do not worry, this is the debt which we all have to pay. My mother has now paid hers and we will pay ours when the time comes and every day brings that time nearer.' And so we went on eating the food together, but with a new sadness.

To a Kikuyu no woman is dearer or more beloved than his mother. For nine months she carries the burden of her child within her until she is relieved in the agony of birth. Then she nourishes and cleans the child until it grows up. My mother had also striven desperately for my education all the days of my youth. It was eight years since I had last seen her and she would never now see the fruits of her struggles. I had nothing, not even a photograph, to remind me of the charity, beauty and wisdom of her face. She had once told me that it was her last and dearest wish that she should see the girl I married and now that could never be. This was the hardest sacrifice I had made in the fight for freedom. It is difficult to explain the quality of my feeling to Europeans. We look upon the relationship between a man and his wife as a partnership involving mutual respect and affection, the purpose of which is the bearing and upbringing of children. This partnership often, but not necessarily, develops into a deeper alliance of the spirit, although it can exist on a lower level only. But we have a saying, *Nyina wa mundu ni ta we Ngai wa keeri*—'The mother of a man is like a second God'—and there is a sanctity about the bond between a mother and her son that transcends other human emotions. There is no greater social crime in our society than abusing or striking a mother, and the shame involved cannot be compared with the consequences of similar treatment of a wife. The news of her death gave me greater pain than all the beatings and torture that I had been subjected to in all the camps put together.

I learnt later that the others had not thought it wise then to tell me how she died, as they felt I might well do something terrible. Afterwards they told me that she first became ill during the twenty-three-hour curfews that were imposed at the height of the Emergency. After treatment by the Catholic missionaries she recovered but later had a relapse and her body swelled up so that even her eyes would not open. Months of dreadful suffering were at last ended by her death.

When the whistle blew for the end of the time with our relatives I returned to the camp and on that night and the following nights the rough prison blanket was wet with the tears so much else had failed to bring forth and I prayed for the soul of my mother.

On 24 June 1958 I arrived at Aguthi (Nyeri) Works Camp from Othaya, and this was the eleventh camp of my detention. It was divided into eight small compounds, each of which held one hundred and twenty detainees. It was surrounded by an electric fence, whose only victim so far had been the lover of one of the warders, who had forgotten to inform her of this obstacle when arranging the meeting. The camp was designed to hold all those belonging to Nyeri District who came from the rehabilitation centres at Mwea, Manyani and Athi River. After staying at Aguthi for a while they were sent to their divisional camps and released to their homes from there. Later in 1958 the Governor decided that many of those who had been convicted of minor 'Mau Mau' offences before a Court should be 'instrumented', which meant that he signed a document remitting the remainder of their sentences and simultaneously signed another document turning them all into detainees so that they could then be put through the 'pipeline' procedure. Many of these people had originally been sentenced to twelve or fourteen years' imprisonment. In the jails they had formed a separate group from the *Mahuru kanga*, who were the ordinary criminals, thieves and pickpockets and so on. *Mahuru* is the word for carrion crows and they were given this name because they could steal and quarrel, fight and commit sodomy with each other: they had no discipline and they were like the vultures who have no shame and eat the filth and garbage and the flesh of dead things. The 'Mau Mau' convicts were a tight society, with high moral standards and stern discipline. Those who were in Nyeri Prison were taken to Aguthi Works Camp in groups of thirty each week. The 'Intake Procedure' employed at the Mwea Camps had now insidiously crept down the pipeline to Aguthi. When the convicts arrived outside the gates they were shown the camp notice board on which was written in large letters MWITEITHIA NIATEITHAGIO, which is to say, 'He who helps himself will also be helped'. They were told that they had fifteen minutes in which to make up their minds whether they were going to help themselves or not. Those who agreed were sent straight inside the camp, the others, who were always the majority, were escorted to the punishment pits. These had no use or purpose except as a means of extorting confessions without leaving any marks. The pits in the red soil were six feet wide, twelve feet long and ten feet deep. The victim had to descend into the hole, dig out some earth and then climb up the side again with the bucket on his head. The act of climbing kept both hands occupied and I remember seeing personally with my own eyes one of the convicts fall back into the pit and the loaded bucket crash down on to his chest. He was badly hurt. When they came away from the pits they looked like red moles, their hair and skins being permeated with the dusty red soil.

When there were too many for the pits, the others were made to run round in the playing-field carrying buckets full of small stones on their heads. When I reached there the African in charge of all these operations was called Micah, nicknamed 'Speaker'. Micah was a brave and courageous man and I admired greatly these qualities in him. He feared nothing and no one. Before the Emergency he had been a trader, and his previous activities had given no indication of any particular leaning to the Government side. Had he fought with the terrorists he would have become a very prominent general, but for reasons I have never been able to understand he went to the other side. A man of about forty years at this time, he retained his business interests in Fort Hall. He used to try to frighten us by saying that he had personally disposed of two hundred terrorists and it was not difficult to believe this. He was one of the originators of the pseudo-gang technique, the groups of mixed loyalists and forest fighters who went back into the forests living and behaving like the gangs. Micah has now left the Government service in which he reached the rank of District Assistant, and runs a transport service. At one time the ordinary people boycotted his bus: they said, 'Do not go into it or you will die.'

One day at Aguthi an intake arrived from Nyeri Prison and I watched from where I was working what was done to them. They were very badly beaten up, especially two of them called Kabugi Njuma and Gachii Karanja. Micah was personally responsible for organizing their treatment, Kabugi died later that same day. Gachii lay in the camp hospital for several days unable to move or speak and he is still a cripple. The next morning I went to help build the Provincial Red Cross Training Centre at Nyeri and while I was there I arranged for a supply of writing paper, and on the next Sunday I went to the camp latrines and sat inside writing a letter describing everything that had happened. Some other detainees kept watch for me in case an officer came to search the place. There was an air of tension in the camp and the senior staff were clearly very worried at the possible effects of the death. I gave the letter to Irungu, one of the drivers, who had been detained with me in Manyani and who knew I would not betray him whatever they did to me. It went to the usual addresses in England and Kenya.

After the inquest Micah was prosecuted and sentenced to two years' imprisonment. As a result of my letter Barbara Castle brought the whole matter up in the House of Commons.[1] In the general amnesty of December 1959, Micah was pardoned by the Governor. Many of us felt, in spite of the verdict, that some of the senior Government officers were shielding behind him. Like Hola, this incident was the inevitable consequence of a system which was rotten through and through. It appeared that the Colonial Government of Kenya had lost its soul and was no longer capable of distinguishing between right and wrong.

[1] *Parliamentary Debates*, 24 February 1959, V. 600. 1036–39, and 28 April 1959, V. 604. 1081–2.

In October 1958 I was moved to the Showground Works Camp near Nyeri Township. Although this camp was not very well constructed, there were no beatings there and we could breathe in the smoke from the fires in our homes, the smoke that came out from the three stones and smelt of goats and ordinary clothes, that leaked out through thatched roofs and hung in a blue mist, breaking the clear morning air over the mushroom clusters of huts that were the villages of our people. Soon after my arrival there the new District Officer at Othaya, John Stein, came to the camp and told us that he was not interested in seeing the people of his division behind barbed wire and we would all be freed. On 9 December 1958 we were taken to Othaya Police Station where Kariithi, a constable, told us: 'You are now free to go to your homes. Each one of you must first go to the office of the Chief of your Location and report that you have arrived. Then you should go to the headman of your village and report to him. You must report every Wednesday to the Chief at his office. You will be required to do the compulsory communal labour, *gitati*, whenever ordered by your headman. If any curfew is imposed you must also obey that, because it is the law. This is all that I have been asked to tell you.'

I walked out of the police station gates free at last. Free, free, free to run, to dance, to shout, and to sing. Odd that the air did not smell different, that the shape of the hills looked the same and that the faces of the people had not changed. I tried a little running and singing and no one stopped me. No more orders and yelling and beating. I wandered gently on the road to my home, joyfully shouting greetings to anyone I met, my friends, everyone in the whole world was my friend today. We were quite a troop by the time we rolled into Kariko Village and Wangui's house. It was ten years since I had last been there.

When we were in detention we used to talk about this first day of freedom. We would kill a goat, a *thenge*, and eat it with the family on the first evening. 'Don't let them kill you a chicken, Mwangi, it's not big enough and it will only mean you will be sent back to detention later. A goat, a real *thenge* he-goat, nothing more nor less.' When Wangui met us she told me that we were going to have a celebration that evening. Before my mother died, said Wangui, she had pointed out a cock that she wanted to be the first meat that I ate when I came home. My heart's joy was quietened a little. The cock must be eaten because it was a bond that joined me with my mother. Anyway, no one could put me back in detention again and the *thenge* could be eaten another day. The great thing was to celebrate my freedom today and to prepare to fight on for my country's freedom tomorrow.

CHAPTER IX

A Political Party is Born

MY first free night's sleep was abruptly interrupted at dawn by a confused trumpeting noise, like the roaring of a lion. When I asked Wangui what on earth it was she told me it was a human voice, shouting through a megaphone and calling the people of the village to forced communal labour. After a snatched cup of tea, I seized a hoe and a shovel and followed my aunt to the Home Guard post at the top of the village. Here all the adult men and women were gathered together in groups and I was told to join one of them, which was sent off to dig some bench-terraces on some fortunate individual's land. There is a place in poor and under-developed countries for group work on public projects which the community cannot otherwise afford, such as schools, health centres and even roads. But the consent of the people must first be obtained and their elected committees must decide which project they wish to undertake. To use such groups without their consent to improve the land of private persons is wrong.

Although it seemed to me absurd after more than five years in detention not to be allowed even one morning at home, I decided to go along and see just what this communal labour, *gitati*, involved. Everyone was given a certain stretch to dig and a woman to remove the soil for him. I worked together with Kamuyu, my cousin's wife, and after my experiences of hard labour in detention I did not find it as difficult as some. The next day the same stentorian alarm clock and the same procedure all over again. This time I noticed the headman detail some women to draw water for him and cut firewood. As he had his own wife, and had the advantage over most of us in that he also received a salary, I could see no excuse whatsoever for this. I inquired and found that the system was in operation in all the neighbouring villages. After four days of this hard labour I felt I had had enough. I was either free or detained: at the moment I was like a donkey tied with a long rope instead of a short rope. The whole country seemed to be in detention with the village as the compound and the works camps as the small cells. We were not released from anything. So I told the headman that my right leg was aching so much that I could not carry on. He gave me a week's sick leave but did not seem happy about doing so.

During the first days of freedom many of the detainees who had previously been released came to greet me and they were very happy to see me still alive since they had heard that I had died at Athi River. There would be anything up to thirty in my house most days, and once we sang together in a hut at evening The Song of Africa and The Song of Kenyatta at Kapenguria.

THE SONG OF KENYATTA AT KAPENGURIA[1]

RWIMBO RWA KAPENGURIA

(This is a song and was what we sang; whether the words were true or not did not, and does not, matter.)

1. Kenyatta in his strength taught the people politics And the hard-core endured to the prisons While the soft-core were conscripted to 'The Little Spears' (Home Guard)

Chorus

Heigh ho! Thus shall there be great rejoicing
When victory comes to our warriors.
Kenyatta is our Leader
The country belongs to the Black People

1. *Andu marutwo uteti ni uhoti wa Kenyatta*
Aria mari ngoro nyumu makiumiriria kuohwo
Na aria mari ngoro huthu makiandikwo tutimu

Chorus (Na Gikeno)

Hahii! Uguo noguo gugakenwo
Ni njamba iria ikahotana
Uthamaki wa Kenyatta
Bururi ni wa Andu Airu

(*Cheerfully con molto spirito*)

[1] The trial of Jomo Kenyatta was heard in Kapenguria before Mr. R. S. Thacker, Q.C.; D. N. Pritt, Q.C., led the Counsel for the Defence. After Kenyatta and the other five accused were convicted, an Appeal was taken to the Supreme Court of Kenya in Nairobi ('The Court of Settlers') where it was dismissed. A Petition for a second Appeal was then placed before the Judicial Committee of the Privy Council in London, and refused.

2. Jomo alone can unite all peoples
He took on himself at Kapenguria the burden of our country:
He was ready to give his soul as a sacrifice for us.
God gave him the victory and all the people rejoiced

Heigh ho!

2. Murathimithia nduriri ciothe ni Jomo
Nake nioneire mathina bururi Kapenguria
Akienda kuruta muoyo wake utuike igongona
Ngai akimuhe uhotani muingi ugikena muno

Hahii!

3. There were forty witnesses at Kapenguria
When they were before the Court they could not prove their stories
They were shamed by Pritt's questions
Thacker said Let us leave here.
The country belongs to the Black People

Heigh ho!

3. Aira mari Kapenguria maari aira mirongo ina.
Riria mathire igoti-ini makiremwo ni ciira
Pritt akimoria cuiria magiconoka muno
Thacker akimera ni tuthii.
Bururi ni wa Andu Airu.

Hahii!

4. From Kapenguria the cause went to Kitale
Pritt adjourned it and flew to London
Until he returned with three more elders
To decide and judge rightly with no colour bar

Heigh ho!

4. Cira wauma Kapenguria ni wathire Gitale,
Pritt akiurugamia akiuga niekwamba guthii
Akinya kwao ruraya agiuka na athuri atatu
Akurora na kihoto hatari karabaa

Hahii!

5. When they looked into the case they decreed that Jomo should be freed
But those that watch over the colour bar rejected this
They said they would take it to Nairobi, to the Settlers' Court

5. Riria marorire ciira makiuga Jomo arekio
Nao arori a karabaa makiregana noguo
Makiuga uguthii Gicuka[1] igoti ria mathetera

---

[1] *Gicuka* is the Kikuyu name for Nairobi. A *cuka* is a white cloth, which in the old days could only be bought in Nairobi. *Gicuka* therefore means Place of the White Cloth.

Heigh ho!	*Hahii!*

6. When it reached Nairobi in the Court of the Settlers
   The Attorney upheld the judgement of Kapenguria
   Pritt said it must go to the Privy Council
   To be judged where there is no colour bar

   Heigh ho!

6. *Riria wathire Gicuka igoti ria mathetera*
   Attorney agitua na hinya toria wa Kapenguria
   Pritt akiuga uguthii ruraya igoti ria muthamaki
   Ukarorwo na kihoto hatari karabaa

   Hahii!

7. When it reached the Privy Council
   The Attorney threw away the files and started to run away
   Pritt said to the judges 'I told you so'.
   Kenyatta is our Leader. The country belongs to the Black People

   Heigh ho!

7. *Riria wathire ruraya igoti ria muthamaki*
   Attorney akirekia bairo akiambiriria gwithara
   Pritt akiira manjanji no nduire ndimwiraga
   Ati uthamaki wa Kenyatta.
   Bururi ni wa Andu Airu

   Hahii!

Next morning the headman reported me to the Chief of Chinga Location, Gachichio Wamiti, who was a tough old man and had formerly been a sergeant-major in the Tribal Police. (He retired in 1961.) Gachichio ordered me to report to the headman the name and business of any visitor that came to my house. Extraordinary as this order may seem I believe there actually is a section in the Native Authority Ordinance (Cap. 97) of the Laws of Kenya that can be stretched to mean this, although I doubt whether the Supreme Court would uphold it.

One evening when, for once, there were no visitors, we sat round the fire and I asked Wangui to tell me the story of the death of my mother. My sorrow had grown a skin by this time and I felt strong enough now to manage the truth. I listened quietly as the sufferings of the time of the curfew in 1955 and 1956 were revealed.

The bell used to ring in the village and some, but not all, were allowed out under guard for one hour to gather food.

Planting and cultivation were well-nigh impossible in those circumstances and much maize was, anyway, destroyed as it was thought terrorists might hide in it. A strip of land one mile in extent along the forest edge was devastated and anyone found there was shot on sight. Because of movement restrictions no one could escape to other parts of the country or bring in food from more fortunate relatives. Famine and death trampled through the land, claiming many of our women and children. It was at this time that my mother, Wanjiku, first fell ill and both my father's second wife, Gathoni, and her daughter, Nyakio, died and thousands of children, desperate in their hunger, ran away to live off the dustbins of Nairobi, breaking up families and creating a social problem whose aftermath is still with us today.

During my few days in the village I planted tea and pyrethrum in the farm which had been allotted to me during the Land Consolidation Process. I found that the area seemed to be about five acres less than it should have been. The produce from these cash crops is of great assistance to my family today. My aunt and the other women in the family tried hard to impress upon me the importance of getting married, especially as I was now an orphan. But my future still seemed to me so uncertain and the likelihood of my re-arrest so probable that I told them that this was not the time when I could think of these things.

After a few days talking to my friends from all over the District I decided that we needed a political party and that I must start one. Unless something were done quickly the bitter antagonism between the loyalists and the detainees would be magnified and we would lose once more the chance of unity, without which our independence would be delayed. From my conversation with the District Officer and the Chief, it seemed to me that the last thing the Government wanted in Nyeri at that time was a political party. This was very short-sighted of them and they would clearly have to be educated away from their Emergency attitudes. I felt flattered when I heard that the Administration were shadowing me to find out what my plans were. They had started to follow me after the letter I had written to Nairobi complaining about the employment of women on communal labour. I had since been busy writing to the Commissioner of Prisons trying to recover for some of the detainees the money and property that had been taken from them in detention. I had considerable success with this and helped my old friend James Thuku Mangothi among others.

I soon heard that the Administration were planning to put me back inside again, so speed was important. I quickly visited my detainee friends in the other three divisions of the District, South Tetu, North Tetu and Mathira. I found tremendous support everywhere for the project, and I decided to go ahead immediately. One morning a man from North Tetu called Kigango came to see me at Kariko Village and told me that Mutahi Chiuki, who ran an eating-house in Nyeri Township, would like me to visit him at Gatitu Village. We talked for a long while and he then took me to see Wanjohi Mungau, who was running a broadsheet called *Habari za Kenya* (News of Kenya), which appeared intermittently, whenever funds allowed, and which took a strong anti-Government line. Wanjohi seemed to me to be an able politician and he at once agreed with our idea of starting a political party in the district. By this time there was a group of about ten of us talking in the small room Wanjohi rented down in the Nyeri *Majengo* (Township), and which served as the newspaper's office. We collected 300 shillings from those present and Wanjohi and I were chosen to draft the constitution and take it down to Nairobi to see certain people there who could help and advise us.

At that time there was a law that everyone going to Nairobi must have a movement pass signed by a District Officer. No one was likely to give me such a thing so we decided to go to Nairobi during the Queen Mother's visit to Nyeri in February 1959, when every policeman for miles around would be lining the streets and for once they would be too busy to watch out for pass offenders. In Nairobi we went straight to the office of Henry Clement Wariithi, a Kikuyu lawyer whose father had been in detention with me at Aguthi Works Camp, and found with him a man from South Tetu called Kaburu, who was working as a clerk at the Royal Technical College. Wariithi later became Jomo Kenyatta's lawyer. They gave us a magnificent welcome and we were speedily in agreement in our political ideas and plans.

The next day we met two officials of the Nairobi Peoples

Convention Party, Elijah Omolo Agar, the Organizing Secretary, and Josef P. Mathenge, the General Secretary. Mathenge, who was the son of a court elder in Othaya and had been sent down from Makerere College, was especially happy to see me and told me that many of the ex-detainees had spoken to him about my troubles and leadership in the camps. Omolo Agar was later deported to Lamu for suspected Communist activities and was not finally released until the end of 1961. The third day we met Tom Mboya, who said he had received all the letters I had written him from detention and that he had been doing his utmost to have my charges investigated and the wrongs put right. We told him of our intention to start a political party and he encouraged us to go ahead with our plans. We discussed the dangers of promoting tribalism by starting a series of district parties rather than a single Colony-wide organization, but we agreed that the Government's law, which only permitted district parties, made it impossible to do anything else at present. Tom himself wanted to expand the N.P.C.P. into the districts, but no one could see a way of doing this legally. He made us free of his house in Ziwani while we remained in Nairobi.

On the fourth day of our visit the N.P.C.P. was holding some traditional dancing in the Kaloleni location of Nairobi and we were invited to attend. Their choirs sang some excellent political songs but the item I remember best was a Swahili lyric sung by the composer, an Asian called H. Ambu Patel. The words beautifully expressed our national aspirations and it contained many references to Jomo Kenyatta and the other African leaders. I also met there John Stonehouse, Labour M.P. for Wednesbury, and he was most interested in my account of my life in the detention camps and in the scar that remained on my right knee after Athi River. He tells about our meeting in his book *Prohibited Immigrant*.

We also saw Dr. Kiano, who represented Kiambu and Fort Hall, and he told us that he was planning to start political parties in those districts. He smilingly said to us in Kikuyu, *Mundu ndatigaga gwake gukihia agathii guthara kwene*, which is to say, 'A man does not leave his burning house to put out the fire in somebody else's'. We laughed at this and he did not give us any more advice, although he promised to meet us again and discuss further the expansion of *Habari za Kenya* into a national newspaper. We spent that final night in Nairobi with Henry Wariithi discussing the form and details of the constitution of our new party, to be called the Nyeri Democratic Party—the N.D.P.

It had been good to see Nairobi again after so many years. Its skyline had changed completely and everywhere tall, gleaming new buildings were growing out of the wood-covered plots, except in the African locations, which were still bursting at the seams in the efforts to contain an ever-increasing population. I noticed most the changes in the people. More and more of our Kikuyu girls were charmingly dressed in beautiful clothes, while the men all seemed to have excellent suits. Politically, Nairobi was clearly going ahead fast with the well-managed N.P.C.P. and the Nairobi African District Congress and it seemed to me very important that the districts should not be left behind. If we could not start branches of a Colony wide organization, we must have district parties and we must have them quickly.

On our return we rapidly produced a final draft of the constitution, using the house of an ex-detainee called Kimunya Kamana at Gatitu Village. (Kimunya now works as a rent-collector for the Nakuru Municipal Council.) This was then typed by Daniel Motoku, who is the son of the old man, Kirori Motoku, to whom I was handcuffed on the aeroplane trip to Lodwar from Kisumu. There were not many educated young people who even then in Kenya's Central Province had the courage to do such things. By the evening of 20 February 1959 the constitution was complete and I had checked the draft and it only now required posting to the Registrar of Societies, so that it could be registered and we could start.

By going to Nairobi without a pass I had been forced to break the law. I had also broken the conditions of the Restriction Order under which we were all placed for six months when released from detention, one condition of which forbade us to leave our locations without informing the Chief. The Administration now knew through their spies what I had been doing and the police were hunting for me. This much my own informers had told me and so I was hourly expecting to be arrested. However, this did not matter provided the N.D.P.

constitution was completed before I was picked up. It was now clear that there was overwhelming support all over the district for a political party that would enable us to speak frankly and openly to the Government and to lay before them in a constitutional and democratic manner our reasonable demands.

At midnight on 20 February 1959 I was editing the next issue of *Habari za Kenya*, when two European police officers came into the room and asked me if I was Josiah Mwangi. I replied that this was correct and they told me to go with them to Nyeri Police Station. I spent that night in the cell with no blankets and it was very cold as this police station is very ancient and was built long before any consideration was given to the comfort of its inmates. *Habari za Kenya* came out the following day and included my editorial on the plans and prospects of the N.D.P.

I was taken to Othaya Police Station where I was interviewed by the new District Officer, Henley. This was the first time I had met him and we did not get on very well together. He told me that since I left detention I had done many things which had surprised the Government. I had made myself a little District Commissioner in the District and he said that he would try to have me detained again (O, why had I not insisted on having a goat killed as well as my mother's chicken?). If this proved impossible, he would not allow me to stay in the division: two big men cannot stay together. I replied that if I was detained again it would not be because I have done anything wrong but because of finding out and speaking the truth. We Kikuyu say *Mai ma mundu matimutigaga*, which is to say a man will drink the water that is his lot and leave the rest for others. If there was still some of my water that remained undrunk in the detention camps then I would have to return to drink my cup to the lees. This was fated and no one, not even he, could change or alter my destiny. Henley was not pleased with my words and the next day he called the District Commissioner, Burton, who came to see me in the police cell. Burton was an honest and kind man, a typical soldier who found politics and politicians distinctly puzzling and not quite cricket. He asked me why I had started a political party and why I had gone to Nairobi without a pass. I gave him the same answers as I had given to the D.O. and they left, talking hard together.

I was removed from the police cell and taken to stay in
Othaya 'Cap. 80' Detention Camp for minor offenders. While
I was there hundreds of people came to see me, to talk to me
and to give me courage to carry on with what I was doing.
Wanjohi Mungau came out from Nyeri and we talked through
the wire together. I told him that the constitution must be
posted off, registered, at once and without fail, to the Registrar
of Societies. Our people make beehives out of a length of the
hollowed-out trunk of a tree. We stop up both ends and then
hang the hive in the branches of a likely tree. When we want
to take honey, we open one end of the hive and put a smoky
bundle of fire in, which drives the bees to the far end of the hive
and as long as this fire is kept in, we can gather the honey we
need peacefully. So I said to Wanjohi in Kikuyu, *Ndukanarute
gicinga mwatu*—'Do not remove the fire from the hive'—and he
understood that we must keep the fire going by posting the
constitution and doing anything else that was required before
registration was granted.

My visitors became such a multitude that Henley decided
to return me to the isolation of the police cell and there I stayed
until, on 27 February 1959, I was taken to Kandongu Works
Camp among the notorious group of rehabilitation centres in
the Mwea division of Embu Division. I was going to be a
detainee again: my leave had finished.

At Kandongu my ordinary clothes and my other possessions
were taken off me and I was issued once more with the white
shorts and the white shirt of the detainee, and I was sent to a
small cell: what a topsy-turvy place Kenya is! But these cells
were not like the Manyani ones. We could move in and out
and wash when we liked. In Kikuyu we say, *Murimu wa mucoka
niguo uragaga mundu*, which is to say, 'It is the second time that
an illness kills you', and I became a little fearful, in view of what
had happened in the past, of my fate. At Kandongu there were
some other detainees who had formerly been at Aguthi where
they refused to work or confess. The D.C. at that time had
ordered them to be beaten for a breach of the regulations and
they had been beaten with a *kiboko*, the whip made out of the
hide of a rhinoceros or hippopotamus, which was itself against
the regulations. There was an inquiry into this. The D.C. later
became a Resident Magistrate in Kenya.

Among my friends there were Kiongo Kiburu, Marungo Ngumi, Q.C. (so-called because of his excellence as a judge), Wahome Kihara and K. Nguru, known as Kapila as he would often take briefs for the defence in the detainees' courts, and A. R. Kapila was the Asian advocate who assisted Pritt in Kenyatta's trial at Kapenguria. We used to swop stories about the different camps we had been in. They told me about the 'Battle of Langata', an open riot against the police and prison warders, when even grenades were used against the unarmed detainees. They fought like heroes on that day and their resistance was only finally put down by tear gas and the throwing of huge jets of cold water on them from the hoses of the Fire Brigade.

They also told me about Embakasi. When the Government could not find sufficient evidence to bring a case against us in the courts, we were detained. But not much evidence was required to convince administrator-magistrates and so in the early days of the Emergency many thousands were convicted and sentenced to terms of imprisonment for taking an oath. While we had been organizing our own resistance in the Detention Camps, our convicted brothers had been doing the same in Kenya's prisons. Of these the most notorious was Embakasi which was built near the site for the new Nairobi Airport. The convicts there felt no more inclination to help the Government than we did and the Government took strong action to force them to work. Kiongo and Marungo told me that life there was so tough that in order to avoid being sent to the runways some would deliberately slash the tips of their fingers: others stabbed the inside of their mouths with pins so as to spit blood and be admitted to the hospital as T.B. suspects. Let us never forget that Nairobi's Embakasi Airport, clean, modern and bustling centre of Africa's communications system, was built on the sweat and blood of our people fighting for freedom and it will remain a permanent memorial to those who died in the prison during its years of construction.

After six days in the camp I read a newspaper report of the Hola Incident, in which eleven detainees died. The newspaper was thrown to my friends by a Kikuyu warder called Mwai, who was very sympathetic. The report said that they had died of drinking poisoned water. I knew too much to swallow this story, especially as none of the warders had apparently been thirsty, in the same way as at Manyani no warder ever contracted typhoid. I decided to write a letter to Stonehouse. Mwai brought me stationery and stamps from the camp canteen and I wrote a long, long letter telling Stonehouse everything that had happened since we had met at the Kaloleni dances, and I ended by asking him to press for an inquiry into the events at Hola as I frankly did not believe the story the Government had put out. I asked the Asian canteen manager, Vergi, to post it for me and he did so. Stonehouse took up the case of my re-detention with the Colonial Secretary, who replied that it had been done in the interests of 'security'.[1]

The Hola incident laid bare to the whole world the policy and methods being used in Kenya's detention camps and the Government appointed a committee under Fairn to investigate what was going on and to make recommendations for the future of these camps. By the time they came to Kandongu, I had been released from the small cell by the Camp Commandant, Louis. He was the kindest and most courteous officer I met in any of the camps and it was not possible that he should ever hurt anyone. We nicknamed him *baba* which is Swahili for 'father', after the habit he had of calling us 'Baba' when he spoke to us. He was a good and humble man and a hard worker, and he looked upon us as human beings in trouble who needed help. We have always been good friends and even today Louis sometimes visits me at my home.

When Fairn came I told him as much as I could remember of what had been happening at all the camps I had been in and what detainees had told me about the other camps. He was clearly intelligent and reasonable and he listened attentively to all I had to tell him.

Shortly after I arrived at Kandongu, the former D.O. at Othaya, Salisbury, came to see me. He almost seemed to be enjoying looking at me behind the barbed wire and he said that he hoped this was the last time I would behave as I had. He said that I had accused him to the Government for making some errors in Othaya, whereas he had at all times worked hard to help the people there. Now I had been brought back yet again for writing letters of complaint to the authorities. Was I

[1] *Parliamentary Debates*, 2 June 1959, V. 606. 6.

quite incapable of keeping quiet, even for a month? If I did
not behave and I continued writing letters this would be the end
of me. I answered him by saying, 'You are playing a match
against me. I can score against you or you can score against
me. You are fighting for your people and I am fighting for
mine. We will always be enemies.'

When I had been there a few weeks some other detainees who
had also failed to squeeze into the pipeline were brought in from
the Mariira Works Camp in Fort Hall District. Among them
were Taddeo Mwaura Ichahuria, who was an elderly man with
an amazing command of English. He had been a true
nationalist almost since birth and he was a teacher of high
quality. His brother, Goddard Mburu, was educated at Fort
Hare College in South Africa, and is now a District Assistant
in the Provincial Administration. Taddeo, whom I loved and
trusted like my father, helped me present our grievances to the
Fairn Committee. He is now chairman of the K.A.N.U. branch
in Fort Hall. Others were Ngugi Mwaganu, brother of Bildad
Kaggia, who was tried with Kenyatta at Kapenguria; Kinuthia,
now secretary of the Kenya Domestic and Hotel Workers
Union; and Mwangi 'Cowboy', one of the strongest and bravest
fighters in the forest. Others were brought in from Nyeri
including Jeremiah Kirumwa Keiru, later my partner in the
National Secretarial Service; and John Michael Mungai, a
close friend to Fred Kubai, also prosecuted at Kapenguria, and
a great nationalist.

They elected me as the camp leader and we organized
ourselves democratically as in the other camps. No one was
beaten at this time and when we wrote letters to the authorities
complaining about the rations, Louis passed them on to his
superiors without abusing or threatening us. We liked him and
we respected the camp regulations.

In another section of the camp, but deliberately and carefully
isolated from us, were many other people who had been recently
detained for being members of a new secret organization called
Kiama Kia Muingi (K.K.M.), which is to say, Society of the
People. It was also alleged to have another name, *Kiama Kia
Rubia*, which means Society of the Rupee (or Two Shillings).
I have already mentioned the intense dissatisfaction of the
ordinary people with the execution of the Government's Land

Consolidation Scheme. This was particularly concentrated in the districts of Fort Hall and Kiambu and it is alleged that some people there started a society which had to remain secret in the conditions of the Emergency and whose object was to collect two shillings a head in order to employ a lawyer to take up some of the disputed cases to the Supreme Court and to write a detailed memorandum of protest to the Colonial Office.

The Government asserted that this was a recrudescence of 'Mau Mau', and by doing so they showed their lack of understanding of either organization. The Kikuyu people had yet again tried with all the constitutional means at their disposal to protest against the forced imposition of a radical change in the system of land tenure when the country was in a State of Emergency. When the Government insisted on carrying it out regardless of public opinion the people were driven once more to secret arrangements. Recent public admissions by the Government of what occurred in Fort Hall during consolidation have done much to vindicate the necessity of their stand. The K.K.M. detainees were not allowed to mix with us, except when they were bringing us food. They were kept working very hard, and earned eight shillings a month as a result. The methods used in some areas, especially in the other Mwea Camps near us, produced the usual crop of false confessions and many K.K.M. detainees had nothing whatever to do with the Society. To some of us it looked almost as if the Government wished to play up and greatly exaggerate the whole affair in order to persuade both the Kenya and the British public of the necessity of keeping the Emergency Regulations on a little longer. Many administrators seemed to wish that the Emergency could become the normal state of affairs.

Kandongu had formerly had one of the worst reputations in Kenya, but it had cooled down as we were now at the beginning of the end of rehabilitation. We did no work ourselves, not even removing our own sanitary buckets. I decided to learn shorthand and Rufus Kinuthia, a shorthand typist himself, gave me daily lessons. Within two months he had brought me up to a speed of one hundred words a minute: this was the greatest benefit I received during my second detaineeship. I would never have had a chance to do this after my final release, because it is very difficult to keep in the swim of African politics, earn one's living and concentrate on studying something all at the same time.

The International Red Cross sent out another Committee of Investigation and I had the pleasure of a second long talk with Philippe Junod, *Muthuri wa Itathi*, whom I had first met at Lodwar. He was accompanied by Dr. Rubli from Zürich in Switzerland. After telling them all our troubles I took them along to be introduced to the other detainees, who were as surprised as I had originally been at their manifest goodness and humility. Before leaving they presented me with a booklet showing how political prisoners or prisoners of war should be treated. I valued it highly and I still have it though I hope it will never need to be looked at seriously in Kenya again. I have been in regular correspondence with Dr. Rubli since that day and when I passed through Zürich in Switzerland on 10 July 1961, I tried to find his home, but what with language difficulties and shortage of time it could not be done.

A few months later, the District Commissioner from Hola, accompanied by one of the staff of the *Atiriri* magazine at Athi River, came to classify us. Several of my friends, including Taddeo, were packed into a lorry with a cage on the back and went off to Galole. The Government had recently issued a circular changing the name of Hola to Galole. They realized that the word 'Hola' would remain a deep reproach to their reputation for all time. I stayed a little longer and I missed Taddeo especially: he had been a good and wise companion to me. One day a European called R. G. Wilson came to see us, accompanied by Rochester. Wilson was a tall, well-built man with a quiet, kind voice. He told us that he had been appointed Special Commissioner in charge of the Detention Camps, and that, providing our behaviour was satisfactory, he would make sure we were released as soon as possible. Rochester greeted me briefly, saying nothing of the past, and they both left the camp. Soon afterwards Rochester was posted to Karaba Camp, still on the Mwea plains, and about fourteen miles from Kandongu. A few days passed and then John Michael was taken there, and three weeks later I followed him.

Karaba was the fourteenth and last of my detention camps. It was not really detention as I was not put inside the compound, but I was told that I was restricted to an area of three square miles round the camp. Karaba is almost as hot as Kowop, although it is situated in less uninviting country. I was given the job of teaching the children of the warders in the Camp School, and I found this very congenial and worthwhile. These children would be growing up into a different, a free Kenya. In the evenings I held a combined class for the educated warders and rehabilitation staff, teaching them English, history, and shorthand. One of my students was Joseph Gaturuku Mathu (an ex-detainee working as a clerk), who is now completing his Cambridge School Certificate by correspondence course, meanwhile working as a typist and editor of our Nyeri newspaper, *Uiguano Witu (Our Unity)*. We stayed in the same house together down at Karaba. Another was James, one of the screeners who classified us at Lodwar. When I started teaching them politics James (my student), with a nervous look at the door, told his teacher, me, that this was not wise.

As a result of the Fairn Committee Report,[1] the detention camps had been taken over from the Prison Department by the Administration. R. G. Wilson, who had been a District Commissioner in Nyanza, put Rochester in charge of the three Mwea camps. Under the new régime there was no beating whatsoever of detainees. Instead we were kept in small huts and the screeners came to speak to the detainees in them. They did not find it easy to converse with what appeared to be a deaf mute from 8 a.m. to 1 p.m. There was a tendency to run out of small talk quite quickly. Anyone who answered at all in reply was now deemed to be rehabilitated and was swiftly taken to his home and released. This was when the Government first seemed to grasp that the whole basis of its confession and rehabilitation had been unsound. All the praise showered by successive Colonial Secretaries on the marvels achieved in the light of the rehabilitation of 80,000 detainees must be assessed in the light of this failure.

It may surprise the reader to hear that I was now on friendly terms with Rochester, who had dealt so hardly with me at Athi River. We say *Arume mekurua matitindaga marakaraniire, kana mamenaine*, 'If men fight, they do not harbour thoughts of malice or hatred between themselves later'. He had been acting under

[1] *Report of the Committee on Emergency Detention Camps*. Supplement to *Kenya Gazette*, September 1. Nairobi (1959).

someone's orders in Athi River, he was now acting under different orders, reasonable and sensible orders in the circumstances. I found I could obey him here. It is surprising how quickly we can forget the past if someone changes and I soon found I had no bad feelings towards him at all.

One day I was called before the Appeal Committee, which investigated the reasons for our detention. I told them that I thought that my conduct had in no way merited my re-arrest and detention and that there was no evidence against me that would be accepted in any court of law. At the end of 1959 we were also visited by Iain Macleod, the Colonial Secretary, who spoke a few words to us all and was shown round the camp. He tried to talk to some of the detainees who were kept by themselves but none of them answered him.

At this time some of the women who had been detained at Kamiti near Nairobi throughout the Emergency were brought to Karaba, among them a daughter of old Senior Chief Koinange, and two Nyeri girls, Margery from Gathaithi Village and Miriam Muthoni, who came from Mumbuini, near my home. Miriam had been sentenced to death for carrying a pistol but the sentence had been commuted and then 'instrumented', and she was now a detainee. We spent many hours discussing the treatment of the women in Kamiti and they left me in no doubt that there were the strongest possible grounds for believing the report made by Eileen Fletcher when she resigned her job in Kamiti.[1] Young girls on life sentences, brutalities by the screeners, and the vile atmosphere of treachery and spying caused by the policy of encouraging weaker women to inform on the others. I hope that one of the women detained will write the full story of Kamiti some day.

During that Christmas of 1959 I produced a Nativity Play, which was performed both in the camp and in the nearest village. It was well received in both places. I taught Rochester's son to act as an angel and to say in Kikuyu the words that the angel spoke to the shepherds on the night that Jesus was born. He did it very well. I approve of the Nativity Play.

[1] *Parliamentary Debates*, 31 October 1956, V. 558. 1418–21. and 31 July 1956, V. 556. 127. See also the speech by Fenner Brockway M.P., in which he uses material from Miss Fletcher's reports, in the short debate on the condition of juveniles in prisons and detention camps in Kenya. *Parliamentary Debates*, 25 June 1956, V. 555. 225–34.

On 8 February 1960 I received a letter from the Attorney-General stating that he had been authorized by the Colonial Secretary to release me on 12 February to my home. I was grateful to him for the trouble he had taken. The warders and rehabilitation staff gave me a special farewell tea party as I had been their teacher so long and on the morning of the 12th I left for Nyeri, reclining comfortably in the back of Rochester's Mercedes. My mind was thinking of only one thing. It was going to be a real plump goat this time: no more chickens!

CHAPTER X

Kenda Muiyuru[1]

THE Administration laid down the red carpet for my return. Burton was still District Commissioner and he took me with him out to Othaya in his own car, talking pointedly on the way about the great economic progress made in the district since my detention, showing me smart new houses springing up everywhere on the consolidated farms and the lines of holes dug ready for coffee seedlings and tea stumps. At Othaya, Burton and I exchanged a few words with the D.O. and I told him of the Kikuyu saying, *Thu ndiguaga haria iikagio*—'The enemy never falls where it is thrown'. But he seemed to have mellowed and gave me a Government Land-Rover to carry me the six miles to my home in Kariko village. There was no reporting to Chief or headman this time and late that evening I knocked on Wangui's door and I was home again. It was too late to organize a celebration that night and so after talking until there was no more wood for the fire we went to bed.

Next day we made no doubt about it at all and my aunt chose the largest and fattest goat she had, all of one colour, black, and we slaughtered and ate it together with the family in a meat-party which no one left unsatisfied. At last I was beginning to feel really certain that I was back for good. Ever sensitive to atmosphere, I had been conscious of a change, slight but noticeable, in the attitude of the District Commissioner and his District Officer. Politics were not quite so dirty a game, they might even be inevitable and help 'the chaps to let off a bit of steam'. Perhaps this really was the end of the barbed wire for me and the beginning of a new, open stage in the campaign for 'Freedom Now'—*Uhuru sasa*. The task that remained was to channel the 'steam' into a party that could govern our country and direct our destiny.

[1] This is a Kikuyu expression. After naming the nine clans, people refer to the tenth as *Kenda muiyuru*.

I had been given a large pink form before leaving Karaba which said that, since I had responded to rehabilitation, I would now be restricted to my 'home area' for an unspecified period on probation so that the effectiveness of my response could be judged in my own location. This sounded like a scientist discussing the effects of a change in environment on newts. They had never screened me during my second time of detention and you cannot rehabilitate a nationalist, so if politics were a crime I was incurable and neither probation nor prison would make any difference.

I spent a few days at home, getting up to date on the family news and checking on the progress on my farm. Then I went around to see what had happened to the Nyeri Democratic Party. I found that both Wanjohi Mungau and his ally, Mugo Muringa, had been restricted to their villages shortly after my arrest and nobody else had been able to do anything. Some of those with no education had tried but the problems of organization had proved too much for them, enthusiastic as they were. It saddened me to hear that Kiambu and Fort Hall already had their parties, whereas Nyeri, which had been first, was now last, and indeed apparently not even running in the race.

Soon after my return Wanjohi's restriction was lifted and the very same day, accompanied by another zealot, Ndegwa Mundia, he came to see me in Kariko. We discussed the general situation and decided to start again immediately with our plans. Although I was restricted to my 'home area' I decided deliberately to court arrest by moving into Nyeri Township from where the organization of the party could be best managed.

In March, Jeremiah Nyagah, Member of Legislative Council (M.L.C.) for Nyeri and Embu, and Dr. Kiano held a public meeting at Othaya. These meetings were being held by M.L.C.s all over the country to explain the results and implications of the Lancaster House Constitutional Conference in London from which they had just returned. As far as my knowledge went this was the first mass political meeting ever held in Othaya.

It was attended by about 7,000 people. Out of nowhere a group of stewards had appeared, all wearing green ribbons in their coat lapels, and among them I recognized some of my friends from detention. Who organized them I do not know

even now, but they included some of the founders of the Nyeri
Democratic Party. Under their guidance the crowd was very
orderly and well disciplined and this showed me both the
necessity for, and some of the powers of, a political organization.
After the meeting I went for a drive with Dr. Kiano, and we
discussed the need for forming not only a Nyeri district party
but also a Colony-wide one. Before he left he asked me to
undertake the job of organizing the district party.

I was not sure what the words 'home area' on my Restriction
Order meant: in one sense all Kenya was my home. So I
decided to test the consequence of moving about freely and I
deliberately went to Nyeri Township and made myself conspicuous. I was arrested the same day and taken back to
Othaya where Henley, the D.O., charged me with contravening
my Restriction Order and I was returned to Nyeri and re-
manded by the Senior District Officer in custody to Nyeri jail.
After a week I appeared before the Resident Magistrate in
Nyeri, Carthew, and pleaded not guilty: I told him that I had
been charged under the wrong section. He flicked over several
large volumes and then said I was quite right and told the police
to go away and get their homework right. In the afternoon they
came back with a charge under a different section of the law
which was certainly valid, so this time I tried telling the judge
that as far as I was concerned, Nyeri District, Central Province,
Kenya, and all Africa were my 'home' and that if this is the area
to which I was restricted I did not understand what I had done
wrong. After considerable further research into his books and
an ominous silence or two, *Bwana Kali*—'Mr. Fierce', as we
called the R.M.—acquitted me. Outside the court my friends
from the town carried me on their shoulders down the street,
pouring rain and angry policemen notwithstanding.

The political situation in the district at this time was
dangerous. No political party had yet been approved by the
Registrar of Societies although several applications had been
made, most of which had been refused, although some had
merely been irritatingly delayed in the hope that they would die
a natural death. At the same time there was considerable
political ferment which had no legitimate outlet and which was
consequently bubbling over into numerous small and dis-
organized groups, none of which were adequately controlled

and one of which might at any ti...
Government would seize upon as ar...
restrictions and curfews on the dist...
themselves Peoples Convention Pa...
Independent Party, Democratic Party...
the ex-K.A.U. Committee organizatic...
plosive position, largely created by the ...
Administration to acknowledge the neces...
parties. Wanjohi Mungau, Tom Gichoh...
meeting at Karatina on 20 May 1960, o...
organizers of the various groups. At th... ...e Kenya
African National Union (K.A.N.U.) was in process of organization in Nairobi and so I told the meeting that the time had
come to forget all these different political parties and disband
them. We must form a District Steering Committee of K.A.N U.,
which would become a branch of the central organization when
its registration had been approved. The leaders of the various
groups then stood up and agreed to disband their associations,
and we set up a K.A.N.U. Steering Committee with myself as
chairman, Wanjohi as vice-chairman, Thomas Gichohi as
secretary, Wambugu Kamuiru as treasurer and five other
officials. This committee worked well over the next few months.

As district chairman I had to attend the meetings held in
Kiambu and Nairobi during the formation of K.A.N.U. There
was some delay over the registration of the party as the
Government would not accept Jomo Kenyatta as president. As
had happened with K.A.U., James Gichuru stepped in to
satisfy the Government and keep the seat warm for Kenyatta.
Many people have been surprised that the Kenya politicians
could not achieve unity among themselves and that we now
have two parties, K.A.N.U. and K.A.D.U. (Kenya African
Democratic Union) instead of one. As I saw the situation
develop during these meetings there were several different
reasons which contributed to this result. The first, and probably
the most important, was the fear of some of the smaller tribes
that they would be dominated by the Kikuyu and the Luo. This
was a natural fear arising out of tribalism, but accentuated in
Kenya by the fact that few politicians had yet been able to
create a non-tribal image: the political strength of most
individual leaders was still dependent on their acceptance by

...be. The Kenya Government with its insistence on
...Political Associations and its long refusal ʒo allow
...C.s to speak in any but their own districts had done much
... prevent the growth of policies, allegiances and images that
could transcend tribal boundaries.

The second reason was the fear of some politicians of the
purposes and motives of others. There were many minor dislikes
but some leaders had an overriding fear of one or two, and were
prepared to sacrifice much to make sure that they did not have
to serve in the same organization with them. The Kenya
Government exaggerated this fear by its refusal to recognize
either that Kenyatta was the only possible generally acceptable
leader, or, if he was not, that nobody else could presume to
usurp his place until he had rejected the offer and opportunity.
So they delayed, until it was almost too late, the settlement of
the relative power positions of the various politicians and they
have also split the country into two groups, when unity is
required above all to face the problems that are in front. How
much the dying embers of the old imperialist 'Divide and Rule'
were also being fanned at this time by money and pressure from
the Katanga and Rhodesian lobbies is not known but the
descent by K.A.D.U. into the bottomless pit of regionalism is
clearly linked with Katanga and the spluttering hopes of some
of Kenya's European settlers.

The third reason is the natural and inevitable ambition of
the politicians. This is not uniquely a Kenya problem but occurs
all over the world. With one party there is only one chairman,
vice-chairman, general secretary, treasurer, and so on. With
two, the possibilities of power and glory seem to be doubled.
(They are not in Africa because few African countries can
afford the luxury of two parties. But the point is that at
first people think they are and although this is clearly not a
fundamental cause, once the first two reasons take any hold
at all it powerfully reinforces them. So two parties were formed,
K.A.N.U. chiefly with Kikuyu, Luo and Kamba support, but
including also some smaller tribes, and K.A.D.U. with the
Kalenjin[1] group and a few other smaller tribes behind it. The
Abaluhya, a powerful and numerically strong group, were split
roughly in half between the parties. We were still awaiting

[1] The groups of Nilo-Hamitic peoples living in Western Kenya.

approval of our registration as a branch of K.A.N.U. when in late May 1960 things became very bad in Nyeri.

In the early part of the month a village headman called Wambugu, a mild and inoffensive man, was killed at Gichiche Village in Othaya about four miles from my home, and his body pushed down a latrine pit where it was found three days later. The Othaya authorities alleged that this was a political murder and since the Special Branch said they had good evidence of oathing and meetings, the acting Provincial Commissioner, Burton, who had been District Commissioner in Nyeri, placed several villages under night curfews. The Government also forbade movement in or out of the area. The D.O., Henley, took a tough line and life rapidly became very unpleasant for my people. The Government did uncover the fact that many people had subscribed money and received receipts marked 'G.M.K.'. Some people said these initials stood for 'Gikumbo Mount Kenya' which was the name of the K.I.S.A. School at Karatina that had been proscribed, and others gave it different identifications. There is no doubt that many people had most willingly subscribed this money in the belief that it was for a school which would be opened and managed by Wanjohi Mungau. I fully approved of his attempts to increase the educational facilities of our people.

The Government took fright at the revelations of what had been going on, and said that there was also evidence of illegal oathing in the Rift Valley and Fort Hall. It therefore announced the pick-up known as 'Operation Milltown' in which about sixty people were arrested and detained at Lamu Island on the coast. These included Wanjohi Mungau, Mugo Muringa and Ndegwa Mundia. A corporal in the police told me that my name had originally been on the list but was removed through the intercession of certain Administrative officials. One of them pointed out that there might be considerable political repercussions in England if I was sent back yet again.

The headman's wife was eventually charged and convicted of the murder of her husband and yet again the bogy of a resurgence of violence, seized on so gleefully, hopefully and often by the Kenya authorities, was laid. The acting District Commissioner had meanwhile gone to Nairobi to meet some of the new K.A.N.U. leaders and Josef Mathenge, a leading figure in

the original Nairobi Peoples Convention Party. He asked them
to come up to Nyeri and hold meetings denouncing illegal
activities and oathing. He promised on his side to persuade the
authorities to allow a K.A.N.U. branch in the district as soon
as possible, so that it would be possible for the political leaders
to control the activities of their subordinates. In June a large
and orderly meeting was held at Ruringu, about a mile from
Nyeri Township, attended by about 15,000 people. James
Gichuru, Josef Mathenge, Arthur Ochwada (a Trade Union
leader from Nyanza), Mwai Kibaki (a former Makerere University economist who became Executive Officer of K.A.N.U.),
Henry Wariithi (a lawyer who was looking after Kenyatta's
affairs) and myself all addressed it, appealing for unity and
condemning secret oath-taking and other similar activities as no
longer necessary at this stage of our political development. I
personally appealed to the ex-detainees to forget the past and
called upon the ex-loyalists to unite with us. Shortly afterwards
the acting District Commissioner licensed another meeting at
which elections for the branch office-bearers were held. The
people shouted my name as chairman but I had already discussed this with Josef Mathenge and decided that it would be
better at this time for him to take this post, so I stood on the
table and told them I did not wish to be chairman. The office-
bearers elected on that day were Josef Mathenge chairman,
Muriithi Wagochi (ex-detainee) vice-chairman, and Wambugu
Kamuiru (ex-detainee) treasurer. The people were not pleased
at my refusal to take office and so elections for the other officers
were postponed and the crowds quietly dispersed. Alvan Kar-
anga, the African D.O. in charge of North Tetu, invited us all
up to his house after the meeting and the acting District Commissioner was also there. It seemed that at last some of the
Administration had realized that we were trying to build, not
to destroy, our country.

    There was a feeling in the country that electing district office-
bearers at mass public meetings was not the best method. So it
was decided to start from the ground up and to elect sub-
location (ward) committees in public, location (parish) leaders
from an electoral college of the sub-location leaders, and
divisional leaders in the same way from an electoral college of
location leaders. The supreme district body would be the

Governing Council, which consists of twelve members from each division and the district office-bearers, who were elected by the Governing Council, although they need not be members of it. I was chosen as organizing secretary with my old friend Eustace Mimamo, who had been a compound leader in Manyani and a strong hard-core. Tom Gichohi, who left his job as a clerk in the Railway (where he had also been a branch official of the Railway African Union), became secretary. Gachuru Ngorano, who had been one of the group of detainees involved in the Hola shambles, became vice-treasurer. Certain things about the management of these elections were not satisfactory but we did now have the nucleus of an organization.

It still remained to encourage everyone to join. We obtained receipt books and membership cards from the central office in Nairobi and began a concerted propaganda drive to enrol members. Within a month we had 35,000 members within the district and were far in advance of any other area in the Colony. Branch officers were established in each division, and it was wonderful to see the old men and women stretching out in orderly queues of hundreds, whatever the weather and in spite of the urgent demands of their farms. Man certainly does not live by bread alone. When they came into the office a divisional official explained to them the objects of K.A.N.U. and the promises they were making and they paid over five shillings and signed or fingerprinted the membership card.

Kenneth Kingori, an educated man who had worked in the Nakuru African Court as Registrar, and whose father was the District Commissioner's driver, had been released from jail on the same day as I. He was elected propaganda secretary and we decided that I should translate into Kikuyu the K.A.N.U. constitution and we would then distribute duplicated copies of it throughout the district. We also issued a duplicated newssheet giving K.A.N.U. news and policy. By September we had a brand-new K.A.N.U. van, brilliant in the red, black and green of the old K.A.U. flag and inscribed with the statements 'Service to one's country is service to God' and 'Jomo Kenyatta is our Leader', and the emblem of a shield and crossed spears used by K.A.U. before its proscription. By this time we had also begun the training of choirs to sing national songs and teams of dancers to bring back the glory and rhythms of olden times.

13

There was an enthusiastic and exciting K.A.N.U. tea party at the Nyeri Stadium, attended by over fifteen thousand, to say farewell to the sixty Nyeri students for whom money had been collected so that they could take their places on the airlift to America, where they would at last have a chance of training themselves to fill responsible posts in our new nation.

We now had a political party but a country is nowhere without economic stability. Certain people in Nyeri Township had been trying for several months to get an association known as the Nyeri African Traders Society registered. The authorities had declined on the grounds that they had little confidence in the office-bearers and anyway there seemed to be at least two factions who thought they were in control of its steering committee. So I approached the District Commissioner and we agreed that if these internal problems could be resolved he would back registration. At the end of July 1960 at a public meeting in Nyeri Township I was elected chairman. Joseph Kingori, a middle-aged firewood contractor and general trader at Kamakwa Market, became vice-chairman. John Kingori, who had a K.A.P.E. (Kenya African Preliminary Examination Certificate) and had been renting a tailor's shop in Nyeri Township, became full-time paid secretary, and Nahashon Gakuu, a wealthy man who owned two bakeries, an extremely honest, English-speaking former hospital assistant, was made treasurer. Thomas Elijah Gikonyo, who became assistant secretary, was the third son of Philip Nganatha, who had been one of the most powerful forces in the Protestant Mission in the area and the inspiration behind the enormous stone church at Wandumbi before he was knocked down and killed by a cyclist in early 1960. One of Thomas's brothers was studying in Addis Ababa, Ethiopia, and all the sons were Catholics. I remember Thomas telling me how at his father's funeral, which was attended by thousands of people, there was nearly a riot because the Catholics said that in his very early youth Philip had been a Catholic and they wanted to bury him according to the Catholic rites. The Protestants were furious as they took the view that, whatever he had been or done earlier, he was now one of their leaders. The night before the funeral the body was guarded by Protestant volunteers at distant Wandumbi and was escorted down to the burial ground by many vehicles. The area round the grave was protected by further massed Protestant ranks and the Catholics were left outside on the road. Mission feeling is very strong in parts of my country but this unseemly squabble over a dead body seemed both indecent and absurd to many of us. It was inspired by the attitude of some European missionaries who counted success by numbers and who were using the corpse as a symbol in their most un-Christian struggle for power.

Thomas Elijah had been active in the infant Trade Union organization in Nyeri and was a keen and true nationalist. He had formerly worked in the Nyeri Marketing Board. The vice-treasurer was a lady from South Tetu, Miss Wanjiru James, who was a produce trader in the Township. The trustees of the Society were Josef Mathenge, M.L.C., and Paul Waithaka, who owned a furniture business. At the annual conference in February 1961 all these officials were re-elected except the secretary and vice-secretary. John Kingori was replaced by Charles Mwaniki Kamara, who worked with the Central Province Marketing Board as a clerk and was a trick-cyclist. Thomas Elijah was in jail for over-enthusiasm on a political occasion, and his place was taken by Wachira Kinguru, a trader from Karatina.

The Society rapidly expanded all over the district and we were able to bring considerable pressure to bear on the district authorities over such matters as the limitation on trading licences, the correct filling in of application forms for transport licences, applications for trading loans and discriminatory conditions for stock trading. I was the only one among the officials who had been detained. The Society had its own small office in Nyeri Township which was always crowded with would-be traders needing help. We Kikuyu are very keen on trading and with the bad unemployment situation many of our people were trying to earn a little money in some business or other.

In September 1960 there was a brawl in a Karatina hotel, which ended up in becoming a major political episode involving many of our district leaders. A European policeman came into the hotel to arrest someone and was roughly treated. He left and returned with reinforcements and tried with them to arrest many of the people there, including Josef Mathenge and our officials. The crowd that had quickly gathered resented this and the situation became ugly when they marched on the police station to release their leaders. Fortunately the people calmed down but it was clearly an incident that should never have occurred. In the explosive political situation in Kenya a little tact and discretion on the part of the police was worth any amount of toughness, manhandling and abuse. In the resulting court case the former acting D.C., who was then climbing Kilimanjaro, agreed to give evidence on behalf of the defence, stressing the excellent behaviour of the local leaders and their control of the enormous public meetings held in the tense situation following Operation Milltown. We sent Eustace Kimano in a K.A.N.U. vehicle to fetch him from the mountain and they drove back to Nyeri through the night. He told the court that he knew no law against shouting *Uhuru* or making the V-sign. Mathenge and the other leaders were fined but not jailed, although Thomas Elijah was convicted and imprisoned later on further charges arising out of the same incident.

As we were eating the *thenge* goat after my second release from detention Wangui reminded me that it was time I married. For several months my political activities prevented any serious consideration of this problem but I had to admit that she was right. I was thirty-one and all my sisters were now married. While working in Nyeri I sometimes had occasion to go to the office of a trade union called the Kenya Distributive and Commercial Workers Union. My concentration on my business there had been disturbed by a most beautiful young lady working as a secretary, typing and filing, and her name was Doris Nyambura, and she was the most beautiful girl I had ever seen. In addition to her charm she was also hard-working and young, being eighteen years old. In Kikuyu country we do not judge a girl by her looks alone, but by her behaviour, her honesty and her personality. She must also like people and welcome visitors with an open heart. Doris had all these qualities. She came from a large family and was the fifth daughter of Gordon Njee and Sephora Mumbi of Riamukurwe Village in Aguthi Location. Gordon was a trader and many years ago had managed a taxi which was one of the first ever run by a Kikuyu anywhere. Harun Muturi, Doris's elder brother, was working as an accountant in an Asian-run printing firm in Nairobi. Her elder sister, Miriam, had married a mechanic working at Nanyuki and they have six children. The second sister, Esther Muthoni, is married to Peter Njoka from Embu, a senior clerk in the Railways, and they have two children. Joyce, the third sister, is married to a driver called Kibara and they have one baby girl. Doris's three brothers, Matuto, Mbogo and Kariuki, and the youngest sister, Mukami, are still schooling at Riamujirwe Intermediate School under the headmaster, Charles Mukora. Charles, who is a friend of mine, is a fine athlete, doing the long jump for Kenya and playing centre-half for the Central Province and, on occasions, for the Kenya soccer team. All these people, after my marriage, had a new special relationship with me and I call them my *Athoni*.

It took me two weeks to get her consent, but I did not mind since I knew that she was making her investigations as I had been and this is a custom. It is not easy for a girl to give her final judgement there and then, even if she feels she loves you enough to die for you. She says, 'I do not agree and I do not refuse', and then later she will come to you and say, 'It is all right, you can now go and see my father'. Things are not so different all over the world. So we went together to her father and he agreed and we now began to think of the marriage. There was a complication because Doris's mother, Sephora Mumbi, had been arrested during the Operation Milltown disturbances because she was alleged to have been implicated in the G.M.K. movement. She was imprisoned for two months and fined a hundred and fifty shillings as well. If she did not pay the hundred and fifty shillings she would have to serve a further two months. Doris told me that she could not marry while her mother was in jail and this seemed very reasonable, but I had to marry and I did not want to postpone the ceremony for several months. After a sleepless night considering ways and means I went to see the acting District Commissioner and I told him my problem. 'I want to marry and my lover's mother is in prison and she says she cannot marry while her mother is in prison.' Although he was a bachelor, he was most sympathetic and, after scratching his head, he finally smiled and said, 'O.K. I'll do it. Take this piece of paper to the court and pay the fine and she'll be released.' He rapidly wrote a letter to the elders, squashing the sentence of imprisonment. I hurried to the court, paid a hundred and fifty shillings, was given a receipt and the release warrant and ran over the hill to Nyeri Prison where a few minutes later my mother-in-law came out of the large clanking gates and greeted me quietly, her eyes wet with her happiness.

There are certain things that we do in our country to increase the bonds between the two families involved in any marriage. People who do not know talk about 'bride-price' and 'buying' wives; these words confuse the purpose and effect of what happens, which is the transfer of cattle and other property from the family of the bridegroom to that of the bride. If the couple do not agree together it is not then so easy for them to divorce each other without good reason. The father of the bride will not lightly gather together all the property he received because of some minor domestic tantrum or lovers' tiff. Great family pressure will be brought on the bride to continue with her marriage as long as it is reasonable for her to do so. It was necessary for me to hand over nine cattle to my father-in-law. One cow equals ten goats, and one goat equals twenty shillings, so each cow was worth two hundred shillings. I had these cattle because when my sisters married we were brought many by the families of their husbands.

In the old days it used to be customary for the bridegroom to be given various tests in the presence of the women of his lover's clan. He was made to carry a full load of firewood or a bunch of bananas or a huge pot of water (*ndigithu*). He never failed because these were tests of the strength of his devotion. The women would be waiting in a hut to see him come staggering in and they would make suitable comments on him, usually full of praise. This is not much done in my country these days and the women told me that my detention had, anyway, exempted me from such ordeals.

There is also another ceremony, which is still kept up in many places, known as *Ngoima*. Six fat sheep (*ngurario*) are skinned and the old men of the wife's clan gather together to eat them with some of the family of the bridegroom. This is another means of strengthening the ties between the groups. Some of these customs are dying out and when educated young men get married today they are often not observed. This one I was myself excused. But I did not avoid the *njohi ya mwana* (the beer party for the child that is lost). As my home was twenty miles away I paid money to Gordon Njee to arrange for people to brew the beer for me. Gordon had to get a permit from the Chief before he could do this. The trouble was that I did not drink myself: my mother's words and advice on this were strengthened, not weakened, in me by her death. Still the old men insisted on my tasting the brew and so I put a little from the *ndua* (calabash) on my tongue and then implored them not to force me to drink any, and they agreed.

It is also a tradition for the bridegroom to give certain gifts to the mother and father of the bride (*muhiki*) to replace those that the bride's father gave to the bride's mother's parents. These gifts would differ from family to family but normally include a *mukwa* (head strap), *kiondo* (basket) and *nguo ya maribe* (women's skin dress embroidered with beads) for the mother and a *ruhiu* (small sword), *itimu ria nduthu* (special spear) and *githii gia ikami* (a man's skin cloak) for the father. Sometimes the father or mother would say that they preferred something else instead of one of these things. If this was the case it would be agreed upon and handed down the generations. For example, I gave Gordon a mackintosh and I shall now expect that when my daughter is married my son-in-law will give me one as well. My lover's parents said that it would be best to commute all the other articles into a sum of money and we agreed on one thousand shillings. They allowed me to pay this in instalments since I had been so prompt with the cattle, and I am still giving it to them.

For an educated man getting married in our country is a very expensive business as we have to comply with both the old and the new customs. Fortunately I still had with me some of the money which had accompanied me to the Three Dry Hills. Having done so much political work it was now going to finance a more social occasion. My family and nearest relatives, together with some of my close political friends, provided the rest. Money was needed for fitting out the three best men with new suits, buying the three bridesmaids new outfits, a reception at Doris's home and my home, a dance at the Ruringu Social Club, photographs, transport and church expenses. The total cost was three thousand shillings. Although my faith had often weakened I was still a Christian, so was Doris, and we decided to get married in the Presbyterian Church at Nyeri. The minister who married us was the Reverend John Kagai, an old man from South Tetu, who used to visit our people in detention although he never came to a camp when I was actually in it. Doris's dress was white flecked with gold, and it looked really wonderful to me. My best men (*Atiiri*) were Josef Mathenge, M.L.C., and John Baptista Wambugu, a senior teacher at Nyeri Secondary School, and leader of the Kenya National Union of Teachers, both of whom were Catholics, and Harrison Thuku, an editor and newscaster in the Mount Kenya Broadcasting Station. The senior bridesmaid was Anna Njoki, daughter of the old man Kirori Motoku, who had been the other link of my handcuffs on the Lodwar flight. The others were Florence Mumbi and Gladys Gathiri, who is now working as a typist in the K.A.N.U. branch offices at Thomson's Falls, and Doris's youngest sister, the schoolgirl, Mukami.

On 10 September 1960 I woke up before the cocks began crowing, very excited at what was going to happen. As the sun stole up out of the ground Wangui called me and soon my three friends came to take me with them amidst much joking and laughter. In the peace of the church I led Doris before the altar and we stood in front of the old man together, answering the questions he asked us. Then I placed the ring (*gicuhi*) on Doris's finger and I quietly told her that we had now created a new person, Mrs. Josiah Mwangi.

The first party, the bride's reception, was held at Riamuk-urwe School, organized largely by the headmaster. The schoolchildren had been excitedly preparing for it for days and there was a huge banner over the entrance saying 'WELCOME' and hung with flowers from the school garden. One of our customs is that the women of a village make a pretence of preventing the bride leaving her home: their sorrow at losing her is usually only consoled by a large 'bribe'. Sure enough as we neared the school I saw hundreds of women barring the way and dancing the '*mikondi*'. They had with them a *gitaruru*, a large basket they used for keeping food in. Our people also throw the grain up in the air from it and blow the chaff away as it comes down. Until this was filled they would not let me through. My assistants had foreseen this, however, and we had with us in the car a bucket filled with a hundred shillings' worth of ten- and five-cent pieces, which we showered into the basket. The dancing ranks opened and we progressed a few yards until the singers closed in on us again. This time we poured in a hundred shillings' worth of fifty cent and shilling pieces and we went jerkily on to the entrance, where we had to pay a final tax of two hundred shilling notes. Our women are stubborn on these occasions. Usually this money is given back to the bridegroom's mother, but this time it went to Doris's parents.

We had a superb two-tier cake, made by Mrs. Diment, the wife of the Community Development Officer in Nyeri, and many of my friends from all races came to eat it with me, including the District Commissioner who had released my mother. This was the time when the Nyeri students were going on the airlift to America and Josef Mathenge took some of the cake with him that evening to Nairobi to eat it with them as they waited for their aeroplane. There was another reception at my own home in Kariko which the whole village joined in and then the dance at the Ruringu Social Club. The next day we went to Mombasa for our honeymoon. We had invited many people to our wedding and the last guests were still coming along in April 1961, seven months afterwards.

On my return to Nyeri, Joseph Kirira, Jeremiah Kirumwa and myself decided to start a business in the Township, to be called the 'National Secretarial Service'. This had been one of our dreams when in detention together. Joseph Kirira became secretary and Jeremiah Kirumwa works supervisor, while I was general manager. There were many sides to it. We composed and wrote letters for those of our people who were illiterate and thus at a great disadvantage when dealing with the Government or the courts. We wrote and published booklets, two of which were completed in 1961, the first on 'Kikuyu customs and teaching before marriage' and the second on 'Democracy in Africa'. We also ran a small class for student typists, boys and girls, and a department for commercial art, designing posters, book-covers and sign-boards. We even secured the agency for certain manufacturers. My two partners were very hard-working and humble people and quickly built up the reputation of the business. Unfortunately we all found ourselves more and more involved in full-time political work and at the end of 1961 we closed down the business to concentrate on the struggle for freedom.

As soon as I was released I had started writing letters to our beloved leader Jomo Kenyatta, then at Lodwar. There were some things he asked for to help him sustain his life in that place and, although I was not rich, I fulfilled every request to the uttermost limit of my ability. When Robinson Mwangi and David Oluoch Okello were released we held a reunion at my house in Nyeri and we were very happy to be together again. We decided to go up and see Kenyatta, who had by then been moved to Maralal, especially as he had told us he greatly wished to meet us. However, 'passes' first had to be acquired somehow and Kenyatta and I applied pressure from both ends until the Ministry of Defence at last gave us permission.

On 26 June 1961 we hired a car in Nyeri and spent that night at Thomson's Falls. Sleep was intermittent, we were tense with anticipation and joy. Before dawn we started on our journey, travelling through the dark over the same old road that led to Kowop. Arriving at Maralal at half past eight we were taken by the police officer in charge of Kenyatta's visitors to the house in which he was living.

There, framed in the doorway, waiting for us, was *Mzee*. He greeted us in a wonderful manner and as he embraced me to him I felt like a tiny chicken being folded under its mother's wings; all my worries and troubles now belonged to him. This would be a small burden indeed for a man who had already taken the suffering of all our people on himself. There are those who say that the Africans of Kenya forsook Kenyatta during the Emergency and that had it not been for Odinga and the other politicians his name would have been forgotten. Nothing is further from the truth. No African who loves his country can ever forget this man who has shown us the way to freedom and who has undergone so much for us. There are a few Africans who hold other things dearer than their love of country; God, peace, wealth, drink or women. These few might genuinely say that they do not like *Mzee*; others might say it through fear. But the living, throbbing, bustling, laughing, crying, bursting mass of our people love him more than anything else they know. He is our chosen leader and he alone will lead us out of the past, out of the deep pits of dark memories to the bright future of our country. Kenyatta does not depend on K.A.D.U. or K.A.N.U., Indian Congress or Indian Freedom Party, New

Kenya Party or Coalition, he is more than any political part
He does not speak of his people as detainees, loyalists, terrorists,
Home Guards, 'Mau Mau', Catholics, Protestants, Muslims,
Asians, Europeans. Kenyatta is greater than any Kikuyu, he is
greater than any Luo or Nandi or Masai or Giriama, he is
greater than any Kenyan, he is the greatest African of them all.
He knows no tribe, no race, he bears no hatred or malice for the
past; he is human and yet wiser than any other human being
I have ever known. They are all his people, his responsibility
and his children: all fellow human beings to love and to cherish,
to correct if they do wrong, to praise if they do right.

We talked all day together and we spoke freely to each other.
Although he wished to hear of our experiences in detention he
did not dwell on the past. He was looking to the future and told
us many of his plans for dealing with the desperate needs of our
people. We gave him some presents, including an earthenware
refrigerator made by some Fort Hall Kikuyu women to a special
design. We had heard he had trouble in keeping water cool in
that hot place. My wife, Nyambura, also sent his wife two pots.
He showed us the hat we made at Lodwar and another his wife
Ngina, who had been detained at Kamiti, had woven for him
since. She took a photograph of us all together. Then we sat
down to eat. When I had finished my plateful, *Mzee* asked me if
I would like some more. I replied that I had eaten enough. He
then turned and said to me in the voice of a father, 'You are not
in detention now. You and I must eat together until this food
is finished.' I told him that I would agree as this was no time
to start disobeying his orders. I nearly split in two, there was
so much to put down. At this time we also met his two charming
daughters, who were schooling at Maralal. In the afternoon we
continued our talks on the political, social and economic future
of Kenya and we discussed my forthcoming visit to England.
He gave me letters of greetings to the Kenya students there and
to other friends of his in London. I was then to go on to Ghana
with special greetings from Kenyatta to Dr. Nkrumah and the
whole people of that country. *Mzee* told me many wise things
that day which I can never forget. When the evening came, and
the time to say farewell, it seemed as if only an hour had passed
since we arrived. We left him sadly but stimulated greatly in
our minds by the privilege of conversation with him.

y, but true, that the Kenya Government still
litating' this noble man. In April 1960 they sent
and the television up to screen him, as if he were
specimen in a zoo. No pipeline would ever be
to contain Kenyatta nor is it possible to thump
ut of such a man. The Government merely con-
their own amazing lack of understanding by their
attempts to ignore him and by their efforts to build up other
politicians in his place. It is a strange thing that even in August
1961 the Governor of Kenya had not yet asked to see the one
man who could have led our lovely country forward in unity.

When I returned from Maralal I discussed my visit to
Kenyatta with Oginga Odinga, M.L.C., who provided the
funds for my trip to England.

While in London I met many of Kenyatta's old friends and
gave them messages from him. I also took Karuga Koinange,
chairman of the Kenya Students Scholarship Fund, a letter
from Kenyatta in which he agreed to become their patron. This
Fund is a body organized by students to try and get help for
students from Kenya who were stranded in England owing to
lack of funds to pursue their studies. I addressed a meeting of
the Kenya students. One day I was invited to visit Oxford where
I had the pleasure of meeting Miss Margery Perham. After a
long talk she suggested to me that I should try to finish this
book, which I had started in Kenya, on my experiences during
the Emergency. She said that many people in England did not
understand what had been happening there. As Dr. Nkrumah
was at this time visiting Eastern Europe, Russia and China, I
agreed that I would do what I could in the few weeks I had
and she very kindly gave me a room in which to work. As I
neared the end my labour was lightened by the great news
on 14 August that Kenyatta was now back at home among his
people in Kiambu.

The struggle for independence in Kenya has been longer
and more bitter than elsewhere. It has been necessary to create
enough strength of feeling among our people to burst through
the position which the Europeans built up over the years of their
power, while we were young in knowledge and experience of
the new politics. Such a feeling does not come from sweet words
of love and charity. So in our desperation and weakness we

fashioned our unity in a harsher mould. We have had to keep this mould far longer than we wished because the Colonial Government has either not seen very far or has been more interested in its own Metropolitan politics than in our future, and the liberation of our leader was criminally delayed. But we shall soon be able to cast it off, and not before time: there are very great dangers in developing an exaggerated sense of opposition in a people soon to be free.

Our leaders must realize that we have put them where they are not to satisfy their ambitions nor so that they can strut about in fine clothes and huge Cadillacs as ambassadors and ministers, but to create a new Kenya in which everyone will have an opportunity to educate himself to his fullest capabilities, in which no one will die or suffer through lack of medical facilities and in which each person will earn enough to eat for himself and his family. This will require responsible leadership, hard work, unity, honesty and a sincere love of our country in all our hearts. Selfish power-seekers will have to go. We have a story in our country that a man and his wife were sitting at the fireplace and the man said to his wife, 'My dear, I am going to buy a cow which I will bring home and it will give birth to a calf and we shall have lots of milk.' 'Oh yes,' replied the wife, 'thank you, my dear husband, and then I shall milk the cow.' Then the husband flew into a rage and said, 'Oh no you won't, otherwise you will kill my calf by starving it,' and he was angry and threw his wife into the fire where her head was badly burned. This husband was a foolish man and he ended up with no cow, no calf, no milk and a badly burnt wife, whom he spent much time taking to and from the hospital. Our politicians must stop fighting among themselves and cure each other of this unseemly hunger for great positions or everything will be lost.

We in K.A.N.U. under our great leader, Kenyatta, do not think in terms of Kenya alone. We are determined to press forward with the concept of an East African Federation, and move on to a Union of East and Central Africa until we approach the great ideal of the Pan-Africanists. None of us can rest quiet while any of our people, whether in Angola, Mozambique, South Africa or the Rhodesias is still under the imperialist's rule. There may yet be further sacrifices needed till they are free and we are ready to undergo them. The present division among African nations into the Casablanca and Monrovia groups is accentuated by the rivalries between the East and West power *blocs*. It is surprising that some of our African leaders have fallen so readily into the trap. We will devote our party and our Nation to the task of achieving unity in Africa as we have in Kenya.

This then is the end of one story and the beginning of another. As I look back over the years I have described in this book it seems to me that there are lessons to be learnt. How could so many people have been so stupid as to cause in Kenya the explosion we called the Emergency? Why even now do the British people haver and dither, apparently creating a similar situation in Rhodesia? These are the big problems, problems that only those who really understand the complex origins of political manœuvres can begin to fathom. But there are the smaller questions. What turns a weak creature into a sadistic bully behind a barbed-wire fence? What strange twists of thought made the security forces think they always had God and Right on their side whatever crimes against humanity they committed? What obstinate streak in their make-up forced experienced and hitherto reasonably righteous administrative officers to pursue policies of torture and brutality leading to the Hola Massacre? How could the Kenya Government ever think it could exile permanently 12,000 of its citizens?

The future historian of these times may well find it difficult to get our side of the story. Many documents vital to his task will be burnt before independence. But in my narrative of the camps and our strange life together inside them he may perhaps see some glimpses of the truth and justice of the movements of unity, and he may begin to understand why we do not regard the soldiers of the forest as 'hard-core', 'terrorists' or 'murderers', but as the noblest of our fighters for freedom. May this book and our new state be a small part of their memorial. Their torture and their pain were the hard travail of a nation.

The Land Consolidation Scheme

'LAND consolidation' is the name generally used to describe the ambitious programme of land reform which has recently been undertaken by the Kenya Government in most of the tribal areas of the Colony and which was initiated in the Kikuyu districts. The various stages began with the measuring and totalling of the areas of an individual's scattered fragments (many people originally owned thirty or more different pieces). After a five per cent. deduction had been made for land for villages, schools, dispensaries and other public purposes, the rest was offered to the landowner in one piece. If he accepted, his new farm was demarcated by surveyors and he was issued with a Freehold Title.

The Kenya Government embarked upon this plan during the Emergency, partly because they felt they had a sufficiently strong administrative control of the Kikuyu districts at that time to put this difficult project through speedily and successfully, partly because they hoped that the opportunity it would give for better farming would supply a release for Kikuyu energies and encourage the development of a stable middle class, and partly to provide the basis for producing the wealth that would be necessary to finance any future development of social services such as health and education.

At first many of the Kikuyu leaders opposed the scheme. They were suspicious of something that had to be forced upon them at a time when the tribe was in turmoil and the ordinary channels of protest were blocked. They were suspicious, too, of such a wholesale reorganization of their lands, a reorganization which could pay scant regard to the religious restrictions inherited from their ancestors as part of their land. The *ahoi* or tenants were deeply worried at the loss of their rights involved in the issue of freehold title deeds to their landlords. There was, too, a feeling among some that with 80,000 of the tribe absent in detention this was not the right time to accept such a scheme.

Others were fearful that it would not be carried out fairly and justly by the colonial régime. Many of these fears were justified. Large-scale corruption was uncovered in the Fort Hall scheme in 1960, many detainees returned from detention only to find they had no land and even today the position and rights of the *ahoi* are not clear. But in districts where the programme has been completed there has been a most marked and dramatic surge forward of agricultural development and opposition to the scheme has dwindled to negligible proportions. Perhaps a major factor in this decrease has been the opening up of the former 'White Highlands' to African settlement.

The policy of collecting the Kikuyu in from their dispersed homesteads into villages, first carried out as a security measure in 1953 and 1954, was thought to be a valuable complement to the consolidation policy and it had been intended to compel anyone with less than three acres of land to continue living in a village after the Emergency. Since few Legislatures in the world would pass a law to this effect and, without legal backing, no one would agree to obey a mere administrative direction on so fundamental a matter, this did not work, and this restriction has now been totally relaxed.

I. Searching suspects picked up in 'Operation Anvil'

II. *Top. En route* for screening
   Bottom. Searching for ammunition during 'Operation Anvil'

III. *Top.* Families waiting to be screened
Bottom. Arriving at a screening camp

IV. *Top*. Nairobi West Screening Camp
Bottom. 'Hooded Men' going to a screening camp

V. *Top*. Arriving for screening at the 'Mau Mau' Investigation
Centre, Embakasi
Bottom. Manyani Camp

VI. *Top.* Aguthi (Mungaria) Works Camp. Note the electrified fence. The Kikuyu proverb means 'He who helps himself is helped'
Bottom. Detainees making bricks at Aguthi Works Camp

VII. The author with his wife, Doris Nyambura,
and son, John Sekou Kariuki

VIII. The author with Mr. Kenyatta

Index

PRINTED IN GREAT BRITAIN
BY EBENEZER BAYLIS AND SON, LIMITED
THE TRINITY PRESS, WORCESTER, AND LONDON

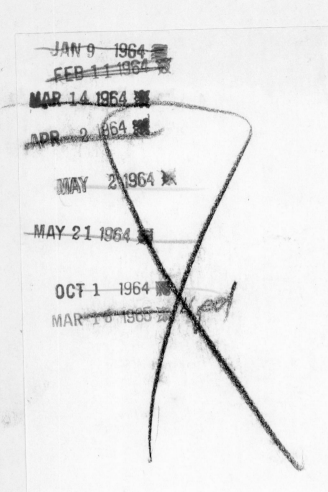